The Ewe-Speaking peoples

of the Slave Coast of

West Africa

Their religion, manners, customs, laws,

languages, &c.

A. B. Ellis

Alpha Editions

This edition published in 2019

ISBN : 9789353956684

Design and Setting By
Alpha Editions
email - alphaedis@gmail.com

THE

EWE-SPEAKING PEOPLES

OF THE

SLAVE COAST OF WEST AFRICA

THEIR

RELIGION, MANNERS, CUSTOMS, LAWS, LANGUAGES, &c.

BY

A. B. ELLIS,

MAJOR, FIRST BATTALION WEST INDIA REGIMENT;

AUTHOR OF "THE TSHI-SPEAKING PEOPLES OF THE GOLD COAST,"

ETC. ETC.

LONDON: CHAPMAN AND HALL,

LIMITED.

1890.

PREFACE.

THE kindly manner in which the *Tshi-speaking Peoples of the Gold Coast,* my first essay in anthropology, was received by the press, has encouraged me to persevere in the task which I had proposed to myself when I commenced to write that book, and which was to show, by examples taken from certain negro peoples of the West Coast of Africa, how the evolution of religion may proceed.

The peoples I had in mind were—(1) The Tshi-speaking peoples of the Gold Coast; (2) The Ga-speaking peoples of the Gold Coast; (3) The Ewe-speaking peoples of the Slave Coast; and (4) The Yoruba-speaking peoples of the Slave Coast; whose languages all belong to one family, and who have apparently all sprung from one common stock. These peoples are situated on the West Coast of Africa in the above order, beginning with the most westerly, and the date of their separation into their present lingual groups must have been rather remote, as Tshi, Ga, Ewe, and Yoruba are now four distinct languages, whose common origin can only be determined by their construction and roots.

The people of these four groups have not progressed equally since their separation. Speaking generally, it may be said that, proceeding from west to east, we find a gradual advance in civilization; the Tshi-speaking peoples being the least, and the Yoruba-speaking peoples the most, advanced. How far this may be due to local conditions and surroundings, I do not pretend to say;

but it appears probable that man would be more retarded
in his progress in such a forested and impenetrable
country as that of the Gold Coast, than when situated
on the comparatively open plains, west of the lower
Niger, which are typical of Yoruba country. However,
whatever may be the cause, as the peoples of these four
groups have not all progressed at the same rate, they
afford us an opportunity for observing how different
religious notions are evolved by the same race when in
different stages of culture.

The religious beliefs of the Ga-speaking peoples
resembling very closely those described in my former
book, I have, for the time being, omitted any description
of them ; and in this volume proceed to the Ewe-speaking peoples, amongst whom the crude conceptions of the
Tshi-speaking peoples will be found to have been considerably modified. Amongst the Yorubas, as I hope to
be able to show at some future date, they are still more
materially changed.

Incidentally, in collecting information concerning the
religion of these peoples, I gathered information respect-
ing other matters—their laws, government, etc.—which
I have included in the same volumes, not with the
intention of putting them forward as complete records
of their social and mental condition, for there is an
immense amount yet to be collected ; but in order to
make a commencement, a starting-point, from which a
systematic and more complete study of these hitherto
neglected peoples may be made.

NASSAU, NEW PROVIDENCE, BAHAMAS,
        July 1890.

CONTENTS.

THE EWE-SPEAKING PEOPLES

OF THE

SLAVE COAST OF WEST AFRICA.

CHAPTER I.

INTRODUCTORY.

THE Slave Coast is that portion of the West African coast situated between the Volta River on the west and the delta of the Niger on the east, the Benin River being taken as the western boundary of the latter, and thus extends from about 30′ east longitude to about 5° 8′ east longitude.

Geologically, the features of this tract are entirely different to those of the Gold Coast. The latter, as has been already stated, is hilly, the coast-line showing numerous small hills; and the country inland rising by successive steps in ranges of hills, which culminate in the well-known Adansi Hills, and the Kwao range more to the east. It is covered with dense and impenetrable forest, and the lagoon system extends over but small areas, such as from the Volta River to the westward towards Ningo. To the east of the Volta, however, that is, from the commencement of the Slave Coast,

B

the lagoon system is almost continuous, and, generally speaking, the whole littoral consists of a ridge of sand, varying in breadth from a few yards to two or three miles, shutting off from the sea the broad stretches of shallow water that are termed lagoons.

From the existence of old sea-beaches lying parallel with the present shore, and which are to be found several miles inland, it is evident that the continent is at this part gaining upon the sea. A sand-bank is formed, and gradually rises above the sea-level, enclosing a stretch of water behind it ; then the bed of this salt lake gradually silts up, partly through the alluvium that is washed down during the rains, and partly through a slow process of upheaval which appears to be in progress ; until at last, instead of a shallow sheet of water, there is a broad sandy plain, whose origin is explained by the old beaches which bound it on the south, by the presence of lagoon shells in large quantities, and by the entire absence of every description of stone and rock. Thus the lagoon lying behind Quittah (Keta),[1] which at the time of my sojourn there in 1878 was from twelve to fifteen miles broad, has since, I have been informed, become much diminished ; and at that time there was, between Elmina Chica and Adaffia, a dry bed more than five miles broad, the soil of which was still too much impregnated with salt to admit of vegetation, showing that the lagoon had been formerly even more extensive.

The cause of the formation of these sand-ridges is at present undetermined. Possibly there may be coral reefs, upon which the sand, swept along the shore by the Guinea current, tends to accumulate ; or it may be

---

[1] Ke (sand), ta (head). Hence, "On the top of the sand."

that their formation is simply due to that current, which, acting constantly from west to east, sweeps the sand into long lines, and obliterating every bay and headland, leaves the coast-line as we now find it, almost a straight line. In 1878 a sand-bank began to appear above water at Quittah, parallel with and about two hundred yards from the existing beach, and, as far as I could then ascertain, it was caused solely by the action of the current. There was at that time an undoubted tendency towards the formation of an outer lagoon, but I am unaware if the movement has since continued.

From the sea the whole coast-line appears low and flat, without any hill to break the monotony of its outline. From six to eight miles inland from Adaffia, after traversing a sandy plain, one finds a steep bank of red earth, running east and west, surmounted by trees, and marking an ancient coast-line ; while to the north-east of Agweh, between the lagoon north of that town and the village of Akraku, there is another broad sandy plain, similarly bounded, and which, though dry at most periods, is still covered with water during the rains. Further to the eastward, however, the encroachments of the land upon the sea have been on a much larger scale. Whydah is two miles from the lagoon, which is about 300 yards broad and waist-deep, and the intervening tract consists of parallel ridges of argillaceous soil running east and west, the depression between every two ridges being almost at the lagoon level, and filled with water during the rains. The highest point in Whydah is scarcely forty feet above the sea-level. North of Savi, which is five miles north of Whydah, is the Nyin-sin swamp, which, now mere mud, is shown in the map

published in Dalzel's *History of Dahomey*, 1793, as a
large lagoon communicating with the Lagos Lagoon, and
Richard Norris (1772) refers to it as a deep and rapid
stream. Beyond Savi the old lagoon bed of alluvial
clay and crystalline sand extends as far as Toffo, which
place is thirty-five miles in a straight line from the sea,
and is covered throughout with remains of lagoon shells,
without a vestige of stone or rock. Just beyond Toffo
occurs a marshy belt, called Ko by the natives, which,
like all these depressions, runs east and west. It is
from six to seven miles broad, and at the lowest point
there is a small stream, in the bed of which rock appears
for the first time. It is undoubtedly an old lagoon bed,
and, according to native reports, it extends from the
Denham Waters on the east to the Togo Lake, or Hacco
Lagoon, at Porto Seguro on the west. It is only to the
north of the Ko that the ancient coast-line is reached,
and the bush-covered, swampy bottoms are exchanged
for open plateaux, dotted with clumps of forest.

According to the maps of the earlier European ex-
plorers, there was, prior to the seventeenth century, one
continuous water-way by lagoon from the Volta to the
Niger Delta, but its continuity is now broken at two
points, namely, between Elmina Chica and Bageida, and
at Godome. The silting up of the lagoon at the latter
place is very recent, for, within the memory of living
men, there used to be water-communication between
Porto Novo and Whydah. It is to be observed that at
these two points no rivers discharged into the lagoon,
and so assisted to keep the water-way open ; while the
Tojeng and Aka flow into the Quittah Lagoon, two
streams into the Togo Lake, the Agomeh, or Monu River,

into the Great Popo Lagoon, the Zunu, or Eso River, into the Denham Waters, the Okpara into the Porto Novo Lagoon, and several rivers, of which the principal is the Ogun, into the Lagos lagoon system. There are but three direct outlets to the sea, as the Quittah Lagoon drains into the Volta River, namely, one at Grand Popo, one at Lagos, and one at Lekki. As might be expected from its comparatively recent formation, the country is, generally speaking, open, and there is but little true forest. The valleys of the rivers are wooded, and the mangrove flourishes in the swamps and along the shores of the lagoons, but the prevailing feature of the country is a grass-covered plain, dotted with clumps of trees and euphorbia.

The climate is not less unhealthy than that of the Gold Coast, and, indeed, is by some authorities considered worse. There are two dry seasons and two wet, corresponding with the movements of the sun, which reaches the zenith about the middle of March, and again about the middle of September. The principal wet season therefore lasts from the middle of March to the middle of July; an interval of dry weather then lasts till about the middle of September, the "little rains" continue till about the middle of December, and the dry season proper completes the remainder of the year. The Harmattan wind prevails principally in January and February.

The inhabitants of the Slave Coast consist of the following tribes and states, commencing with the most westerly, and on the sea-front.

1. Awuna, whose territory extends along the sea-coast from the Volta to Kiedje, a village about five miles

east of Quittah, and comprises the islands and northern shores of the Quittah Lagoon, and the left bank of the Volta for some forty-five miles inland. The small states of Avenor and Ataklu, to the north of the lagoon, are dependencies of Awuna.

2. Agbosomi. From Kiedje to about twelve miles to the east. The territory of this tribe formerly extended as far west as Quittah.

3. Aflao, or Flohow. From Agbosomi to about six miles to the east. Its capital is Danú.

4. Togo-land. From Aflao to Bageida.

5. Geng. From Bageida to the river Akraku. This territory is divided into the districts of Porto Seguro, Little Popo, and Agweh. Gliji was the former capital of the whole.

6. Great Popo. From the river Akraku to about three miles east of the village of Arlo.

7. Dahomi. From Great Popo to Kotonu. The kingdom of Dahomi extends inland about one hundred and twenty miles; the Zunu, or Eso River, is considered its eastern boundary, and the Monu, or Agomeh River, its western; but these only have reference to the southern half of the kingdom, for to the north and north-west its limits are undefined, and to the north-east it extends certainly as far as the sources of the Yewa, and perhaps beyond. Its broadest part is to the north, and at the south it narrows to about thirty miles. Agbomi, the capital, is about sixty-one miles distant from Whydah by road, and about fifty-one miles as the crow flies.

8. Kotonu, which occupies about five miles of seaboard.

9. Fra. From Kotonu to Pogi.

10. Appa. From Pogi to Badagry.

To the east of Appa are the old states of Badagry, Lagos, and Lekki, which have for some years been blended into the colony of Lagos. These states are inhabited by Yoruba-speaking peoples, and so do not come within the scope of this volume.

Inland to the north of the territories of the above-mentioned tribes are the following—

11. Anfueh. North and north-west of Awuna. Its capital is Peki.

12. Krepe. West of Anfueh.

13. Ewe-awo. North of Anfueh.

14. Agotine. East of Anfueh.

15. Krikor. South-east of Agotine.

16. Máhi, or, less properly, Makki. This is the most north-easterly territory occupied by the Ewe-speaking peoples, and the distance to which it extends inland is unknown. It lies north of Dahomi, and is supposed to extend to the west of that kingdom in a broad belt to Krikor and Agotine. Little, however, is known about it, and it is probable that it is inhabited by semi-independent tribes, such as the Aja and the Attakpami, who live immediately to the north-west of Dahomi.

17. Ewemi. North of Kotonu. This state is subject to Dahomi.

18. Porto Novo. North of Fra.

Of these tribes 1, 2, 3, 9, 10, 11, 12, 14, and 15 are under British rule ; 4 and 5 are German ; 6, 8, and 18 are French. The boundary between the German and French territories is a meridian passing through the west point of the island of Bayol, in the lagoon, and

runs inland as far north as the ninth degree of north
latitude.

All these tribes speak dialects of one language, the
Ewe, with the exception of the people of Agotine, who
speak Adañme, the language of Krobo and of the inhabitants of the right bank of the lower Volta, and
which is a dialect of the Ga language. The Agotines, a
small tribe, appear to have emigrated and settled in
their present locality about the period of the destruction
of the old kingdom of Accra by the Akwamus in 1680.
At the same date others of the inhabitants of Accra fled
to and settled at Little Popo, where they still inhabit a
distinct quarter of the town in which the Ga language
is spoken. With the exception, then, of these two
foreign colonies from the west of the Volta, the Ewe
language prevails from that river for a distance of 155
miles eastward along the coast, and inland to an
unknown distance, probably about 200 miles. It is
also spoken in seven towns on the right bank of the
Volta, namely from Agrafo on the south to Bato on the
north, where the people of Ewe stock have migrated
across the river. Its approximate area will be better
understood by a reference to the map.

Low in the scale of civilization as are the Ewe-
speaking peoples, they have in some respects advanced
beyond the condition in which we found the Tshi-
speaking peoples of the Gold Coast ; for though both
have been, and are still, obstructed in their progress by
climatic influences, yet the more open character of the
country occupied by the former, where the different
communities are not shut off and separated from each
other by vast tracts of impenetrable forest, has facilitated

the interchange of ideas, and rendered them more
amenable to civilizing influences. The interior of the
country of the Slave Coast, especially in Dahomi, has
moreover been known to Europeans for a longer period
than that of the Gold Coast. The Prah was crossed and
Ashanti visited for the first time by a European, Mr.
Bowdich, in 1817; whereas an Englishman resided at
Agbomi, the Dahomi capital, from 1708 to 1726; and
during the latter part of the eighteenth century it was
customary for all the European residents of Whydah,
English, Dutch, Portuguese, and French, to proceed to
the capital and remain there during the celebration of
the Annual Customs; and without attributing too much
to the influence of these personages, most of whom, if
not all, were slave-traders, it may reasonably be supposed that the frequent contact with individuals of a
more advanced race had some beneficial effect upon the
natives. And this contact was so frequent that in the
preface to Dalzel's *History of Dahomey*, 1793, we find
the remark that "the short interval from Whydah
beach to Abomey is perhaps the most beaten track, by
Europeans, of any in Africa."

The Ewe-speaking peoples of the Slave Coast present
the ordinary characteristics of the uncivilized negro.
In early life they evince a degree of intelligence which,
compared with that of the European child, appears pre-
cocious; and they acquire knowledge with facility till
they arrive at the age of puberty, when the physical
nature masters the intellect, and frequently completely
deadens it. This peculiarity, which has been observed
amongst others of what are termed the lower races, has
been attributed by some physiologists to the early

closing of the sutures of the cranium, and it is worthy
of note that throughout West Africa it is by no means
rare to find skulls without any apparent transverse or
longitudinal sutures.

Like most inhabitants of the tropics, whether black
or white, the negroes of the Slave Coast have more
spontaneity and less application, more intuition and less
reasoning power, than the inhabitants of temperate
climates. They can imitate, but they cannot invent, or
even apply. They constantly fail to grasp and generalize
a notion. Thus M. Borghéro says, concerning these
very tribes—"A negro learns more easily, and in less
time, a rule of arithmetic, but when it becomes a
question of applying that rule to something besides
mere figures, of establishing some conclusion by the aid
of that rule, he is very much embarrassed; while the
European, who will have taken a much longer time to
learn the rule, will be able to deduce the general law
without difficulty, and obtain from it a variety of prac-
tical results. This difference is manifested throughout
his entire life." They are usually deficient in energy,
and their great indolence makes them easily submit to
the despotism of kings, chiefs, and priests ; while they
are as improvident as they are indolent.

Many of these moral deficiencies may be attributed
to the relaxing influences of a hot climate, which besides
being primarily inimical to physical and mental energy,
causes on the other hand a greater amount of intensity
whenever the state of indolence is overcome, to which
the savage outbursts of passion and the frantic excesses
of the negro in moments of excitement are due. Others
may be ascribed to the social condition and the general

sense of insecurity. Where life is uncertain, of what advantage is it to prepare for the morrow ? Where any improvement in condition is only likely to arouse the cupidity of an irresponsible chief, why seek to improve it ? Hence we find a great indifference to the future, and the masses regard everything not bearing immediately upon their necessities with an apathy which, in its turn, prevents them from learning by experience. The chiefs are arrogant and tyrannical, and the people servile. The latter rarely go straight towards the end they wish to attain, but seek to compass it by subterfuges and devious methods. Concealment of design is the first element of safety, and as this axiom has been consistently carried out for generations, the national character is strongly marked by duplicity. The negro lies habitually ; and even in matters of little moment, or of absolute indifference, it is rare for him to speak the truth. Concurrently with this grows up the habit of concealing resentment of injuries, and the gratification of revenge by the secret and safe agency of poisons.

As a result of all these inimical influences the energy of the whole people has degenerated into idleness and sensual enjoyment, and it will take centuries to raise them, for nature exercises a paramount influence on the development of the human being, which is the more powerful the nearer a people is to a natural state, for in civilized communities he gradually learns how to combat it. In all this, however, we see the effect of external conditions, and there is no reason for supposing that the white races had originally a greater mental endowment than the black. If they have succeeded in arriving at higher results in the same period of time, it is only

because they have been more happily situated. But at
the present time most Englishmen, especially those who
are interested in the promulgation of the different
forms of the Christian religion, appear to think that, if
that religion is imposed upon the negro, a civilization
approximately equivalent to that of Europe will then
ensue almost at once as a matter of course. They hold
the view that our civilization is the outcome of our
religion, whereas the converse is the truth. Moreover,
the pagan negro who is, to use the stock phrase, converted to Christianity, is not thereby raised to the
European moral standard. Moral characteristics transmitted by heredity cannot any more be effaced by a
simple change of belief than can physical ; and the converted negro invariably and necessarily lowers the new
religion to the level of his own mental culture. In any
case, however, we are now some 2000 years in advance
of the negro, and that is a gap which cannot be cleared
at a bound. Any endeavour to force upon him our
artificial conditions of existence must fail, for racial
character cannot be suddenly transformed ; and, even if
it were possible to impose our civilization upon him, it
would not be lasting, for the various transitional stages
between his position and ours would have been wanting.
Civilization must be gradual in order to be permanent;
for it is only as each successive forward step is won that
the racial character becomes strengthened, and capable
of making a further advance.

CHAPTER II.

RELIGIOUS BELIEFS.

IT is in their religious development that the supe-
riority of the Ewe-speaking peoples over the Tshi-
speaking peoples is most apparent. In other respects
they are much on the same level; but they have
undoubtedly taken a step in advance in their conceptions concerning their gods. On the Gold Coast we
found a multitude of village gods, a few tribal gods,
and none at all which were worshipped by the Tshi-
speaking peoples as a whole ; but amongst the Ewe-
speaking peoples we find a different state of affairs,
which may probably be in a great measure due to the
greater facilities for the interchange of ideas possessed
by those people. Their gods are more concrete. Instead
of a thousand different villages possessing each a god,
each of whom resembles all the others in general attributes and functions, but is believed to be essentially
separate and individual, we find on the Slave Coast the
same gods, worshipped under the same name, in every
town and in every considerable village, represented by
images modelled on a common plan, and possessing in
every case identical attributes and functions. On the
Gold Coast there are no general objects of worship,[1] few

[1] The gods which I have, in my former work, styled "General
Deities," are not worshipped by the whole of the Tshi-speaking tribes.

tribal, and many local ; while on the Slave Coast, though there are still many local and tribal objects of worship, there are also a great number of gods who are worshipped by the Ewe-speaking peoples as a whole. It will hardly be disputed that, as the village community is necessarily antecedent to the tribe, the village god must be an earlier conception than the tribal god. Hence, the possession of a number of general objects of worship by the Ewe-speaking peoples, clearly marks a step made by them in the evolution of religion in advance of the condition in which we found the Tshi-speaking peoples.

It seems that the local gods, as they exist now on the Gold Coast, have been classified on the Slave Coast, and different types produced, which are everywhere recognized and accepted. As each of these gods is represented by a particular kind of image or by particular paraphernalia, a stranger, upon entering a village, sees objects which are familiar to him, and knows to what gods the various shrines are dedicated ; but a native of the Gold Coast, on entering a strange village, would know neither the names nor attributes of the local gods whose shrines he might see. Doubtless this consensus of ideas has been brought about by the priesthood, who are on the Slave Coast possessed of an organization such is as yet unknown on the Gold Coast ; but though the chief objects of worship are thus known and defined, there is still an absolute toleration, and every man is at liberty to worship any one god, or as many as he pleases.

I have already stated the conclusions to which my investigation of the religious notions of the Gold Coast negro brought me; but as they are scattered here and there throughout the volume on the Tshi-speaking people, it will perhaps be as well to recapitulate them here concisely. Shortly stated, they are as follows—

Partly through dreams, and partly through the condition of man during sleep, trances and states of syncope, the Tshi-speaking negro has arrived at the conclusions—

1. That he has a second individuality, an indwelling spirit residing in his body. He calls this a *kra*.
2. That he himself will, after death, continue his present existence in a ghostly shape. That he will become, in short, the ghost of himself, which he calls a *srahman*.

Now 1 has very frequently been confounded with 2, though they are essentially distinct. The *kra* existed before the birth of the man, probably as the *kra* of a long series of men, and after his death it will equally continue its independent career, either by entering a new-born human body, or that of an animal, or by wandering about the world as a *sisa*, or *kra* without a tenement. The general idea is that the *sisa* always seeks to return to a human body and again become a *kra*, even taking advantage of the temporary absence of a *kra* from its tenement to usurp its place. Hence it is that any involuntary convulsion, such as a sneeze, which is believed to indicate that the *kra* is leaving the body, is always followed by wishes of good health. The *kra* can quit the body it inhabits at will, and return to it again. Usually it only quits it during sleep, and the occurrences dreamed of are believed to be the adventures of the *kra* during its absence. The *srahman*, or ghost-

man, only commences his career when the corporeal man
dies ; and he simply continues, in the ghost-world or land
of dead men, the existence the corporeal man formerly
led in the world. There are, therefore, in one sense,
three individualities to be considered—(1) The man ;
(2) the indwelling spirit, or *kra;* (3) the ghost, or *srahman*—though in another sense the last is only the
continuation of the first in shadowy form.

This belief in an indwelling spirit, or " soul," as it is
generally termed, though that word is not at all applicable, and its use has led to serious misconceptions,
is almost universal amongst uncivilized races, and the
manner of its origin is now very generally acknowledged.
Shortly stated, man arrives at the belief that living men
have a second individuality by dreaming about living
men, whom he afterwards finds not to have taken part
in, or to be conscious of, the occurrences of which he
dreamed ; and that dead men continue to exist in their
former shapes by dreaming of dead men.

The bulk of the evidence yet collected with regard
to uncivilized tribes goes to show that, more generally,
these two existences appear to be considered as one, and
that the shadowy being or ghost which continues in the
dead world the existence of the living man, is no other
than what was the indwelling spirit or *kra* of the latter ;
but this is far from being universally the case.   As Dr.
Tylor has shown,[1] the Fijians distinguish between a
man's " dark spirit " or " shadow," which goes to Dead-
land, and his " light spirit," which stays near where he
dies ; the Malagasy say that the *saina,* or mind, vanishes
at death, but that the *matoatoa,* or ghost, hovers round

[1] *Primitive Culture,* vol. i. p. 434.

the tomb ; the Algonquins believe that every man has two " souls," one of which abides with the body at death, while the other departs to the land of the dead ; and the Karens distinguish between the " la," or " kelah," which may be defined as the personal life-phantom, and the " thah," which is the soul. The Navajo Indians have a similar belief, for Dr. Washington Matthews says,[1] —" The suppliant is supposed, through the influence of witchcraft, exercised either in this world or in the lower world when in spirit he was travelling there, to have lost his body or parts thereof—not his visible body, nor yet his soul, his breath of life, for both of these he knows himself to be still in possession of, but a sort of spiritual body which he thinks constitutes a part of himself." These appear to be instances of a belief fairly parallel with that held by the Gold Coast negro, and doubtless a more careful examination will discover many more ; for Europeans, holding as they do, the belief in one " soul " only, are naturally prone to misconceive a native's idea of two " souls," unless, which is rarely the case, they are aware that such a belief is known to exist amongst certain peoples.

The Tshi-speaking negro does not limit the possession of a ghost, or soul, to man, but extends it to all objects, inanimate as well as animate ; and, acting logically upon this belief, he releases these ghosts, or souls, from their material parts, for the use of ghost-men in Dead-land. At the death of the chief he buries with the corpse, weapons, utensils, food, gold-dust, and cloth, for the use of the ghost-chief ; just as he cuts the throats

---

[1] *The Prayer of a Navajo Shaman,* p. 19. Reprinted from the *American Anthropologist,* vol. i. No. 2, April 1888.

of the chief's wives and slaves in order that their ghosts or souls may be released from their bodies, and enabled to continue their attendance upon their lord in Dead-land. In this respect his belief is similar to that held by every uncivilized people of the past or present; but he has gone beyond this, and just as he believes himself to have a second individuality, or indwelling spirit, so does he believe every living creature, and every object not made by human hands, to have similarly a second spiritual self, or indwelling spirit. He holds that just as when the man dies, the *kra* of the man enters a new-born child, and the ghost-man, or soul, goes to Dead-land, so, when the bush is torn up and withers, the *kra* (so to speak) of the bush enters a seedling bush, or a seed, and the ghost-bush goes to Dead-land.

Similarly, the *kra* (so to speak) of the sheep, when that sheep is killed, enters a new-born lamb, and the ghost-sheep goes to Dead-land for the use of ghost-men; but whether that ghost-sheep's career definitely terminates when it is killed and eaten by ghost-men we do not know: the negro has not pushed inquiry so far as to ask if there is anything beyond.

Not only does in Dead-land the ghost-man live in a ghost-house and use the ghosts of such implements, &c. as have been placed at his disposal; but Dead-land itself, its mountains, forests, and rivers, are, the Tshi-speaking negro holds, the ghosts of similar natural features which formerly existed in the world. The trees, as they die in the earthly forest, go and join the ranks of the shadowy forest in Dead-land; and though the negro has not perhaps witnessed or even heard of the destruction or disappearance of such features as

ountains, lakes, or rivers, &c., yet since they are in Dead-
nd, as his dreams testify, he decides that they came
be there by a similar process of destruction or decay.

The belief that animals, trees, plants, and inanimate
bjects have ghosts is, as has already been said, uni-
ersal amongst uncivilized peoples, who, in this respect,
re more logical than the modern European believer in
pparitions, who claims a ghost for man, but denies it
r inanimate objects; though it would be curious to
quire, since ghosts are not usually believed to appear
aked, what it is they wear if not the ghosts of clothes.
ut while all uncivilized peoples are known to believe
at inanimate objects have ghosts, it has not, as far as
know, been ascertained whether they believe, as does
he Tshi-speaking negro, that while they are in existence
this world also, such inanimate objects have spiritual
dividualities, or, so to speak, *kras.* The question does
ot seem even to have been referred to in the text-books
f Anthropology, and yet there are, beyond doubt,
any different peoples, widely separated, who do hold
his view. For instance, Dr. Washington Matthews
ays, of the Hidatsa Indians [1]—" They worship every-
hing in nature. Not man alone, but the sun, the
noon, the stars, all the lower animals, all trees and
lants, rivers and lakes, many boulders and other
eparated rocks, even some hills and buttes which stand
lone—in short everything not made by human hands,
vhich has an independent being, or can be individual-
zed, possesses a spirit, or, more properly, a *shade.* To
hese shades some respect or consideration is due, but
ot equally to all. For instance, the shade of the

[1] *Ethnography of the Hidatsa Indians,* p. 48.

cotton-wood, the greatest tree of the upper Missouri
Valley, is supposed to possess an intelligence which
may, if properly approached, assist them in certain
undertakings ; but the shades of shrubs and grasses are
of little importance." I venture to think that future
investigation will show that most uncivilized peoples
hold this belief, and that it has hitherto been overlooked, is, I imagine, due to the *kra* and the ghost
having been confounded together—to the second having
been considered the first when finally separated from
its tenement.

This belief in every animate and inanimate natural
object having two individualities besides its tangible
one, will perhaps help to explain much that is still
obscure as to the origin of Nature Worship. It must
be borne in mind that the *kra* is not the soul, for
the soul, in the accepted sense of the word, is "the
animating, separable, surviving entity, *the vehicle of
individual personal existence,*[1] whereas every *kra*
has been the indwelling spirit of many men, and
probably will be of many more. The *kra* in some
respects resembles a guardian spirit, but it is more
than that. Its close connection with the man is
indicated by the fact of its nocturnal adventures
during its absence from the body being remembered
by that man when he awakes. The latter even feels
physically the effect of his *kra's* actions, and when a
negro awakes feeling stiff and unrefreshed, or with
limbs aching from muscular rheumatism, he invariably
attributes these symptoms to the fact of his *kra* having
been engaged in some struggle with another, or in some

[1] Dr. Tylor.

severe toil. If, moreover, a man dreams of other men, he believes that his *kra* has met theirs; consequently the *kra* is held to have the outward appearance of the man whose body he tenants. Hence the *kra* is more than a mere tenanting, or guardian, spirit. It has, though doubtless only in a shadowy form, the very shape and appearance of the man, and both the mind and the body of the latter are affected by, and register the results of, the *kra's* actions.

The Theory of Animism is divided into two parts— (1) That which treats of the souls of individual creatures, capable of continued existence after the death or destruction of the body; and (2) That which treats of spiritual beings, who are held to affect and control man's life and the events of the material world. For the origin of the belief in souls we have the explanation already referred to, namely, that it originated through dreams, and the condition of man during sleep or suspended animation, an explanation which is now very generally accepted. For the origin of the belief in the spiritual beings we have no such satisfactory explanation, and I therefore venture to put forward what may be called the *kra* theory; which, even if it will not apply to other peoples, will possibly explain how the negroes of the Gold and Slave Coasts of West Africa came to believe in the existence of such beings.

The Tshi-speaking negro believes that every natural object or feature has what we may call its *kra*. Not to multiply instances, rivers and trees, let us say then, have *kras*. Some day a man falls into a river, and is drowned. The body is recovered, and is found to present no external injury which in the experience of

man would account for death. What then caused the
death? asks the negro. Water, alone, is harmless:
he drinks it daily, washes in it, uses it for a variety of
purposes. He decides, therefore, that water did not
cause the death of the man, and having an entity, a
spiritual being, ready to hand to whom to attribute the
disaster, he concludes that the river's *kra,* its indwelling
spirit, killed the man. This alarms him. If one man
can be dragged down and killed by the river-spirit, why
not another—himself perhaps? He seeks how to mollify
this powerful being, and a worship is established. Another time a tree falls in the forest and kills a child.
How was this? Trees do not commonly fall down and
kill people. On the contrary, they ordinarily stand
firm, and even the strongest men cannot uproot them.
He follows the same train of thought, and arrives at
the same conclusion. Evidently the tree's *kra,* the
tree-spirit, cast down the tree on the child. The tree-
spirit must be propitiated; something must be done to
keep it quiet. Whether the notion of a *kra* had hitherto been restricted to man, and the negro now extended
it to all Nature to account satisfactorily for such accidents ; or whether he had already formed the belief that
all natural objects and features possessed *kras,* and such
accidents only served to prove to him their malignity
and power for evil, the result would be the same. In
either case, that form of religion which we term Nature
Worship would ensue.

The indwelling spirit of a natural feature or object
is not, it must be observed, regarded as being inseparably
bound up with that object, but can quit it and return
at will, just as the *kra* of the human being can quit the

body it tenants. It can wander about, and, at a later stage of belief, can enter the image made to represent it, or the priest, who then becomes inspired; but its ordinary dwelling-place is the natural object or feature of which it is the indwelling spirit.

These are the actual ideas of the Tshi-speaking negroes of the Gold Coast at the present day, and they can also be found in the beliefs of the Ewe-speaking peoples, though there overlaid to a certain extent by ideas of a later growth. Naturally those indwelling spirits which time and experience show to be innocuous are not much regarded; as with the Hidatsa Indians, "the shades of shrubs and grasses are of little importance"; and in course of time the belief becomes centred on those spirits which are believed to possess the power and the desire to injure. Thus we find, generally speaking, that the objects whose indwelling spirits are worshipped, are such as rivers, lakes, the sea, mountains, &c., localities in which accidents are more likely to occur; or such phenomena as lightning, storm, and earthquake, which are frequently accompanied by loss of life. Proceeding on the same lines the Ewe-speaking negroes have given pestilences a spiritual individuality, and on the Slave Coast the small-pox is a god who is much dreaded. Possibly, too, in this way, the worship or reverence paid to beasts of prey, such as the leopard, the crocodile, and the shark, may be accounted for. It may originally have been a propitiation of the indwelling spirits of such creatures. However, the actual ideas of the natives of the Gold Coast being as I have stated, we have here a possible explanation of the origin of Nature Worship; viz. the belief

in the gods of rivers, rocks, mountains, lakes, etc., grew
up alongside of, and in consequence of, the belief that
man has in his body an indwelling spirit called a
kra.

I am aware that the origin of Nature Worship has
by some anthropologists been ascribed to Ancestor
Worship, to the fear and respect felt by the living for
ghost-men, but I do not think this will apply to West
Africa.   On the Gold and Slave Coasts sacrifices and
appeals for aid are sometimes made to the dead, but the
dead are certainly not considered gods by the natives.
The fact that they are shadowy men, or ghost-men,
appears to me to be never lost sight of, and they are
in an entirely different category to the gods of natural
features.   They seem to be considered as guardians or
protectors, a view which is supported by the word for
ghost-man, " *srahman*," and which being compounded
of *srah*, to watch or guard, and *oman*, family, community,
village or tribe, affords fair evidence of what the original
conception of a *srahman* was ; while the primary idea
concerning the gods of natural features was, and with
regard to the great majority of them still is, that they
are beings who must be propitiated in order that their
malignity may be averted.

It may be urged that the intention and object of
prayers addressed, say, to a chief who has been dead
for some considerable time, might be forgotten and
distorted ; and that, through a confusion of ideas, and
in consequence of these prayers being usually, if not
always, offered at the spot where the chief was buried,
the ancestral ghost might become identified with that
spot, and so come to be considered a *genus loci*, or

indwelling spirit of some natural feature. No doubt this is possible, and it may sometimes have happened, but not frequently, I think. Considering the invariable practice of the negro of burying the dead in the earthen floors of the huts, it is difficult to understand how the ghost of a man so buried could come to be identified with a river, a mountain, or a tract of forest. It could not generally be that the hut, in which the man lived and in which he was buried, stood near to some such feature. Ordinarily it is the deepest pools of rivers, the most hidden recesses of the forest, the cliffs or more inaccessible parts of mountains that are believed to be the dwelling-places of local gods, and these are situations where it is improbable that man would have dwelt. How could the awe and respect felt for a dead ancestor become developed into the dread of a being supposed to dwell in some such locality? And the confusion of ideas would have to take place not three or four times only, but thousands of times, for the local gods of the Gold Coast alone may be numbered by tens of thousands. Besides, I have found that the people of the Gold and Slave Coasts do not address prayers to chiefs or ancestors who have been dead for any considerable time. Whether they believe that they have been too long absent from earth to have preserved any interest in its affairs, or whether it is that they simply are forgotten, the fact remains that except in the royal houses of Ashanti and Dahomi, where the bones of former rulers are carefully preserved, the negroes do not ask for assistance from remote ancestors. On the whole then I cannot think that, in West Africa, the gods of natural features are simply deified dead men :

the other explanation of their origin seems more in accordance with existing facts.

A belief in a local god, the god of a river, lake, or mountain, once established, the rest follows easily. Propitiatory offerings are made to him, and it becomes important to ascertain what pleases and what displeases him. Then, as I have elsewhere shown, persons are set apart to make this a study, or to tend the offerings; and in this way arises a priesthood. The priests, naturally, for their own ends, endeavour to magnify the importance of the god ; they wish to emphasize the necessity for their office. They attribute to him superhuman powers and a cruel disposition, but allege that they know how to mollify him. Perhaps up to this stage the people had no clear idea as to what the god's moral and physical character was like ; they feared something that possessed the power to injure, but had no clear conception of it. The priests rectify this omission, and having first supplied the god with moral attributes, next furnish him with a shape, an image, a tangible object to represent the absent god, who remains in his river or mountain, but who enters the image to receive the homage and sacrifices of his worshippers. They give him a name also. Thus, reduced to form and substance, the career of the god is assured. He is no longer a vague, shadowy being, varying according to individual notions.

This is the stage in which we left the Tshi-speaking peoples of the Gold Coast. The more important local gods have been supplied with tangible representations, but the great majority of them are still undefined in the popular mind, and the belief in every animate and

inanimate object having a second individuality as well
as a ghost is still in full vigour.

Next the priesthood becomes better organized.
Possibly the priests see that it is prejudicial to the
success of their profession to have one set of men in one
village worshipping, say, a lightning-god with one set
of ceremonies and paraphernalia, and another set, perhaps in a village only a few miles distant, worshipping
another lightning-god, whose functions are essentially
the same as the first, with totally different ceremonies.
They see it would be better to have some common plan ;
and by degrees they contrive to blend five or six hundred
local lightning-gods into one general lightning-god, who
is everywhere represented by the same sort of image,
and who is everywhere served with the same ceremonies.
This is the stage of religious development the Ewe-
speaking peoples of the Slave Coast have now reached ;
the gods of similar type have been aggregated, while
those of the Gold Coast are still segregated.

As a consequence of the blending together of a
number of individual gods of the same type into one
general god of that type, there ensues a loss of the idea
which caused a belief in the existence of the individual
local god to arise. These local gods, originally held to
be the indwelling spirits of certain local features or local
phenomena, are severed from their local habitats and
centred in one general god, with the inevitable result
that the notion of the indwelling spirit disappears. Thus
we find on the Slave Coast that the General Deities are
not the indwelling spirits of natural features ; they are
beings independent of any tangible abode. This change
was probably materially forwarded by the priests having

represented that the god entered the image, and that consequently sacrifice and prayer might be made before the image instead of in the actual habitat of the god, as was done before images came into use. The result of years of such a practice would necessarily lead to a weakening of the tie between the god and his habitat, to an obscuring of the notion of the indwelling spirit. But although the original conception has been lost sight of by the Ewe-speaking peoples with regard to the gods that are worshipped generally, yet, as there are still a great many local gods left, it has not altogether disappeared. It has really only been limited to the lower grades of gods, and there is abundant proof of its existence.

This state of affairs gives us a curious example of how the development of religion may proceed. The local gods of the Slave Coast are on the decline, for they cannot compete with the renown of the general gods, who are supported by a well-organized priesthood. In the next stage of development they will lose ground still more, they will become water-sprites, gnomes, and wood-nymphs ; then they will only linger in the popular imagination as elves or fairies, and finally they will disappear. In the meantime the general deities will have been struggling together for supremacy, or, in other words, their priests will. The less powerful or renowned will first drop out of the race, and their number will continue diminishing until there are only two or three ; the survivors assimilating to themselves the functions of those who disappear. The last stage is reached when there is only one god left, who combines in himself the attributes of all those he has survived.

This stage lasts a long time, for the priests being all interested in the same god, there is no rivalry between gods which tends to damage both, and man has seen so many gods pass away that he clings despairingly to this last one. But this stage, like all the preceding ones, is bound to terminate, and finality is only reached when the last surviving god has been pulled down from his pedestal and disgraced.

The generic terms used by the Ewe-speaking peoples for gods and superhuman or supernatural agencies of all kinds, are *edrŏ* and *vŏdu*, which thus correspond to the Tshi term *bohsŭm*, the Ga term *wong*, and the Yoruba term *orisha*. The word *vŏdu* is that most commonly used in Dahomi and by the eastern tribes, and *edrŏ* by the western. *Vŏdu* appears to be derived from *vŏ* (to be afraid), or from *vŏ* (harmful), and *edrŏ* from *drŏ* (to direct, judge, or execute). From the latter are a number of derivatives, such as *drŏnu*, witchcraft; *drŏnu-wola*, witch or wizard; *drŏive*, dream or vision (literally, place or region of the gods, or mystical region); *kudrŏ*, to dream (literally, to attain a godlike or mystic condition). The accent (~) in the above indicates a highly nasal intonation, and *ẘ* represents the aspirated *w*, or *hw*.

The term *vŏdu*, it may be mentioned, is still used at the present day in the West Indies, in the so-called Vaudoo, or Vaudoux worship of the negroes of Hayti, at which, according to the testimony of Spencer St. John,[1] a human victim is still offered, and where the old python *culte* of Whydah still survives in the worship of a non-venomous snake of the island. It may also be traced in Louisiana, under the same name, Vaudoux, but the *culte*

---

[1] *Hayti, or the Black Republic.*

has there degenerated into a number of insignificant superstitious practices, nothing remaining of the original but the name, and even that a recent American author has proved, to his own satisfaction, is derived from the Pays du Vaud. That the term *vŏdu* should survive in Hayti and Louisiana, and not in the British West India islands, will surprise no one who is acquainted with the history of the slave trade. The Tshi-speaking slaves, called Coromantees in the slave-dealer's jargon, and who were exported from the European forts on the Gold Coast, were not admitted into French or Spanish colonies on account of their disposition to rebel, and consequently they found their way into the British colonies, the only market open to them; while the French and Spanish colonies drew their chief supply from the Ewe-speaking slaves exported from Whydah and Badagry.

For the sake of convenience, I propose describing the gods of the Ewe-speaking peoples in the following order—

(1) General Deities ; that is, gods worshipped by the Ewe-speaking peoples as a whole.

(2) Tribal Deities ; that is, those worshipped by one or more tribes.

(3) Local Deities.

CHAPTER III.

GENERAL DEITIES.

I. MAWU.—The god who ranks first in the religious system of the Ewe-speaking peoples is named Mawu, a word which, besides being a proper name, has also the meanings of sky, firmament, and rain. It is derived from *wu* (to stretch over, or overshadow), and the god himself is no other than the indwelling spirit of the firmament, the deified canopy of the heavens.

The Ewe-speaking peoples, like most uncivilized races, imagine the earth to be flat; they have mentally divided the horizon into four quarters, namely, in front, behind, to the right, and to the left, and so come to fancy that the earth is square; while they believe the whole to be enclosed by the heavens, which is to them a solid and tangible roof to the earth, stretching over to the four corners and there joining them. The universe is to them contained as it were in a rectangular box, with an arched top, the top being the sky and the bottom the earth ; and their four points of the compass are *Anyi-go* (lower-side), North ; *Dsi-go* (upper-side), South ; *Wu-go* (sea-side), East ; and *We-go* (Ewe-side), West.

Wherever man believes in a plurality of gods it is

natural that he should imagine that they differ from
each other at least as much as individual men differ;
that some are more powerful than others, and that one,
answering to his own king, chief, or other earthly ruler,
is the most powerful of all; and in selecting the god
who is to fill the latter position, what is more natural
than that he should assign the chief place to the, to
him, huge and solid mass of the sky, which encompasses
the earth like a vast roof, and which, if the sky-god
were ill-disposed, could so easily crush out all earthly
life ? The firmament, the sun, or the moon, appear
obviously the nature-gods that uncivilized man would
consider the highest, in preference to such terrestrial
objects as the sea, rivers, mountains, &c.; and in West
Africa the bias of the negro mind appears to have been
almost universally in favour of the first.

Mawu, then, is regarded by the Ewe-speaking peoples
as the most powerful of the gods, but he is not a supreme
being or creator. Although he is the chief, he is but
one of many independent gods. I am aware that this
is not the view commonly held by the German missionaries, who are the only class of Europeans who ever
seem to try to discover what the religious beliefs of the
natives really are. They are of opinion that Mawu is
held to be the lord of the terrestrial gods, who are
subordinated to his control, and some even go so far
as to say that he created them ; but though one may
occasionally obtain from natives who inhabit the sea-
coast towns, and who, having all their lives been in
contact with Europeans, have become familiar with the
European notion of a creator and supreme god, state-
ments that go to corroborate this, yet it is evident that

this is a modification of the more original conception of Mawu, and is due to European influence ; for natives who have not been subjected to that influence distinctly hold the view that Mawu, though the most powerful, is simply one of many gods, each of whom is perfectly independent in his own domain, and subject to no control whatever. The genuine native idea is that each god is quite independent of every other, and free to act as he pleases. Thus Khebioso strikes with lightning, Sapatan sends the small-pox, and Legba excites sexual desires without any reference or subordination to Mawu or any other god. Hence it is that the native finds it necessary to worship every god to whose actions he is exposed ; for to offer sacrifice to one or two only would not guarantee him from the consequences of the anger of those he had neglected.

But though Mawu is considered the most powerful of all the gods, sacrifice is never directly offered to him, and prayer rarely. He is in fact ignored rather than worshipped. The natives explain this by saying that he is too distant to trouble about man and his affairs, and they believe that he remains in a beatific condition of perpetual repose and drowsiness, the acme of bliss according to the notion of the indolent negro, perfectly indifferent to earthly matters. It is a question as to how far this belief may not be due to the fact that the firmament, though sometimes obscured by the clouds of Khebioso, always remains the same, outspread, calm, and serene, and that no disaster or misfortune can be referred to it. To this belief may be undoubtedly attributed the absence of sacrifice to Mawu. To the native mind, a god that works no evil to man, and is

D

indifferent to his welfare, is one that it would be a work
of supererogation to mollify or appease, while there are
so many other gods who either work evil and have to be
appeased, or are special guardians and have to be lauded.
Mawu controls the rain supply, and keeps a vast store
of water in the firmament, which he lets out at will.
This seems to be his only function with regard to man ;
and as the seasons on the Slave Coast are regular and
well-defined, and there is rarely either flood or drought,
the natives do not often find it necessary to address
him. The following reply made by a chief of the Tobas
to a missionary who had said his God was good and
punished wicked people—" My god is good likewise, but
he punishes nobody, satisfied to do good to all," might
fairly well be applied to Mawu ; and if we were to substitute " satisfied to leave every one alone " for the last
part of the sentence, it would be exactly in accordance
with the ideas of the Ewe-speaking negroes.

I have said above that sacrifice is never offered
directly to Mawu, and this requires some explanation.
The indirect sacrifice consists of the indwelling spirits of
domestic fowls and other birds sacrificed to the terrestrial
gods, and which are believed to ascend to Mawu, and to
be, as it were, his portion of the sacrifice, the body
being that of the terrestrial gods. The explanation of
this notion seems to be as follows.   In the imaginations
of the Ewe-speaking negroes, there is, under the blue
sky, which is the roof of the world, and extending from
it to the earth, a region termed *khekheme*, a word which
may be translated " free air region." This region is
traversed by birds alone of all earthly creatures, whence

[1] Hutchinson, *Chaco Indians*, in Tr. Eth. Soc., Vol. iii. p. 327.

a bird is termed *khe-vi*, "child of the free or open air."
On this account birds are considered to some extent as
mysterious creatures, and there are a variety of superstitions about different birds, which will be stated further
on, while their indwelling spirits are regarded as having
some connection with, or relation to, Mawu, because it
is they alone who soar up into *khekheme*, and approach
his dwelling-place, the sky. A small bird, a variety of
the oriole, that soars like a lark, and makes a whirring
noise by striking its wing-feathers together, is sacred to
Mawu.

Christianized natives, and natives who have been
much in contact with Europeans, have very generally
confused the Jewish god, Jehovah, with Mawu ; while
Roman Catholic missionaries have imagined Mawu to
be a surviving recollection of the former. For this reason
they term themselves Mawu-no—"Mawu's priests," in
opposition to the *Vōdu-no*, or *edrō-kosi*, or priests of the
native gods ; but Protestant missionaries have been
more cautious, and generally translate Mawu as "the
unknown god." This mutual mistake arose very
naturally. The ordinary unscientific Christian, although
he may have abandoned the notion that the sky is a
material tangibility, still holds, somewhat illogically,
that his God dwells in the sky. He also believes that
he controls the rain-fall, and he still addresses prayers
to him for rain ; while, not very long ago, before the
phenomenon of rain was understood, the Christian idea
was like that of the negro at the present day, that there
was a vast store of water above the blue firmament,
which Jehovah let out at will. The Ewe-speaking
natives, then, on learning that the God of whom the

missionaries spoke, had the same dwelling-place and the same functions as Mawu, very naturally concluded that Jehovah was only a foreign name for Mawu ; while the missionaries, by a similar process, conceived Mawu to be an obscure recollection of Jehovah.

This blending together of Mawu and Jehovah is one of the chief causes of what are called relapses into heathenism.   A negro, on being converted to Christianity, does not any the less believe in the existence of the gods of his country ; on the contrary, he is still convinced that they are absolute entities, a belief which some of the missionaries are simple enough to share ; only, instead of calling them gods, he now calls them devils, and instead of sacrificing to them, he relies upon Mawu-Jehovah to protect him from their machinations. While all goes well he remains in this state of mind ; but, directly he meets with misfortune or ill-health, then inevitably recurs to him the latent notion of Mawu's indifference to human affairs ; and attributing the misfortune or sickness to one of the god-devils, he thinks it would only be prudent to propitiate him by a little sacrifice and worship.   He calls in a native priest, and the relapse is complete.

While upon the subject of this god, I may as well say that, from additional evidence I have since collected, I now think that the view I expressed concerning the origin of Nyaukupon, the parallel god of the Tshi-speaking peoples, was incorrect ; and that instead of his being the Christian God, borrowed and thinly disguised, I now hold that he is, like Mawu, the sky-god, or in-dwelling spirit of the sky ; and that, also like Mawu, he has been to a certain extent confounded with

Jehovah. It is worthy of remark that *nyan-kum* means "rain," and *nyan-konton*, "rainbow," while the word *nyankupon* itself is as frequently used to express sky, firmament, thunder or rain, as it is as a proper name.

II. KHEBIOSO.—Khebioso, whose name is often abbreviated to So, is the lightning-god, and the word itself is sometimes used to mean lightning, though the more correct term for that is *so-fia*. On the Gold Coast the lightning is wielded by the sky-god, Nyankupon, but here it has been made the weapon of a separate entity, who is much feared, since he strikes with lightning those who offend him.

The name Khebioso is compounded of *khe* (bird), *bi* (to let go light, or throw out light), and *so* (fire), so that it literally means the bird, or bird-like creature, that throws out fire. As the thunder-cloud rolls along in *khe-kheme*, "the free-air region," and as that region can, to the native mind, only be traversed by birds, the Ewe-speaking negroes imagine that Khebioso is a flying god, who partakes in some way of the nature of a bird. The general idea seems to be that Khebioso is a bird-like creature, hidden in the midst of the black thunder-cloud, from which he casts out the lightning; and by some, the crash of the thunder is believed to be the flapping of his enormous wings. This belief in the lightning-god being bird-like does not stand alone. The Mandans of North America believed that lightning and thunder were caused by the flashing eyes and flapping wings of the terrible Heaven-bird, and the Tupi tribes of Brazil hold similar views.

On the Slave Coast, as is generally the case elsewhere, flint implements of the Stone Age are believed

to be thunderbolts, and are consequently called *so-kpe,*
(*kpe* = stone). After a building has been struck by
lightning, the priests of Khebioso, who at once run to
the spot to demand that the inmates should make
amends for the evident offence they have given their
god, almost invariably produce a flint arrowhead, or
axe, which they of course bring with them, but pretend
to have found in or near the building. As Dr. Tylor
says,[1] the fact that siliceous stones actually produce a
flash when struck, gives a key to the widespread belief
that flint implements are thunderbolts.

Besides his priests, Khebioso, like most of the gods
of the Ewe-speaking peoples, has a number of women
consecrated to his service, and who are commonly
termed the "wives" of the god, the native name for
them being *kosio.* They take care of the various
shrines of the god, but their chief business is prostitution. Khebioso is said to have fifteen hundred "wives"
in Dahomi alone.

Worshippers of Khebioso may generally be distinguished by an iron arm-ring, which is often ornamented
with zigzag lines like our conventional sign for a flash
of lightning. It is worn as an amulet, with the idea
that the god may by its means discriminate between
those who worship and those who neglect him, and so
spare the former.

A house ignited by lightning may not be extinguished, for the obvious reason that to do so would be
to act counter to the wishes or decrees of the god ; and
might, in consequence, bring down his anger upon the
entire community. A native who infringed this law

[1] *Primitive Culture,* vol. ii. p. 262.

would probably be put to death, and Europeans even
are expected to observe it; a most unusual exception,
for in all other cases the natives are quite indifferent as
to what white men do or say about the gods. In
March 1863, lightning struck the quarters of the French
Catholic missionaries at Whydah, and set fire to them.
The inmates naturally extinguished it, and the principal,
M. Borghéro, was brought before the Yevo-gan (captain
of the white men), to answer for his conduct. He was
ordered to pay a fine to the priests, as an offering to
pacify the god, and upon his refusing compliance was
imprisoned ; but was subsequently released upon payment of a fine to the Yevo-gan, instead of to the priests
of Khebioso.

Even if a house be struck by lightning and not set
on fire, such an accident itself carries with it very
serious consequences to the inmates ; for it is at once
invaded by a mob of priests and worshippers of the
lightning-god ; who, while pretending to search for the
holy *so-kpe*, the thunderbolt, strip the house of everything portable, and secure their plunder in the large
wallets always worn by followers of Khebioso. In
addition, fines and compensation are demanded ; for the
fact of the house having been struck is proof that the
inmates must have been guilty of some act or omission
which has angered the god. If the fine imposed cannot
be paid—and the priests are generally very extravagant
in their demands—imprisonment or slavery follows, and
it is not at all uncommon for a whole household to be
enslaved in consequence of such an accident.

When lightning strikes and kills a man, no search
is made for the *so-kpe*, possibly because the conditions

afford no opportunity for plunder, but the priests and
" wives " of Khebioso seize the body, with loud cries
and shouts of " Khebioso has killed him—He was in-
famous, he was evil, and Khebioso has killed him. He
struck him, and he is dead—the wretch, the monster,"
drag it off by the heels to the market-place, or some
open space in the town, and there expose it on a platform. Strictly speaking, a person killed by lightning
may not be buried, but it is usual for the priests to
allow the body of a free man to be ransomed. If the
person killed be a slave, the " wives " of Khebioso cut
pieces of flesh from the corpse as it lies on the platform,
and chew them, without swallowing, crying to the
passers-by—" We sell you meat—good meat." It is
said that in times past the priest and " wives" of
Khebioso used to eat the bodies of all persons killed by
lightning, and the above practice certainly looks like a
survival of such a custom. At the present day the
priests often declare that they are going to eat the
body, but, as far as I have been able to ascertain, the
threat is never carried into effect, and is apparently only
made so that the relatives of the deceased, shocked at
the idea of the corpse being desecrated, may be induced
to give a larger ransom.

Directly the growl of thunder is heard in the distance, the priests and wives of Khebioso rush into the
street, and testify their joy at the approach of their god
by the most extravagant dances, and by loud and
unearthly shouts and cries; and their wild shrieks,
resounding in the darkness of the night in the interval
of oppressive stillness between two thunder-claps, are
heard with terror by the shuddering natives cowering in

their huts. This practice, while it tends to inspire the uninitiated with awe, also enables the priests and "wives" to see if any houses are struck; and, even if a house is not struck, it is easy for them, amid the darkness and general horror, to declare that such a one has been struck, and to produce the *so-kpe* as proof.

Saturday is sacred to Khebioso, and is kept as a holy day by his followers, who pass it in eating, drinking, and dancing. The food at these repasts consists chiefly of mutton and male kola-nuts. For sacrifice, the heads are torn off fowls, and the blood sprinkled upon the ground of the sacred enclosure, which is always surrounded by a hedge or fence made of a shrub with broad, cuneiform leaves, which is sacred to Khebioso, and is called So-yan, or A-yan. A leaf of this shrub held in the hand will, it is believed, prevent a musket from bursting.

III. LEGBA.—Legba, Elegba, or Lekpa is a phallic divinity whose worship is very prevalent throughout the Slave Coast. The phallus is seen everywhere, in front of houses, in the streets and public places, sometimes alone, but more frequently in connection with the image of Legba, to whom the organ is sacred, and whose principal attribute is the exciting of sexual desires. The name Legba may perhaps be derived from *le* (to seize), and *kpa* (to carry off), or it may merely be borrowed from the neighbouring Yoruba-speaking peoples, who have the same god. Both peoples attribute sexual desires to possession by the god, and the derivation of the name in Yoruba appears to be *Egbe* (body), and *gba* (to seize, and carry off).

The image of Legba is made of red clay, and rudely

represents the human figure, generally male, rarely female, and always entirely nude. It is always represented as squatting down and looking at the organ of generation, which is enormously disproportionate. The head is sometimes of wood, rising like a cone; the mouth extends from ear to ear, and is garnished with the teeth of dogs, or with cowries to represent teeth; the eyes are also represented by cowries. The arms of the figure are invariably immensely long, while the legs are short and the feet large; sometimes it is only the head, arms, and trunk of a man, the legs, from mid-thigh down, being omitted. Feathers are frequently planted on the head and chin to represent hair. When female, the figure is provided with long pointed breasts, and the other necessary adjuncts. The image is always seated in a dwarf temple, circular in shape as a rule, covered with thatch, and open at the sides. Anatin-kpo, or knobbed bludgeons, rude imitations of the phallus, are planted round the figure, with their knobs in the air.

He-goats and cocks are the offerings considered most acceptable to Legba, on account of their amatory capacities, and, next to these, dogs. Ordinary sacrifices, however, are palm oil and blood, with which the figure is smeared. On extraordinary occasions a human sacrifice is offered, the victim is disembowelled, the entrails placed in a dish or calabash before the image, and the body suspended on a tree or post in front of the shrine, where it is suffered to remain till it rots and falls to pieces. The turkey-buzzard is sacred to Legba, and at almost every house-door is to be seen a small clay saucer, called a Legba-zen, or Legba-pot, in which is placed, morning and evening, a little food for the bird.

Circumcision (*awá-dsodso*), which is performed on boys between their twelfth and seventeenth years, seems to be connected with the worship of Legba, it being, apparently, an offering of a portion of the organ to the god. The operation is very rudely performed, and on account of it being deferred to so late an age, not unusually has fatal results. It is performed by all classes, and no woman would have intercourse with an uncircumcised male. Excision, which is so prevalent in northern West Africa, is here entirely unknown. In Dahomi, and the eastern Ẃe-states generally, on the contrary, the clitoris and the nymphæ are artificially elongated, the operation being performed by women specialists, and a woman in the natural state is an object of ridicule. This custom, which, like circumcision, is connected with the worship of Legba, was first noted by Bosman, about 1702. It is worthy of note that among the Tshi-speaking tribes, where there is no trace of phallic worship, there is also no circumcision; amongst the Ga-speaking tribes there is a little phallic worship, and circumcision is generally observed; while amongst the Ẃe-speaking tribes, where phallic worship is prevalent, circumcision is universal, and alongside of it is this operation performed on women. It certainly looks as if, in this part of the world, there was an intimate connection between the worship and the rite.

Erotic dreams, which, amongst the peoples of the Gold Coast, are, like all other dreams, attributed to the adventures of the *kra* during his absence from the body,

are here, amongst the eastern Ewe-tribes at least, very
generally attributed to Legba, who is supposed to
have possessed the body during sleep.   In this, perhaps,
we have a key to the belief in such nocturnal demons as
the *incubi* and *succubi*, who disturbed the peace of mind
of monks and nuns in the Middle Ages; and to the
possibility of conception through supernatural possession
by a god during sleep.

In certain processions in honour of Legba, the phallus
is borne aloft with great pomp, fastened to the end of a
long pole.   The worshippers dance and sing round it,
and the image is waved to and fro, and pointed towards
the young girls, amidst the laughter and acclamations of
the spectators.   Sometimes the phallus is concealed by
a short skirt, or petticoat, which a man causes to fly up
by pulling a string.

The mysteries of Legba and the excesses committed
during them are of a nature which does not admit of
any description here.   It will be sufficient to say that
the "wives" of Legba, that is the women dedicated to
his service, give themselves indiscriminately to the worshippers of the god, as, according to Strabo, was done
by the Armenians in the worship of the phallic deity
Anaitis; and that at the commencement of the ceremony
the priests cause the worshippers to drink a mystic
draught, containing powerful aphrodisiacs.   The mysteries
almost invariably take place at night, and usually in the
"bush," at some little distance from human habitations.

Besides exciting desires, Legba removes barrenness.
A sacrifice is offered, and the worshipper anoints the
organ of the figure with palm-oil, in order that the
required fertility may be attained.

In addition to his primary attribute, Legba is the god of discord, who delights to make mischief and foment quarrels. In illustration of this propensity there is a popular tale to the effect that, having observed how friendly two neighbours were together, and determining to make them quarrel, he put on a cap, one side of which was white and the other bright red, passed between them as they were working together in a plantation, gave them " good-day " so as to attract their attention, and then went on. When he had disappeared, one of the two friends said—

" What a fine white cap that man had ! "

" White ? " replied the other. " It was red."

" Not at all," said the first. " It was white, I saw it plainly."

" So did I," rejoined the second. " It was red."

And so they bandied words till the quarrel waxed warm, and finally ended in a fight, in which one man fractured the skull of the other with his hoe.

In his capacity of a mischief-maker Legba can, if bribed by a sufficient offering, be induced to take up the quarrel of a worshipper, and work evil upon the unconscious offender. Hence it is common for natives who wish to revenge themselves upon some one who is too powerful to be attacked openly, to sacrifice a he-goat, or dog, anoint the image with palm-oil, and pour out a copious libation of palm-wine, informing the god that the injury is now left to him to be redressed. To the native mind, if the person indicated be not most powerfully protected, calamity will soon overtake him.

At the court of Dahomi there is a special body of servitors whose duty it is to have charge of the king's image of Legba. They are known to Europeans as the " King's Devils."

IV. Dso.—This deity is the god of fire, and the word is also used to mean fire itself. Fire-worship, as it exists among the Ewe-speaking peoples, does not appear to be a feeling of awe or reverence for any particular fire or flame, but rather an adoration of fire generally as a manifestation of the fire-god, a superhuman and commonly invisible being of the ordinary type, who manifests his displeasure by conflagrations and by accidents through fire. There is no sacred fire kept up, whose extinction is regarded as unlucky, nor is there, as far as I have been able to ascertain, any ceremony of putting out fires at certain seasons and rekindling them. Fire seems to be regarded to some extent as a means of purification from sacrilege, and an example will be found in the description of the python worship in the chapter on Tribal Gods.

When a house is first built it is usual to place a pot containing fire in one of the rooms, and to offer sacrifice to it, in order to put the house under the protection of Dso, so that it may not be destroyed by fire. In former days the man in whose house a destructive fire originated was always put to death, as a warning to others ; because the danger of a conflagration spreading to other houses being so great, everybody had an interest in Dso being properly served and propitiated, so that he might not find it necessary to manifest his displeasure by setting fire to the house of a negligent servitor. At the present day the person in whose house a fire originates is made responsible for all the damage caused thereby, but in the remoter districts it is said the old death penalty is still sometimes enforced. During the Customs of 1772, when Mr. Norris was at Agbomi, a fire broke out in one of the palaces, and as soon as it was extinguished he called on the king as a mark of respect. He found him much excited; several heads, to the number of twenty at least, lay scattered about, those of the women who had lived in that part of the palace where the fire originated, and who had been put to death in consequence; and he sold nineteen more women to Mr. Norris, for exportation, as a punishment.

Dso-vodu, or *Dso-sesa* are the amulets worn in honour of Dso by his worshippers, or placed on their houses. Those worn by individuals consist of necklets or armlets made of a cord of twisted fibre, smeared with red earth, with beads or small stones attached; and those for houses and property, of a country grass-rope, also smeared with red earth, with dead leaves attached at intervals. These latter are placed round the object they protect. The idea of the natives is that the fire-god will see by these tokens that they are faithful to him, and that he will consequently spare them and their property.

It is a common practice for a person whose property has been stolen to take a lighted stick from a fire, and wave it round the head till it is extinguished, praying the while that the thief may die as the fire dies in the stick. It is not clear, however, whether this practice has any connection with the worship of Dso, though, according to some natives, Dso is the agent whose assistance is invoked to procure the death.

V. Anyi-ewo.—Anyi-ewo is the rainbow-god, who manifests himself in the form of a serpent, and only appears, it is believed, when he is thirsty and requires water. At such times he is seen by man with his tail resting on the ground, and his head raised up into the sky, above the clouds, to where Mawu keeps his store of rain. He drinks prodigious quantities of water, and all that he spills falls down like rain. When he has drunk enough, he goes down again to the edge of the world and there rests.

The notion of the rainbow only appearing when it is thirsty, comes evidently from the fact that the rainbow is never seen except in company with rain. The Karens of Burma[1] have a similar belief, and the common saying when a rainbow appears is, " The rainbow has come to drink water ; " while the Zulus have almost exactly the same notion as the Ewe tribes, for they believe that the rainbow is a snake, and when it touches the earth, they say it is drinking at a pool.

Most travellers in West Africa have called this god Dañh ; but *dà* (as the word is pronounced by the western Ewe tribes) or *dañh* (as it is pronounced by the eastern) means any snake, and not the rainbow snake alone. His proper name is Anyi-ewo—*anyi* (lower part, or underneath), *ewo* (a large snake)—" Great snake of the Underneath," because he ordinarily lives underneath, or over the edge of the world, and only comes up into the sky when thirsty. In Whydah and Porto Novo he appears to have another name, which Captain Burton writes Aydo-whe-do, and the French missionaries Aïdo-wedo and Aïdo-Khouédo. This, I believe, has the same meaning as Anyi-ewo, which is the name by which the god is universally known by the western tribes ; but as I have lost a vocabulary I had collected of words of the

[1] *Journal As. Soc. Bengal*, 1865.

eastern dialect, I am unable to speak positively. Speaking from memory, I think that Aido-wedo is a corruption of Aïdó-ewo-dò : *aï* (earth, or under-part), *dó* (edge), *ewo* (a large snake), *dò* (large), and hence means, "The great snake of the under-edge."

Popo beads, the aggry-beads of the Gold Coast, curious mosaics whose origin is undetermined, and which are much valued by the negroes, are believed to be made by Anyi-ewo. His excrement is believed to have the power of transmuting grains of maize into cowries ; whence comes the notion commonly held by Europeans in West Africa, that Anyi-ewo confers wealth on man.

The temples of Anyi-ewo are usually painted with the colours of the rainbow, in stripes, and in the middle of the prism a snake is often rudely drawn. His messenger is a small variety of the boa, but only such individual snakes of this kind as are declared by the priests to be his messengers are free from molestation, and all others may be killed with impunity. When one of these boas has been declared a messenger, palm-leaves are scattered about his habitat, to warn natives of his sacred character ; and henceforward he is free of the locality, and may seize and devour the fowls of the villagers unmolested.

Anyi-ewo, like many others of the gods of the Slave Coast, has his own distinguishing pottery. His consists of a snake, rudely fashioned in clay, with two small red feathers for horns, coiled up in a shallow earthen pot, or calabash. This is whitewashed, and placed commonly under silk-cotton trees.

VI. HUNTIN. } These gods are the indwelling spirits
VII. LOKO. } of the silk-cotton and odum, or

E

poison, trees respectively, and the first seems to answer to the Srahmantin of the Gold Coast. Trees which are the special abodes of these gods—for it is not every tree of these two varieties that is so honoured—are seen surrounded by a girdle of palm-leaves; and the sacrifices made, usually fowls, but on extraordinary occasions human victims, are fastened to the trunk, or laid against the foot.

When Bosman wrote (1770), Huntin was the second of the three chief gods then worshipped in the kingdom of Whydah, and, like the two others, had a province under his protection. After the conquest of Whydah by Dahomi, in 1727, the god was relegated to a somewhat lower position; but he still has a numerous priesthood, and large numbers of " wives " scattered throughout the country. Both he and Loko are chiefly sacrificed to in time of sickness.

Loko has only a few " wives," but he has his own distinguishing pottery, namely, a clay pot, full of small holes like a cullender, and another with a very narrow neck. Water is offered to Loko, and is contained in the second pot, which is generally seen at the foot of the tree beside the first pot, but separated from it by an iron rod planted in the earth.

A tree distinguished by a girdle of palm-leaves may not be cut down or injured in any way, and even silk-cotton and odum trees that are not supposed to be animated by Huntin or Loko, cannot be felled without certain ceremonies being performed; they being considered to appertain to these gods to some degree, or to be under their protection. A negro who wishes to cut down one of these trees must first offer a sacrifice of fowls and palm-oil, to purge him, as it were, from the proposed sacrilege, and to omit to do so is a punishable offence. A few years ago, indeed, a native of Porto Novo, in the service of a European, who cut down a silk-cotton tree by his master's order, was arrested and beheaded by the king without trial, although the man pleaded that he thought the necessary propitiatory offering had been made.

The owl is the messenger of Huntin and Loko, and any one who wishes to be revenged upon an enemy can go to a tree which is the abode of one of these gods, offer sacrifice, and invoke the god to send his messenger to eat out the heart of the offending person by night.

The owl is believed to proceed on this mission night after night, and gradually devour the heart, whence it is that the word for owl is *khedome-ku—khe* (bird), *dome* (body), *ku* (to kill), "Bird that destroys the body." Natives believe that wizards and witches assemble at the foot of these trees by night to worship Huntin and Loko, and whenever an owl is seen in a house it is believed to have been sent by a dabbler in black art to kill one of the inmates. The only mode of escape in such a case is to catch the bird and break its legs and wings, which has the effect of breaking the legs and arms of the person who sent it.

Throughout West Africa, from the Senegal to the Niger, the silk-cotton tree is regarded with reverence, and believed to be the abode of a god or spirit ; this general consensus of opinion being no doubt due to the stupendous size attained by these trees, which tower far above all others of the forest. It is by no means unusual to see silk-cotton trees which measure 100 feet round at

the base, and rear a stately column from 70 to 100 feet
high before a single branch is thrown out ; while the
branches frequently extend laterally from 40 to 60 feet.

VIII. AIZAN.—This god is the protector of markets,
public places, gates, and the doors of houses, and here
performs the functions of the multitudinous local
market-gods of the Tshi-speaking peoples. He is represented by a cone of clay, large or small indifferently,
with a stone or a clay saucer at the apex or base, on
which are poured daily small offerings of palm-oil, palm-
wine, and food.

IX. HOHO.—This god is the tutelary deity of twins,
who are called *Hoho-vi*, and their mother *Hoho-no*. He
is, of course, only worshipped by twins, so that shrines
of Hoho are not very common : he has no " wives."
The pottery of Hoho consists of small double pots,
called Hoho-zen, either like two pipe-bowls, or two
miniature, decanter-shaped pots joined together ; and an
iron utensil, called the Asen, consisting of two small iron
cones fastened to an iron rod about six inches long, is
also peculiar to Ho-ho.

A woman who bears twins is now honoured amongst
the Ewe-speaking tribes ; but if the old travellers were
correctly informed, such a birth was considered a scandal
in the former kingdom of Whydah, the people believing that no woman could have two children by one
man.

X. SAPATAN.—Sapatan is the small-pox god, who lives
in deserts and the hidden recesses of the forests. His
symbol is a large staff, marked with red and white
blotches, and flies and mosquitoes are his messengers.
He is at all times much dreaded, and during an outbreak

of small-pox his priests are able to dictate any terms they please to the terrified people.

It is worthy of note that the Ewe-speaking peoples have no earthquake-god, corresponding to the Sasabonsam of the Gold Coast. This is probably because there are only two occasions on which earthquake shocks are known to have been felt on the Slave Coast, one in 1778, and one in 1858; for it is only in countries where earthquakes occur with some frequency that we find a belief in an earth-shaking god. The earthquake of 1778 threw down portions of the palaces in Agbomi, and the Dahomis, according to Dalzel,[1] applied to the Europeans at Whydah for an explanation of the phenomenon, they having not even a tradition of such an occurrence. The whites, thinking to reform the king, informed him that it was the manner in which their god showed his displeasure, and that sometimes the earth opened and swallowed entire towns and even provinces, with their inhabitants; but this did not produce any change in the king's conduct, no doubt because he thought, like all other pagan negroes, that the god of the whites concerned himself with white men alone. The second earthquake occurred on 10th July, 1858, and when Gelele, the Dahomi king, asked the priests to explain what it was and whence it came, they declared that it was caused by the late king, Gezo, who was impatient to have his retinue in Dead-land swelled by the ghosts of fresh human victims.

[1] *History of Dahomey*, London, 1793, p. 206.

CHAPTER IV.

TRIBAL DEITIES.

I. Dañh-gbi.—This deity is the python, which is worshipped in the kingdom of Dahomi, especially at Whydah ; at Agweh, at Great and Little Popo, and in the kingdom of Porto Novo. *Dañh*, as has been before said, means " snake," and *gbi* or *gbe* is a contraction of *agbi*, " life," so that the name Dañh-gbi, implies " Life-giving snake." The snake itself is not worshipped, but rather its indwelling spirit; the outward form of the python being considered the manifestation of the god.

This serpent *culte* appears to have originated at Whydah (We-ta),[1] and from the testimony of the early voyagers the python was the chief god of the old king-doms of Ardra (Allada) and Juida (Whydah). Although the worship of the python has now extended through Dahomi, it is evident from the history of the conquest of the sea-board states by that power, that at that time it was a strange religion to the Dahomis. In 1726, when Guadja Trudo marched to invade the kingdom of Juida, the army found its progress arrested by the lagoon or swamp which runs east and west to the north of Savi. There was only one fordable spot, and that of

[1] *We* (house, household), *ta* (head, summit).

so narrow a front, that five hundred men might easily have defended the passage against the entire army; but the Juidas had confided the defence to their tutelary deity, the python, and the Dahomis, on discovering this, crossed the swamp without opposition, killed the snake, and captured Savi. The conquerors treated the serpent deities of the Juidas with utter contempt. According to Snelgrave [1] they seized the sacred pythons, saying, "If you are gods, speak and try to defend yourselves," and then disembowelled, roasted, and eat them. However, with that absolute toleration in matters of religion that prevails in uncivilized communities, the Dahomis did not prohibit python-worship, and the remnant of the Juidas who escaped the slaughter of Trudo's conquest, continued it; with the result that after a few years the Dahomis adopted its worship themselves.

Tradition has it that the people of the kingdom of Juida advanced the python to the dignity of the principal national god, on account of the signal services it rendered when they were on the point of being vanquished by a powerful army that threatened their independence. Overwhelmed by superior numbers, they were giving way and the foe was already shouting victory, when suddenly Dañh-gbi appeared in the ranks, caressed the faltering soldiers with his tail and head, and reanimated their courage; so that, when the chief priest raised the god on high in his arms, and showed him to the army as a guarantee of victory, the Juidas rushed forward in a frenzy of enthusiasm and swept all before them. On this account, continues the tradition,

[1] *History of the Conquest of Juida.*

a splendid temple was built for Dañh-gbi at Savi, in
which the priests preserved the individual python who
had led them to victory.

This temple with its inmates was destroyed by the
Dahomis at the capture of Savi, since which the chief
seat of the worship has been the town of Whydah; but
many people believe that the original python, that
turned the tide of battle in favour of the Juidas, still
lives. The popular idea is that he is hidden in a gigan-
tic tree, which is growing somewhere in the depths of a
vast forest. Every morning the snake climbs to the
topmost branch of the tree, wraps his tail round it, and
hangs head downwards towards the earth, to measure
his length. When he has grown long enough to touch
the ground, he will be able to reach the sky and climb
up into it.

Dañh-gbi is the god of wisdom, and of earthly bliss.
He is also the benefactor of mankind, for the first man
and woman that came into the world were blind, and
mankind would have been blind to this day had not
Dañh-gbi opened their eyes. The white ants are his
messengers, and their nests may often be seen surrounded with palm-leaves, to show that they are in his
service. Whenever a native sees a python near a nest
of white ants he at once informs a priest, who then
places round it the protecting circle of palm-leaves, for
nests not so encircled are not free from molestation.

Dañh-gbi has his special offerings, iron rods bent so
as to give the appearance of the serpentine curves or
concentric folds of a snake, and a rude, bell-shaped
image of iron. These are considered representations of
Dañh-gbi, the former representing the male python, and

the latter the female, and are constantly to be seen on the shores of lagoons, the banks of streams, or near springs or pools, for the god loves the neighbourhood of water. Near these are calabashes, or covered earthen vessels, containing water and other offerings.

The Dañh-gbi-we (House of Dañh-gbi), or Python Temple at Whydah, consists of a circular hut thatched with grass, a privilege accorded to shrines and temples only, standing in a small oblong enclosure near the middle of the town. Inside the fence are a few sacred trees, a small round hut containing an image of Legba, and, on the ground, calabashes and earthen vessels containing water, maize-flour, palm-wine, cowries, fowls, and other offerings made by worshippers. Several long poles of bamboo are planted in the fence, and the long strips of white cotton floating from these indicate the sacred character of the locality. The snakes, usually about fifty in number, have free exit from the temple, holes being left in the mud walls to allow of them passing in and out; and they can move about the town, or even go into the bush, the only occasions upon which they are carried back to their abode, being when they have entered some profane spot, such as the house of a European. In such a case, a priest goes to fetch the errant god, purifies himself by rubbing certain fresh green leaves violently between the palms of his hands, and then prostrating himself before the reptile, takes it up gently in his arms and carries it home.

Opposite the Dañh-gbi-we are the schools or seminaries of Dañh-gbi, in which any child who may happen to touch, or be touched by, one of the pythons, has to be kept an entire year, at the expense of the parents,

and taught the songs and dances peculiar to the worship.
In old days adults were similarly liable, particularly
women, and not even the daughters or wives of the
most influential chiefs were exempt f.om this penalty
for having come in contact with the python-god. The
scandals that resulted from this practice, however, and
the decline of the priestly power, have caused it to fall
into desuetude of late years.

Unlike the variety of boa which is regarded as the
messenger of the rainbow-god, certain individuals only
of which are to be treated with respect, every python
of the Dañh-gbi kind must be treated with the utmost
veneration, wherever met. A native of Whydah who
meets a python in his path, prostrates himself before it,
rubs his forehead on the earth, and covers himself with
dust, in token of humiliation. "You are my master;
you are my father; you are my mother!" he cries to
the god. "My head belongs to you; be propitious to
me." Amongst the Ewe tribes who follow this worship,
a native who kills a python, even by accident, is by
custom liable to be burned alive, and a European to be
beheaded. Fifty years ago a native was invariably
burned to death for such an offence, but at the present
day, though the appearance of carrying out the old
sentence is preserved, the culprit is allowed to escape
with life, and a heavy fine is imposed. A small hut of
dried grass is built, usually near the lagoon, the guilty
man thrust inside, the door of plaited grass closed on
him, and the hut set on fire. As the culprit is un-
bound, he has no difficulty in bursting out of the frail
tenement long before the flames can reach him; but he
does not escape scot-free, for the snake-worshippers, who

are waiting outside, have the right to beat him with clubs and sticks, till he has purified himself by reaching running water.

L'Abbe Bouché mentions a case of this kind that came under his notice. A young negress, slave to the Chacha,[1] accidentally crushed the head of a python under a door, and the priests demanded her as a victim. The Chacha could have settled the matter by paying a certain sum, for his position placed him above all ordinary rules, but he preferred to keep his money, and a hut of straw was accordingly built, on one side of an open space near the temple of Dañh-gbi; and the young girl, and five men who had been guilty of the same offence, having been shut up in it, it was set on fire. They, of course, at once broke out, and the *mosio* of the Chacha, placing themselves round the girl, and four of the men, who had bribed them, escorted them safely through the crowd, which did not dare to attempt to strike them for fear of striking the *mosio*. All its rage then was vented upon the fifth man, who had neglected, or been unable, to offer a bribe. He was furiously assaulted with sticks, his head and back soon streamed with blood, and he only escaped by jumping into a palm-oil cask that lay in the shallow lagoon.

Even in former days Europeans were rarely put to death for molesting the python-deity, a heavy fine being almost invariably substituted; but Europeans have been slain on account of Dañh-gbi. Des Marchias (1731) tells a story of a Portuguese, who, when leaving Whydah, secreted a python and put it in a box,

___

[1] The Chacha is the chief of Whydah who has the superintendence of commerce.

intending to take it to Europe; but the canoe in which he was going off to his ship was upset in the surf, he drowned, and his sacrilege exposed; and as soon as the news spread, an excited mob invaded the houses of all the Portuguese established in Whydah, plundered their property, and even killed one or two who had not had time to take refuge with the other Europeans. The popular fury was only calmed by means of considerable presents. The same traveller mentions also the case of a newly-arrived Englishman, ignorant of the local superstitions, who killed a python that he found in his bed, and who was only saved from the mob by the king taking the case into his own hands for adjudication.

Dañh-gbi has numerous "wives," probably to the extent of two thousand. They are called Dañh-si, except at Agweh and the Popos, where Dañh-wi is the more common term. Dañh-gbi marries these "wives" secretly in his temple, and the mysteries of the initiation are unknown, but it is of course the priests who consummate the union. The ordinary duty of the "wives" is to bring water for the pythons, and to make grass mats, but at the festivals they decorate the temple, make the sacrifices, and look after the food and drink of the dancers. The *fêtes* are usually kept up all night, and are horrible orgies at which the "wives" give themselves up to the most unbridled libertinage. It is the god, they say, who possesses them and makes them act thus: it is he also who makes them pregnant.

Of late years the worship of Dañh-gbi has somewhat fallen from its former high position, and it is apparently on the decline. This is shown by the mitigated penalty now imposed for killing pythons, and also by the fact that the processions in honour of the god, which were formerly held annually, and celebrated with great pomp, having now almost entirely ceased. The temple is now only visited once during the year by the Yevogan, or viceroy of Whydah, shortly after the Annual Customs, when he presents a bullock, goats, fowls, rum, &c. to the priests, and invokes the good offices of the god in behalf of the king and the crops.

In former times, on the eve of the day for the public procession, the priests and Dañh-si went round the town, announcing the approach of the festival, and warning all the inhabitants, white and black, to close their doors and windows, and to abstain from looking into the streets. Death was the punishment of any one who was detected peeping out, even through a crevice; and report says that more than one European who violated this prohibition, and were secretly denounced by their native servants, fell victims to poison. The natives never ventured to disobey the injunction of the priests, because, apart from the fear of punishment, they believed that if they set eyes on the god in the procession their bodies would at once become the prey of myriads of loathsome maggots. Fortunately for us, many Europeans seem to have found their curiosity too much for their prudence, for we have abundant evidence of what used to occur.

On the morning of the great day all the priests and "wives," armed with clubs, rushed furiously through all the quarters of the town, beating to death every dog, hog, or fowl they came across—for dogs annoyed Dañh-gbi by barking at him, hogs killed and eat him, and fowls pecked at his eyes. After this slaughter, the python, which had been carefully reduced to a condition of torpidity by a hearty meal, was placed by the priests in a silk hammock, carefully covered from sight by a large piece of silk or damask, and the procession was then formed. First came a body of priests and "wives," armed with clubs, probably to destroy any straying dog, hog, or fowl that had escaped the massacre; and, following them, a number of men beating drums and blowing horns. Next came the hammock containing the god, borne by eight men, round which danced four priests and four "wives," all stark-naked, singing songs in his honour; and another body of priests with clubs brought up the rear. In this order the streets of the town were paraded throughout the entire day, and at nightfall an orgy was held in the temple enclosure. According to some, this procession was designed to remove all sickness from the town. The last took place in 1857 or 1858.

The other festivals held in honour of Dañh-gbi were not secret, and the populace could take part in them. There were three held every year, when oxen, sheep, fowls, &c. were sacrificed, and the day was passed in dancing, singing, feasting, and drinking, amid the sounds of barbaric music. On these occasions the priests drank rum mixed with blood.[1] Shortly before the immolation of the victims for sacrifice, the "wives" used to simulate possession by the god, and placing on their heads small bowl-shaped clay pots, would walk, with strange contortions of body and shaking of head, to the lagoon, crying out that the god was leading them, and that was why the pots did not fall. After filling the pots with water, they returned in the same manner.

[1] This is still done in the Vaudoux ceremonies in Hayti.

Public processions in honour of Dañh-gbi were also formerly held in times of pestilence, war, or drought, and on such occasions human victims were sometimes sacrificed. The god was paraded with great pomp, amid volleys of musketry and the sound of horns and drums ; and offerings of all kinds, merchandise, cowries, rum, &c., were made to propitiate him. The principal ceremony, however, was that which followed the succession of a new king of Dahomi. It was presided over by the mother of the king, and repeated three months later under the direction of the Yevo-gan.

II. W̓u.—This god is the Ocean, the junior of the three principal gods formerly worshipped in the old kingdom of Whydah, and whose worship has since spread into Dahomi. His name is generally spelt Hu, but the proper pronunciation is with the aspirated *w̓* (*hw*)—*w̓u*. All along the western portion of the Slave Coast, the natives, like those of the Gold Coast, see in the roar and motion of the surf a multitude of gods, each of whom is worshipped in his own proper locality, so that there are two or three local sea-gods to almost every village along the shore ; but at Whydah and its neighbourhood this is not the case, and W̓u appears to be considered the god of the sea generally, and not of some portion only.

Although W̓u was the junior of the old Whydah triad, at the present day his chief priest, the W̓u-no, takes precedence of all other priests in Whydah. When the surf, which is nearly always so bad as to render landing difficult even in surf-boats, becomes so bad as to stop all commerce, the W̓u-no goes in procession to the beach, and invokes the sea to be calm. " Oh, W̓u ! W̓u, the

terrible ! Wu, the immense ! be less angry. If you
want rum, if you want cowries, if you want palm-oil—
here they are : " and the offerings, thus enumerated are
cast into the waves. So little change has taken place
since 1693, that the ceremony witnessed by Captain
Phillips in that year, when, at the complaint of the
head-men, the king of Whydah sent the Wu-no to
pacify the angry sea-god, answers equally well for the
present day. Says Phillips [1]—" Accordingly he sent his
fetish-man with a jar of palm-oil, a bag of rice and corn,
a jar of pitto,[2] a bottle of brandy, a piece of painted
calico, and several other things, to present to the sea.
Being come to the sea-side, he made a speech to it,
assuring it that his king was its friend, and loved the
white men ; that they were honest fellows, and came to
trade with him for what he wanted; and that he
requested the sea not to be angry, nor hinder them to
land their goods; he told it that if it wanted palm-
oil, his king had sent it some; and so threw the jar
with the oil into the sea, as he did, with the same
compliment, the rice, corn, pitto, brandy, calico, &c."

The king of Dahomi occasionally sends an ambassador
to Wu, in the person of a man who is carried in a hammock, with all the paraphernalia and state of a chief,
from Agbomi to the sea-shore, then taken out to sea in a
canoe and thrown overboard. Mr. Bernasko, a mulatto,
and native Wesleyan missionary, met such a *cortége* on
13th July, 1860, when on his way to Agbomi. The
ambassador was riding in a hammock dressed as a chief,
with a large umbrella canopy, and a chief's stool. The
people told him, " the poor man was going to be thrown

---

[1] Astley's *Collection*, vol. ii. p. 411.   [2] Maize beer.

into the sea, to join the two porters of the sea-gate, to open it for his (the king's) father to enter in and wash himself."

The temple of Wu at Whydah is a circular hut, thatched with grass, near the large market. It is filled with the usual skulls, bones, and other relics of offerings.

III. LISSA.} Lissa, or Lisa, is the spirit of the Sun,
IV. GLETI. } which is called *ge* in the Awuna dialect, *wo* in the Anfueh, and *whi* in the Ffon, or Dahomi dialect. He is worshipped in Dahomi and the eastern Ewe states. His emblem is a pot of red clay with a cover, both striped with white, and having on the top the image of a chameleon (*agāma*), which is the messenger of Lissa. This pot is usually seen placed on a small mound, and filled with water. Offerings of food are sometimes made to it. The male chameleon, as represented on these pots, is distinguished from the female by its figure being curved.

Lissa has his "wives" (*Lissa-si*): they are distinguished by long strings of black and white beads, and on ceremonial occasions carry iron rods curved in serpentine undulations.

This god is sometimes called Dsi, or Se; but *Dsi* means really "spirit," or "heart," and is not a proper name.

Lissa married Gleti, the Moon, sometimes called Dsinu, or Suñh. They had a vast number of children, but as the young suns, when they grew up, tried to follow their father in his daily course across *khekheme* (free-air region), he became jealous of them, and so fell upon them and killed several, while the rest fled into the sea. The daughters did not try to emulate their

F

father, hence they still accompany their mother by night, while their father travels by day alone. The word for "star" in Ewe is *gletivi*, literally "moon's child"; or in the Anfueh dialect *wuletivi*, which seems to mean, "the children scattered about." According to some natives Lissa and Gleti made man.

Husband and wife do not always agree, so it sometimes happens that Lissa leaves his course to follow Gleti and beat her. When he is doing this, his black shadow comes across Gleti and obscures her light. This is the manner in which the natives explain eclipses of the moon, and at such times they throng the streets, beating drums, shrieking and shouting out—"Leave her —Be off—Go away "—in order to frighten the sun and make him leave the moon alone. This procedure always has the desired effect, as, after a time, the shadow goes away, and the moon is seen to be at peace.

On the Gold Coast and in the western Ewe states there does not appear to be any sun-worship, nor any moon-worship, properly speaking, though the new moon is generally saluted. In central and eastern Ewe, however, the new moon is always greeted with salutations, cries of welcome and expressions of respect, while at Agweh the priests and "wives" of the various gods announce its appearance by chants and processions in the street. In Dahomi the moon has her "wives," who wear, over one shoulder, long strings of cowries threaded back to back, each pair being separated by a black seed.

V. NATI.—This is a marine god, worshipped generally along the coast between Kotonu and Bageida. At Whydah he is considered a subordinate of Wu. He is the store-keeper of W̊u, and takes charge of the fish, hence he is especially worshipped by fishermen.

VI. AVRIKITI.—This is another marine god, whose worship prevails over the same area as that of Nati. He steals the keys of W̊u's stores from Nati, and supplies man with fish ; hence he also is a special object of worship for fishermen. He has numerous " wives " in the districts where he is worshipped.

Avrikiti is represented by a clay figure of a man in a sitting posture, covered round the loins with a strip of calico. There is a notable image at Agweh, on the beach, to which, on a day towards the end of October, the chiefs and principal men of the town proceed, and eat a meal before it. Towards the end of the repast they are attacked by the boys of the town, who pelt them with limes and oranges till they take to flight, a curious custom which requires explanation.

VII. NESU is the tutelary deity of the royal family of Dahomi, and hence of the kingdom, throughout which his worship is general. His shrines, called Nesu-ẘe— " Houses of Nesu," consisting of long sheds open at the sides, are to be seen adjoining the royal palaces and public buildings. According to tradition, his worship was established by Guadja Trudo about 1720.

Nesu has a number of " wives," who are distinguished by armlets and long necklaces of cowries, in which the shells are separated by red and black seeds. Water is largely used in the rites of Nesu, which are performed in secret, and one of the chief duties of the " wives " is to fetch water for this purpose. While so employed they are guarded by Amazons. Before changing his residence from one palace to another the king always sits in a Nesu-we, and offers sacrifice to propitiate the god.

VIII. Bo.—This god is the protector of persons engaged in war, and in the eastern Ewe states, throughout which his worship prevails, he takes the place of the various village war-gods, which are found in the western Ewe states as well as on the Gold Coast. His image represents a man squatting upon the haunches, with the virile organ largely developed and turgescent, and his temples, *Bo-we*, are found at town gates, markets, and other public places. In Dahomi, soldiers, who are under his special protection, wear horse-tails and strings of cowries in his honour.

Bo has a variety of objects peculiar to his worship, such as—(1) The *Bo-sio*, small clay images representing the human figure, male or female indifferently, with the distinguishing characteristics made very prominent. They are painted black, red, or blue, and some of them are attired in white caps and waist-cloths. (2) The *Asi-'avi*, a peculiar axe, made usually of brass, carried by the priests of Bo on ceremonial occasions. (3) The *Bo-so*, fasces, or bundles of sticks, from four to six feet long, painted red and white in alternate stripes, or spotted with the same colours. (4) An iron figure of the tortoise (*logoza*), carried on ceremonial occasions on the top of iron rods. (5) The *Bo-kpo*, or Bo-staff, a crutched stick, which is supposed to ward off all the evils incidental to travelling. It is carried in the hand by persons on a journey, and when not in use is planted in the ground. There is always a little skirt, called *avo* (cloth), fastened round it below the crutch, which conceals the yolk of egg and other substances smeared on

the stick, as on the sticks used by priests on the Gold
Coast. (6) A fringe of dried palm-leaves, called Azan,
tied round a person or object, places him or it under the
protection of Bo. It is believed that a man with such
an amulet cannot be injured in war, and if taken prisoner
cannot be killed. It also protects the wearer against
witchcraft.

Dahomi being essentially a military kingdom, Bo, as
the guardian of warriors, is much honoured throughout
the kingdom, and is perhaps worshipped more than any
other god. The Dahomis have a custom of adopting
mystic names, which are commonly called "Names of
the Bo-võdu," and are designed to show that the individuals who adopt them are under Bo's protection. The
king is specially protected by this god, and a stick
appertaining to Bo, called Kafo, and which is wrapped
in a white linen case, surmounted with a plume of white
feathers, is usually carried before him when he goes out.

In Dahomi the Bo temples (*Bo-we*) are frequently
elaborately decorated, and Captain Burton thus describes
a group of them that he passed between Kana and
Agbomi [1]—" A heap of ashes, the usual sign of entering
a great fetish place, points to a white village of Bo-hwé,
tabernacles, or fetish hovels, under huge cotton woods,
beginning at about 350 yards from the town gate. . . .
The nearest fetish huts are six in number, and are disposed across the road ; a neat compound for spiritual
meetings rising from the grass on the right hand. The
hovels contained effigies of chameleons, speckled white
and red ; horses, known only by their halters ; squatting men, like Day and Night at masquerades, half

[1] *Mission to Gelele*, vol. i. p. 287.

mud-coloured and half spotted; others brown all over, and grinning with cowrie-teeth; and the largest, a huge chalked gorilla, intended to be human, and completely disgusting."

The same author further describes the contents of a temple belonging to the house in which he lived while at Agbomi [1]—" There were two sets of grotesque figures ranged in a row opposite one another. That to the south numbered six. 1. A bit of iron-stone clay stuck round with feathers, and planted on a swish clay step, a couple of inches high. 2. A little Bo-doll in a cullender, or perforated pot. 3. An earthenware basin with a circular base, surrounded with the Azau, or fetish palm-girdle, and the Asen (Sein ?), or Twin-iron, stuck in the ground before it. 4. A Mon-gbo, or sheep-fetish, very easily confounded with—5. An Avun, or canine, provided with any number of claws. Finally, No. 6 was an awful-looking human face in alto-relief, flat upon its base, a swish square, with a short stake planted behind it, three small earthen pots rising from its wrinkled forehead; its huge gape of cowrie teeth, and eyes of the same, set in red clay, were right well calculated to frighten away, as it is intended to do, witchcraft from the devotee.

" The other set occupied three sides of the dwarf roofless hut ruin, and embraced everything necessary for man's welfare. A red clay kpakpa, or duck, with a line of feathers round its neck, and an artificial tail, if duly adored, makes the prayerful strong. A Bo male image, half black, half white, even to the wool, and hung with a necklace of beasts' skulls; with a pair of Hohozen, or twin-pots, two little double pipkins of red clay, big

---

[1] *Mission to Gelele*, vol. i. p. 299, *et seq.*

pipe-bowls, united like the Siamese twins, and covered with whitewashed lids to guard the water offering, would guard Sedozau and his brother from the ills to which twin-flesh is heir. . . . Defence against disease was secured by a clay parallelogram, puddinged half with cowries and half with pottery-bits stuck edgeways, and supporting an Asen-iron and an Asiovi, or fetish axe; by a red clay Bo-man with a beard of poultry-feathers, and the left side stuck with fragments of earthenware; and by a Bo-pot containing a heap of black earth rising to a ball, and supporting a fetish iron. . . ."

There were several other things in this hut, amongst them a specimen of the pottery peculiar to the rainbow-god, so that, although the articles belonging to the worship of Bo predominated, this was not properly speaking a Bo-shrine, but rather a family temple, in which the owners had collected the paraphernalia of several gods who might be useful to them, as for instance, of Hoho, for they were twins.

IX. The CROCODILE, called *elo, lo,* or *adopra* by the central and western Ewe-speaking tribes, and *jalodeh* at Porto Novo, is worshipped at Bageida, Porto Seguro, Savi, Porto Novo and Badagry. In the days of the former kingdom of Whydah there were two pools of water near the royal palace at Savi, in which crocodiles were bred, and a numerous priesthood was set apart for their service; but at the present day offerings to the crocodile are as a rule only made by persons whose avocations take them upon the lagoons, by those about to journey by canoe in the lagoons, or by members of the clan of which the crocodile is the totem, and it has no temples, or priests, or regular offerings.

It is not uncommon for canoe-men to sing chants in praise of the crocodile when they are upon the water, and l'Abbé Bouche gives [1] a specimen, sung by his canoe-men when he was travelling on the lagoon near Porto Novo. It is curious, in that it shows how the natives believe their gods to be influenced by flattery. These men, as long as they were upon the water, and within reach, so to speak, of the crocodile, lavished upon him the most extravagant praise, the object of course being to flatter and please him and induce him to leave them unmolested, though, directly they got on shore, they would have but little regard for him. The invocation or chant, which like most native ones consisted of a solo and a short chorus, the former by the head canoe-man, was as follows :—

Chorus. " Jalodeh, good deity ; guide us, shield us from harm."

Solo. " You are great, you are strong, oh, Jalodeh! If you chose you could rival Shango [2] in power. But to be cruel and terrible seems to you unworthy of a god, and you prefer to make yourself renowned by the benefits of your protection.

" We trust in you, oh, Jalodeh !—be propitious to us."

Chorus. " Jalodeh, good deity ; guide us, shield us from harm."

Solo. " You are so strong that people fear you even when they love you. But you, what have *you* to fear? The spear cannot pierce your skin, the musket-ball glances off and is lost. One can do nothing against you.

[1] *La Côte des Esclaves*, p. 222 et seq.
[2] The Yoruba lightning-god.

Nothing can resist you. He whom you protect has no need to watch ; he sleeps tranquilly when your eye is upon him.

" We trust in you, oh, Jalodeh !—be propitious to us."

Chorus. " Jalodeh, good deity ; guide us, shield us from harm."

Solo. " See in the canoe this traveller come from the land of the whites. Let no harm come to him in your lagoon, or he will believe that you are as mischievous as Legba. If he were to die, people would believe that we had not taken care of him. Show the white man that you protect men ; guide us without accident."

Chorus. " Jalodeh, good deity ; guide us, shield us from harm."

Solo. " I remember . . . . I was a child. . . . My mother led me to the lagoon and plunged me in the water. I did not know there was any danger ; I advanced, and I fell into a hole. You were there beside me, and my mother was frightened. But you, you caressed my little legs, and made me go back to a safe place.

" Jalodeh, oh, best of gods, guide us. I will always honour you, if possible, more and more."

Chorus. " Jalodeh, oh, best of gods, guide us. Always, if it is possible, we will honour you more and more."

The native idea concerning the crocodile seems to be that it is the abode of a spirit, apparently of one that has been, to use the Tshi term, a *kra* in a human body, and which, in default of a human tenement, has been obliged to use the body of a lower animal. Indwelling spirits, in these reduced circumstances, are considered to be, as a rule, though not invariably, malignant ; hence they enter, by ehoice, the bodies of creatures that prey upon man.

Some natives say that it is not every crocodile who is thus tenanted by a malicious spirit, but that, as it is impossible to know beforehand which is and which is not, it is both wiser and safer to propitiate all. Others seem to think that the indwelling spirit can pass from crocodile to crocodile at will, and others again that all crocodiles are the outward and visible sign of such inward and spiritual beings ; but there must naturally be much diversity of opinion upon such a subject, there being no established standard of orthodoxy ; and precision eannot be expected. On one point, however, they are all agreed, and that is that every erocodile who kills a man is actuated by a malignant indwelling spirit. Of course, in the districts in which it is reverenced or worshipped, the erocodile may not be molested. The whole worship may be the outcome of totemism.

X. The LEOPARD.—This animal is regarded as saered in Dahomi proper, that is in the territory north of the *Ko*, and is specially worshipped by the royal family. In the dialect of Dahomi a leopard is ealled *kpo*. As the leopard is the totem of one of the Ewe clans, this worship may also be the outcome of totemism.

Theoretically, a man who kills a leopard is put to death ; according to Commander Forbes [1] he was sacrificed to the offended deity ; but really the culprit escapes by paying a fine, and performing certain ceremonies to propitiate the god ; but no leopard-skin may be exposed to view. As in the case of the crocodile, the leopard is

---

[1] *Dahomey and the Dahomans* (1851), p. 171.

believed to be animated by an indwelling spirit ; so that when a man kills a leopard, he does not destroy that which he worships. What be does is to deprive it of its corporeal tenement, a sufficiently serious offence, and one that requires expensive atonement.

Shrines exhibiting rude effigies and fresco drawings of leopards are very common in Dahomi, and at these offerings and prayers are made to the god. Leopards' claws are considered valuable amulets, and are much prized. At the Dahomi court some of the king's wives, usually the youngest and best-looking, are distinguished by the title of " Leopard Wives " (*kpo-si*), and on state occasions wear striped cloths.

The foregoing are the tribal deities of the Ewe-speaking peoples, whose worship is most widely diffused. Every tribe and every state has its own proper tutelary deity, but as these resemble, generally speaking, the gods of similar position and power on the Gold Coast, it will be unnecessary to give any detailed account of them. There is one of these, however, whose worship is peculiar, viz. the tutelary god of the Awuna or Añlo tribe, whose residence is at Awuna, the capital of the kingdom, and who lives in a separate house, which must always be kept in utter darkness. No one but the chief priest may enter this house and commune with the god ; hence nothing whatever is known about him, and hence also the chief priest, as the mouth-piece of the deity, and promulgator of his decrees, is really the chief power in the tribe. The chief priest carries daily offerings to the god, prefers petitions to him, asks him the causes of calamities, and brings back the answers, which he is able to make what he pleases.

In Dahomi, Ewemi, and Porto Novo, Ugun and Ife
are worshipped, the former as the God of Iron, and the
latter as the God of Divination, his priests, called
Buko-no, being very numerous. Both of these, however, properly belong to the Yoruba-speaking peoples,
Ugun, or Ogun, being the god of the river of the same
name which flows into the Lagos lagoon, and Ife, or Ifa,
of the Yoruba town of Ado; and any description of
these will more properly belong to the next volume of
this series.

Wuo, the spirit of the Harmattan wind, is regarded
as a god by the eastern Ewe-speaking tribes, but he is
not worshipped. He is believed to be shut up in a
cave, under the charge of a keeper named the Wuo-
hunto, who at certain seasons opens the door and lets
out Wuo to annoy mankind. This dry wind appears to
natives of the tropics very cold and cutting, hence the
belief that the Wuo-hunto, before opening the cave,
carefully oils himself from head to foot to save his body
from being cut by the keen blast.

CHAPTER V.

LOCAL DEITIES.

THE majority of the local deities of the Slave Coast
are similar in all material respects to those of the Gold
Coast that are described in Chapter V. of the Tshi-
speaking peoples ; they belong in fact to the same level
of religious culture, and are the indwelling spirits, the
kras, so to speak, of lagoons, streams, pools of water,
tracts of bush or forest, rocks, hills, etc., or of reefs,
rocks in the sea, or portions of the sea-shore.

From the very nature of their being, from the very
fact of their being the spiritual individualities of natural
features, they have a more restricted sphere of influence
than the general and tribal deities ; for the general
deities may practically be regarded as omnipresent
throughout the territories of the Ewe-speaking peoples
as a whole, and the tribal deities throughout those of
the tribe or tribes who worship them ; since both are
worshipped daily, over large areas, in communities widely
separated. Of course the negro mind cannot conceive
the possibility of the same god being present in several
places at once, a conception which belongs to a higher
stage of religious development than that which he has
attained ; but the native never asks himself questions of

this kind, and as each group of worshippers believes that the god is, for the time being, in the image or shrine before which they are offering their prayers and sacrifice, the general and tribal gods may be taken as being, to all intents and purposes, omnipresent. The local gods, on the other hand, being each identified with some distinct natural feature or object, so that the god cannot be thought of except in connection with it, are naturally only worshipped by those who live near, for people at a distance are absolutely unaware of their existence; and although this connection with a local object gives the local god a certain fixity of tenure in that locality, yet, in another way, it tends to shorten his career. For instance, a small village community, accustomed to worship the indwelling spirit of a pool close by, is destroyed in the inter-tribal wars or forced to migrate, and this god disappears from view—no one lives near him, to fear him or to desire to propitiate him; there is no one to worship him, and his existence is forgotten. As a set off against this, however, new ones are constantly appearing. A family settles near some stream, hill, or prominent rock, and imagination and superstition, assisted perhaps by a priest, soon find an indwelling spirit, a local god; who may, if the conditions are favourable, arrive at some eminence, and, if they are unfavourable, relapse into oblivion.

On the Gold Coast the local gods are the chief objects of worship in their several localities; they are the beings with whom the inhabitants of those localities are most closely connected, and whom it is of paramount importance to propitiate; but on the Slave Coast the local gods are relegated to a much inferior position, a man's first duty being to the general gods, next to the tribal, and lastly to the local. The general and tribal gods have each their own proper priesthood, their shrines, images, and various paraphernalia, and most of them have their "wives"; but the local god has, as a rule, no image or tangible representation other than the local feature or object he inhabits, and two or three priests at the most. The result of this is that the general and tribal gods are more stable, while the local have a tendency to be ephemeral.

Every general, tribal, and local god, with the exception of Mawu, has his holy day, on which a festival is held in his honour on a scale proportionate to the number of his worshippers. These festivals always commence with a sacrifice, and if any living creature is immolated, the blood is usually smeared on the image or his paraphernalia, or scattered about the temple, amid the loud beating of drums and cries of " Hu, hu," made by the worshippers at regular intervals by striking the palm of the hand against the open mouth. After the offering the drums strike up the rhythm peculiar to the dance (*edrŏ-ge*) sacred to the god, and the dance commences. Rum and palm-wine flow copiously, the dance is followed by a feast, and before nightfall the festival has become an orgy. In the case of general gods it is sometimes prolonged over three or four days.

The blood of the living sacrifice is regarded as the portion of the offering which specially belongs to or is particularly acceptable to the god, because the natives suppose it to be the vital principle, a primitive belief that still survives in the saying, " The blood is the life." In the case of non-human sacrifices, it is usual for the priests and worshippers to cook and eat the body of the offering at the feast. When Captain Snelgrave witnessed the sacrifice of the Whydah prisoners in 1727, at which time four thousand victims are said to have been slain, the interpreter told him "that the blood was devoted to the Fetische, the head to the king, and the body to the common people." The latter part of this meant that the heads, or skulls, were the king's perquisite, to be used for the decoration of his palace walls; and Snelgrave was of opinion that the bodies were actually cooked and eaten by the Dahomi soldiery.

Prayers that are addressed to the god are not in any stereotyped form, but worshippers ask for what they want in natural language, with a certain amount of added adulation, just as they might prefer a petition to a chief. These people, in fact, have not reached that stage of religious development in which prayers are always put forward according to certain formulas, which, becoming traditional, are after a time believed to have some peculiar efficacy of themselves, and to be as it were incantations or charms. It is only the local gods who can be addressed directly by persons desiring their aid; the higher deities must be addressed through the medium of a priest, and the more eloquent the priest the more he is in request.

In Dahomi, temples and shrines alone may be thatched with grass, all other buildings being covered with palm-thatch. Both temples and sacred groves or tracts of bush are distinguished by the long streamers, usually strips of white calico, which flutter at the end of tall poles or from the branches of trees. The temples themselves are nearly always small huts, circular in shape, and so low that a man cannot enter without bending nearly double. The images of the gods are placed inside, usually on a raised rectangular platform of clay; and before them are the earthen pots and vessels, smeared with the blood, eggs, and palm-oil of countless offerings. Many of the images have long since, owing to exposure to the weather, become mere heaps of rubbish, but no one would dare to remove the sacred dust.

The most absolute tolerance prevails with regard to the worship of the gods, and it is considered quite natural that opinions should differ concerning the choice of a god. Sacrilege or insults to a god, however, are always resented and punished by the priests and worshippers of that god, it being their duty to guard his honour; but where the sacrilege is committed by a European, it is usually regarded with unconcern. For instance, Captain Phillips (1693-4) having observed, at the palace door of the king of Whydah, a large wooden image which, the natives assured him, gave forth oracular utterances, went there one night in order to hear one. After waiting a long time without anything having happened, he thrust his walking-stick into the mouth of the image, and then fired a pistol-ball into its left eye, without the natives in any way resenting it; they merely expressing surprise that the god did not kill him. The reason for this indifference with regard to the actions of Europeans, appears to be that it is generally held that the gods of a country are only concerned about the actions of the people of that country, a notion that would probably arise from a belief in the local gods, each with its limited sphere of influence

G

but that it is not always shown, the attack made on the
Portuguese in Whydah, on account of the sacrilegious
attempt on the python-god made by one of their
number, clearly proves.

Detailed descriptions of so many local gods of the
Gold Coast have been given in the first volume of this
series, that it will be unnecessary to do more here than
give a short account of some of those of the Slave Coast,
which present novel features.

On the Gold Coast nearly every sea-coast town, or
village to which Europeans have been in the habit of
resorting for trade, has its "Slayer of white men," but
there are no protectors of white men such as are found
in Whydah in the gods Dohen and Ajaruma, and formerly
in Nabbaku; and whose existence may possibly be
accounted for by the great importance that is there
attached to commerce. Of these, Dohen brings ships
and Englishmen to the English fort when that building
is empty, and protects Englishmen generally. He is
worshipped in the fort, where beans, and occasionally
sheep and fowls, are offered to him. Ajaruma's sole
function is to protect Europeans: his shrine is in the
English fort, and he is represented by a tree and a clay
pot. Nabbaku was a former protector of Englishmen,
who is now forgotten. He is described by Dalzel as
"the titular god of the English fort in Whydah."[1] The
English fort, it must be noted, like those of the French,
Dutch, and Portuguese, was simply a fortified trading
establishment, belonging to a company formed for
trading in West Africa. It was built by permission of
the native king, and was not in any sense a Govern-

---

[1] *History of Dahomey*, p. 92.

ment building. It seems that the shrines of two of
these gods were on the piece of ground on which the
fort was subsequently built ; and the merchant-governors
permitted their worship to be continued after the area
was enclosed.

AGASUN is a local deity of Agbomi, whose *culte* is
peculiar in that his high-priest, the Agasun-no, is the
chief priest in Agbomi, and ranks next to the king.

The next two are curious in having each a legend
which professes to give an account of the origin of the
local god. Both of the pieces of water concerned, however, are in the extreme east of the territory occupied
by the Ewe-speaking tribes, and the inhabitants of
that part have been influenced to a very considerable
degree by their Yoruba-speaking neighbours, who have
progressed much further in their religious development.
Originally, it seems, the deities of these two lagoons
were, like all such gods, considered their indwelling
spirits—indeed by natives who have not been so much
subjected to foreign influence they still are so considered ;
but, in the case of the inhabitants of Porto Novo, this
idea has gradually been obscured, and the existence of
the gods is now accounted for in the manner stated in
these legends. It is fairly clear that these legends are
the result of intercourse with the Yoruba-speaking tribes,
for there is not, as far as I have been able to discover,
a single legend in vogue amongst the central and
western Ewe tribes that professes to account for the
origin of any god ; while amongst the Yoruba tribes
there are scores. In fact, the former, like the peoples of
the Gold Coast, do not require any legends, for the
origin of their gods is explained to them by the, to

them, simple and reasonable idea of every natural object having, like man, an indwelling spirit; and it is only when this idea is lost sight of, as it is amongst the Yoruba-speaking peoples, that another explanation has to be sought.

The first of these two is the god of the Denham Waters, called "House of the Mother" (*No-we*) by the natives, a name which is explained as follows :—" Long ago, on the spot where the lagoon now is, but which was then dry land covered with dense forest, there lived a priestess. One day this priestess gave birth to a child, but instead of being full of joy, as women always are, and caressing it, she refused to suckle it and threw it out of the door. The child, thus abandoned by its unnatural mother, immediately began to run about in the forest, calling upon all the gods, but more particularly on the lightning-god, to protect it; and invoking them to destroy the forest and his mother's house, to show that, though she despised him, he was acceptable to them. The lightning-god listened to this appeal, and he destroyed the forest, burning it up with lightning, and changing it into a deep lagoon."

The natives have a superstitious dread of the waters of this No-we lagoon. If a criminal ventures upon its surface, he will, they say, be sucked down and killed; and misfortune will surely overtake any one who takes up its water in the hollow of his hand, or who, after having filled his calabash with water from it to drink, throws out the residue.

This lagoon, it may be observed, formerly communicated with the sea, and the memory of this opening is still preserved in a number of local songs. The Dahomis, when they advanced to attack Appa in 1778, having no canoes with them, closed the channel with thousands of baskets filled with sand; since which time the old bed has silted up to such an extent, that a plain some four miles broad now separates the lagoon from the sea.

The second god is TOGBO, the deity of the most northern of the three narrow lagoons or creeks that connect the Porto Novo lagoon with the Denham Waters. The native name of the creek is Tochi; by Europeans it is commonly called the Ewemi canal. The part of the creek in which the god resides is used by the inhabitants of Porto Novo and the surrounding districts for the purpose of carrying out the ordeal by water. Persons charged with an offence, and who declare themselves guiltless, are thrown into the creek, if the evidence brought against them is insufficient to establish the charge. The case, in fact, is referred to the god for decision. If the accused be innocent he will save him, if guilty he will slay him. The laity are forbidden to reside in the neighbourhood, and priests alone have habitations there.

It is rarely that a person submitted to this ideal is found innocent. Probably there is a powerful undercurrent which sucks down even a strong swimmer; but natives who have been converted to Christianity declare that the priests spread nets under the water, so that those whom they have beforehand condemned may become entangled in them and held down. A native trader of Porto Novo, named Todjinu, whose wealth had excited the avarice of the king, was compelled to undergo this ordeal, and, being an unusually powerful man, was able to struggle to the shore. The priests and the king were naturally dissatisfied with this result, and a little later Todjinu was again compelled to submit to the ordeal to clear himself from a trumped-up charge of treason ; but this time the priests caused him first to drink a potion they had prepared, and he was drowned without a struggle. This was what was required : the *vōdu* had killed him, he was consequently guilty, and his property was confiscated.

The accused is ordinarily taken to the middle of the creek in a canoe, and then thrown into the water. If he should be drowned, the body is exposed next day on a raft near the bank, it being placed there, say the priests, by the god. This practice is accounted for by the following legend :—A poor woman, who was in great destitution, and had two young children to support, used to go to the bank of this creek to earn a livelihood by cutting wood in the forest to sell in the town. While she was thus employed in the forest she used to leave her children to play on the bank of the creek. One day, however, when she returned there with her load of wood the children were nowhere to be seen. She called to them, but there was no reply ; she sought for them high and low, but they were nowhere to be found. They had either been stolen, or had fallen into the water and been drowned. The mother returned to the town, which she filled with her lamentations, and thenceforth, day after day, she came to the creek to mourn.

Once day, as she was sitting on the bank, bewailing her loss, she was surprised to see her two children in the creek, swimming towards her like fish, but with their bodies out of the water as far as the waist. As they came near they cried—

"Weep no more, mother. We are happy here. The *vŏdu* used to see thee toiling day by day for our sakes, and he took pity on thee. He saw we were a burden to thee, and he took us to his home under the waters, where we have fish to eat every day in abundance. We live in a house under the waters, and the little fish play with us. Listen now to what the *vŏdu* says, 'Go and tell the king of Adjassi (Porto Novo) that he must build a temple to him on this bank and offer him sacrifices. He, in return, will decide for him all cases that are doubtful, or difficult to prove. Let the accused be thrown into the water, and if he be innocent he will hold him up; but if he be guilty he will drag him down to the bottom, and cast his body upon the bank next day.'"

Having delivered their message, the two children dived under the water, and their mother returned to Porto Novo, where she recounted what she had seen and heard. In consequence, a temple was built as the god had directed, and priests were appointed to tend the offerings.

Every year after that, the waters used to open, and all the people used to go to offer presents to the god in his palace under the waters. From the lagoon they used to pass on to the sea, where they ate and drank, danced and sang, and enjoyed themselves, and then returned home, the sea and the lagoons closing up after them. Now, however, the waters open no more, for a wicked king of Dahomi, hearing of the annual opening of the waters, sent down a number of his women-soldiers, as if to take presents, but with secret orders to seize the female water-spirits, and bring them to

Agbomi to be made Amazons. This the Amazons did,
and when the people and the water-spirits were all
dancing together and enjoying themselves, they seized
the females. They tried to bind them, but the water-
spirits changed themselves into drops of dew, and
slipped through their fingers. Since this the waters
have always remained closed.

The next four are instances of the deification of man
by the eastern Ewe tribes, of which we have no example
either on the Gold Coast nor amongst the western Ewe
tribes. Two out of the four are deified kings, and with
reference to what has been said with regard to ancestor
worship in Chapter II., it may be remarked that in
no one of these cases, which are all I have been able to
find, has the fact that these demi-gods were formerly
men been lost sight of.

The first is Adanlosan, or Adanzan, a king of Dahomi,
who flourished at the beginning of the present century,
and whose cruelty, licentiousness, and rapacity are
commemorated in a dozen songs and legends. He was
dethroned by his brother Gezo in 1818, and the action
which was the immediate cause of his downfall will
serve as an illustration of his character. His nephew,
a little child, son of his brother Owo, was playing in a
court of the palace, throwing pebbles in the air, when
one of them happened to strike Adanlosan, who immediately ordered the boy to be taken out and slain.
Accustomed as the officials of the court were to the
king's outbursts of rage, this order seems to have been
received with consternation ; and Gezo, the next brother,
who was close at hand, was sent for to beg for the child's
life. The news spread through the town, and an excited

crowd composed of Gezo's and Owo's adherents thronged outside the palace. Adanlosan, in spite of all appeals for mercy, remained inflexible, and one of the executioners had already laid hands on the boy, when Gezo rushed upon his brother and felled him to the ground. At the outcry that was raised, the crowd outside burst in; a few of the king's women who strove to oppose them were soon scattered or slain, and the tyrant was secured. As the royal blood may not be shed, Adanlosan, bound hand and foot, was walled up in a small room, and left to die of starvation; while, in order to avoid setting a bad precedent of rebellion, Gezo and those who acted with him circulated a report that the king, being old, had shut himself up in this room in order to become a *vŏdu*, so that he might remain with his people and protect them. They erected a temple to him, and appointed priests for his worship, while it was announced that future kings were never to undertake any affairs of importance without first consulting him.

The Dahomis of the present day say that Adanlosan is not dead, that he never died, but became a *vŏdu* during life, and that he often may be seen in the palace at Agbomi.

The next is Ajahuto, a former king of Porto Novo, who is chiefly remembered because he murdered his father-in-law. His temple is in the palace at Porto Novo, and human victims are, it is said, still sacrificed to him annually. Young girls who are dedicated to his service are obliged to remain virgins; they have charge of the temple and make the daily offerings. As a mark of honour they are not required to prostrate themselves before the king regnant, but this privilege is apparently not considered by native girls a sufficient compensation for the sexual restriction, as, of late years, there has always been some difficulty in finding candidates for the position. About 1880 one was put to death for unchastity.

Both Adanlosan and Ajahuto were terrible to their subjects during life, and the fear with which they were regarded has seemingly led men to seek to propitiate them after death, but the remaining two are worshipped as benefactors of mankind. They are Kpati and Kpasi, two local gods of Whydah. According to the local tradition, Kpati was the first native of Whydah who succeeded in bringing a ship to anchor before the town, which feat he accomplished by making signals to it with a cloth tied to a long stick. He was assisted by Kpasi, and when the captain of the ship landed they led him to the town. This, continues the tradition, was the commencement of that trade which afterwards made Whydah the chief port of the whole West Coast of Africa; for, before that, vessels used to pass by without seeing the town, which lies some two miles inland.

The Yam, or Harvest Custom, is held very generally by the Ewe-speaking peoples, more particularly by the western tribes. As on the Gold Coast, it appears to be a festival held as a thanksgiving to the gods for having protected the yam crop, and suffered it to arrive at maturity; but here its ceremonies are largely mixed with the rites of phallic worship.

CHAPTER VI.

AMULETS, OMENS, AND VARIOUS SUPERSTITIONS.

AMONGST the Ewe-speaking peoples there are no
gods similar to those described in Chapter VIII. of the
Tshi-speaking peoples—the tutelary deities of individuals,
termed *ehsuhman*, and which are believed to be animated
by indwelling spirits—their place being here taken by
the *võ-sesao*, or amulets, of which every god has his
own description, and two of which have been mentioned
under Khebioso and Dso in Chapter III. These *võ-sesao*
are believed to owe their virtue to being consecrated
to, or belonging to, the gods, and the special property
of a *võ-sesao* is not dependent on an indwelling spirit.
They enable the god to recognize and protect his people,
just as the blood on the door-posts of the Jews enabled
their God to recognize their habitations when the first-
born in Egypt were slain (Exodus xii. 13). On the
Gold Coast, the possessor of an amulet, derived as they
all are from a *suhman*, offers small portions of food and
drink to it; but amongst the Ewe-speaking peoples
neither prayers nor sacrifice are offered to *võ-sesao*,
though they are regarded with a certain amount of
reverence. The priests of a god alone possess the
requisite knowledge for the manufacture of amulets

consecrated to that god, and they sell them at a high
price; while, if the amulet should fail to defend the wearer
from the danger which it was its peculiar attribute to
avert—if, for instance, an amulet consecrated to the fire-
god should fail to protect the wearer from a disaster
by fire—they are never at a loss with some excuse to
account for its inefficacy.

The word *sesa* is derived from *sa* (to bind, or
fasten), which verb is used solely with reference to
amulets, the priests who supply them binding or fasten-
ing them on the persons or property of those who buy
them. From the fact of these *vŏ-sesao* being sold, *sa*
gets also the meaning of "to sell," but only with
reference to amulets; and as they enable the god to
discover his followers, the word *sesa* gets a secondary
meaning of "discoverer," as in *sesa-la*, "one who dis-
covers." *Vŏ* is a contraction of *vŏdu*, which has already
been explained.

Vŏ-sesao are usually worn round the neck or on the
arm, or are tied on to houses and household property;
but crops, standing on cultivated patches in the bush,
are, in the absence of the owners, left under the protection of such amulets, generally fastened to long sticks
in some conspicuous position; and, so guarded, are quite
safe from pillage. Food and palm-wine, also, may
often be seen placed by the side of frequented paths,
left there by the owner for sale, under the protection
of a *vŏ-sesa*. A few cowries placed on each article
indicates its price, and no native would dare to take
anything without depositing its stipulated value, for
fear of the unknown evil the god to whom the *vŏ-sesa*
belonged might bring upon him.

Besides amulets of this description, which may be considered, as it were, badges of the different gods, there are preparations of another kind, made also by the priests, which are believed to have various uses. With these, as with the first kind, the special property of the amulet, or charm, is believed to be derived from the god from whom the priest obtained it; but, as a rule, any god can issue these, and each kind is not peculiar to one god only. These preparations are also called *vō-sesao* by the eastern tribes, but amongst the western their more common designation is *eka*. The following are some of them :—

(1) A dog beaten to death and hung by the heels to a scaffold in the market-place prevents disease.

(2) An amulet made of the teeth or claws of animals, especially of beasts of prey, protects from beasts of prey.

(3) *Tibuli* is the name of a charm much used by thieves. It is believed to render the thieves invisible, and to send the occupants of the house they wish to rob into a deep sleep.

(4) A rude effigy of the head and trunk of a man, the former composed of a calabash and the latter of grass, dead leaves, or palm-branches, fastened to the top of a pole and planted opposite to the entrance of a house, protects the inmates from injury.

(5) A human tooth and a Popo bead, strung on a string and worn round the neck, is a Bo charm against sickness.

(6) Another defence against sickness is a flat rectangle of clay, dotted over half with cowries and half with pieces of broken pottery.

(7) The tail of a horse, cow, or goat, is an amulet much in vogue amongst the soldiery of Dahomi; for, carried in the hand and waved to and fro in front of the body, it causes the bullets, slugs, and other missiles of the foe to deviate to the right and left.

(8) *Damiki* is the name of an amulet worn as a protection against headache.

Magic powders are very numerous. One kind, when blown against a door or window, causes it to fly open, no matter how securely it may be fastened; another, when thrown upon the footprints of an enemy, makes him mad; a third, used in the same way, neutralizes the evil effects of the second; and a fourth destroys the sight of all who look upon it.

Magic unguents (*iro*) are not uncommon. They and the powders are obtained from the priests, and must be rubbed on the body of the person who is to be influenced by them. Some are believed to compel a man to lend money, but their more common property is to constrain the unwilling fair to listen favourably to the amorous proposal.

The Mohammedan negroids from the north also do a profitable trade in Dahomi, and amongst the north-eastern tribes, by the sale of amulets. These amulets consist of a sentence or verse from the Koran, written on paper and sewn up in leather. The natives frequently smear them with blood, palm-oil, or the yolk of eggs, and stick feathers on them; for these, being obtained from no priest, and deriving their power from no god, are regarded more like the *eh-suhman* of the Gold Coast, though the natives deny that they believe them to be animated by an indwelling spirit.

A charm for procuring the death of an enemy is a tree-stump, from three to four feet high and one foot in diameter, though the size varies considerably, wrapped round with palm-leaves and strips of calico, and adorned with a string of cowries hanging from the top. To set this power in motion the performer hammers the top of the stump with a stone, while pronouncing the name of the person it is intended to do to death. This does not appear to be a charm proper, and some natives affirm that it is a mode of invoking the gods Huntin and Loko, though the great majority say it is not.

Among omens the following may be mentioned :—

It is a bad omen for a dancer to slip and fall when performing before the king of Dahomi, and, up to the reign of Gezo, any dancer who met with such an accident was put to death. In old times a similar superstition prevailed concerning the rudge bridges leading across the ditch to the gates of Agbomi, and any one who lost his footing on one of them lost also his head.

The flocking of the hooded crow (*corvus senegaliensis*) is a bad omen, and denotes impending war. This bird is believed to be a " man-eater," like the owl ; where it lays its eggs no rain will fall, and potent charms for the injury of one's fellow-men can be made from its feathers.[1]

[1] The belief that the crow affects the rain-fall is found in South Africa, amongst the Makololo. Livingstone says (*Missionary Travels and Researches in South Africa*, p. 559) that when there is no rain, the nest of the crow is sought for and destroyed, in order to dissolve the charm with which it is supposed to seal up the windows of heaven. A bird, called Mokwa Reza, whose cry, " *pula, pula* " ("rain, rain "), is believed only to be uttered before a heavy rain-fall, is said to throw the eggs of the crow out of the nest, and to lay its own

The cry of the black-and-white kingfisher is a good omen when heard to the right, a bad one if heard to the left.

To sneeze is a bad omen. Amongst the western Ewe-speaking tribes this involuntary convulsion is regarded as an indication that something is happening to the indwelling spirit, usually that it is about to quit the body; and as that affords an opportunity for a homeless indwelling spirit to enter the body and cause sickness, the omen is bad. Amongst the eastern tribes, though the notion of the indwelling spirit has been to some extent confused with that of the ghost-man, the old superstition still prevails; and in Dahomi, when the king sneezes, all present touch the ground with their foreheads, and utter prayers to avert the omen.

It is a bad omen for a cock to crow in the middle of the night, and the bird is immediately killed in order that the omen may be fulfilled at its own expense.[1] In Dahomi, even during the day, cocks may not crow in a street, market, or other public place, and any bird who does so is confiscated to the priest. In consequence of this custom, which the natives are unable or unwilling to explain, cocks always appear gagged by a cord, or thong, placed between the mandibles and fastened behind the head.

Divination is a function peculiar to the priests, and is usually performed by throwing things on the ground, and drawing inferences from the position in which they

---

instead. In this hostility of the rain-bird to the crow we perhaps find the key to the notion that the crow's eggs cause a drought.

[1] Livingstone (*loc. cit.* p. 577) mentions a similar superstition amongst the Makololo. His men killed any cock that crowed before midnight, accounting it guilty of *tlolo* (transgression).

fall. A number of short sticks a few inches in length, or of pieces of knotted cord, or a handful of cowries or nuts are the articles generally used. A less common mode is to impale a fowl or animal, and make the required deductions from the length of time it lives. Amongst the eastern Ewe tribes divination is always practised according to the rule of Ife, the Yoruba God of Divination.

Ordeals are resorted to when human ingenuity fails to elicit the truth of a charge, and it is really a transfer of the burden of a decision to the gods. One example has been given in Chapter V. in the case of the god Togbo, but the most common ordeal, as on the Gold Coast, is the drinking of a decoction of odum wood.

The following superstitions concerning certain birds and animals are curious.

(1) The flickering appearance of the air near the ground in hot days is called "Fire of the Tortoise," and is believed to be caused by a subterranean fire made by the tortoise to burn the roots of the trees and kill them.

(2) A small black-and-white bird, a species of wagtail, is called in Dahomi the King's Bird, and may not be killed. The Yoruba women are believed to be able to converse with it. According to tradition, a king of Dahomi was greeted by a flock of these birds on returning from a victorious campaign, and in consequence took them under his protection.

(3) It is believed that any town in which the wild cat beats its tail three times on the ground will shortly be deserted.

(4) The "Fool-bird," or "African Pheasant," called *Wu-tu-tu* by the natives, from its note, is believed to have malign powers and to make muskets burst. A tawny-coloured antelope, caled *kravi*, also has this power,

H

if he chance to see the piece before it is discharged. These two superstitions are examples of how the native seeks to find an explanation for every occurrence. To him there is no such thing as an accident.

(5) It is believed that the porcupine, before going to look for food, shakes its quills in order to divine what the result of its search will be.

Owing to a confusion between objective and subjective connection, which appears to be very common amongst uncivilized peoples, the Ewe-speaking natives believe that there is a real and material connection between a man and his name, and that by means of the name injury may be done to the man. An illustration of this has been given in the case of the tree-stump that is beaten with a stone to compass the death of an enemy; for the name of that enemy is not pronounced solely with the object of informing the animating principle of the stump who it is whose death is desired, but through a belief that, by pronouncing the name, the personality of the man who bears it is in some way brought to the stump. In consequence of this belief the name of the king of Dahomi is always kept secret, lest the knowledge of it should enable any person to do him harm, and the names by which the different kings have been known to Europeans are aliases, called by the natives *nyi-sese*, literally "strong names," and which are, as a rule, the first words of sentences denoting some quality. Thus Agaja, the name by which the fourth king of the dynasty was known, was part of a sentence meaning "A spreading tree must be lopped before it can be cast into the fire," and Tegbwesun, the name of the fifth king, the first word of a sentence meaning, "No one can take a cloth off the neck of a wild bull." Gezo was the first word of a sentence meaning, "The red bird is not afraid of the bush," and Gelele that of one meaning, "Bigness which there is no means of lifting." It appears strange that the birth-name only, and not an alias, should be believed capable of carrying some of the personality of the bearer elsewhere, since the latter preserves the subjective connection just as well as the real name; but the native view seems to be that the alias does not really belong to the man.

Since the name even of a person, should it fall into bad hands, may be used to the detriment of the bearer, of course anything that has belonged to a man, especially anything that has formed part of or has come out of his body, such as hair-clippings, nail-parings, saliva, or the fæces, can be used for a similar purpose. Some nail-parings that belonged to a man recall that man to the mind of the native ; and the subjective connection being thus unbroken, he believes that the objective connection, which was terminated when those parings were cut, is still also unbroken ; and that anything that is done to them will be felt by the body to which they belonged. Hence it is usual for pieces of hair and nails to be carefully buried or burned, in order that they may not fall into the hands of sorcerers ; and whenever a king or chief expectorates, the saliva is carefully gathered up and hidden or buried.

This confusion between subjective and objective connection is further illustrated by the tooth or claw amulet, whose special property is to save the wearer from the fangs or claws of beasts of prey ; in the flesh of the elephant being believed to make those who eat it strong ; and in the practice which, it is said, still

survives amongst the Amazons of Dahomi, of eating the
hearts of foes of conspicuous courage, in order that some
of the fearlessness that animated them may be trans-
ferred to the eaters. In former days, according to
report, the hearts of foemen remarkable for sagacity
were also eaten, for the Ewe-speaking negro holds that
the heart is the seat of the intellect as well as of courage.

The Ewe-speaking tribes, like the people of the Gold
Coast, are totemistic, and the different communities are
heterogeneous ; that is, members of several, in some
cases of all, of the clans are found in each community.
Owing to the loss of a portion of my notes, I am unable
to give a complete list of the totem-clans, and can now
only remember the following :—

1. Kpo-dó (*Kpo*, leopard ; *dó*, people, clan, or tribe),
Leopard Clan.

2. Ordañh-dó (*Ordañh*, snake), Snake Clan.

3. Dzáta-dó, or Jáhnta-dó (*Dzáta*, or *jáhnta*, lion),
Lion Clan.

4. Téhvi-dó (*Téhvi*, a variety of yam), Yam Clan.

5. Elo-dó (*Elo*, crocodile), Crocodile Clan.

6. Eddu-dó (*Eddu*, the monkey with long black
hair), Monkey Clan.

Kó is sometimes used instead of *dó*. It equally
means "people, clan, or tribe."

The usual reverence is paid by the members of a
clan to the animal or plant from which the clan takes
its name. It may not be used as food, or molested in
any way ; but must always be treated with veneration
and respect. The general notion is that the members
of the clan are directly descended from the animal, or
plant, eponymous.

CHAPTER VII.

THE INDWELLING SPIRITS AND SOULS OF MEN.

THE supernatural or superhuman beings who have
been described in Chapters III., IV., and V., and who
may be designated gods proper, are, to the native mind,
in quite a different category to those which are the
subject of this chapter, viz. the Indwelling Spirits and
Souls of Men. It is true that the gods were, I think,
fashioned by the negroes on the primary conception of
an indwelling spirit of man, which conception was afterwards extended to all nature, to explain satisfactorily
its phenomena; every natural phenomenon, feature, or
object being believed to have an indwelling spirit, which,
like the indwelling spirit of man, would grant protection,
or at all events would not work evil, if properly propitiated. But though the gods are in manner of origin thus
closely related to the indwelling spirits of men, they
seem soon to have been considered as quite a different
class of beings. This was perhaps due to the evidence,
to the native mind, of their superior power. Any fatal
accident or minor calamity that occurred, or does now
occur, in connection with any phenomenon of nature or
natural feature, is attributed to its god, or indwelling
spirit; and since the evil is wrought in spite of the

indwelling spirit of the man, the presumption to the
native mind is, that the former is the more powerful.
The wider area of power possessed by the gods would
perhaps also tend to their gradual elevation in the mind
of the negro to a class superior to that held by the
indwelling spirits of individual men; but in any case,
although amongst the Tshi-speaking peoples the original
notion has not been lost sight of, and the gods are still
believed to be indwelling spirits, the fact remains that
even there they are considered a class apart from the
indwelling spirits of men ; and amongst the Ewe-speaking peoples, where many of the gods have been separated
from their habitats, this idea has naturally become
strengthened.

The Ewe term corresponding to the Tshi *kra* is *luvo*,
which, like it, means the indwelling spirit of a living
man, whose ordinary abode is in the living man, but
who indulges in temporary absences, usually during
sleep, and whose adventures during such periods of
absence are the occurrences dreamed of by the man.
Like the *kra*, the *luvo* existed before the birth of the
man, and has probably been the indwelling spirit of a
long series of men : after his death it becomes a *ñoli*, or
luvo without a tenement (the Tshi *sisa*).   For a short
interval after the death of the man the *ñoli* lingers near
the grave in which is interred the body it formerly inhabited ; after which it usually enters a new-born human
body, and again becomes a *luvo;* but, failing a human
body, it can enter that of an animal.   If it should not
succeed in entering the body either of a man or of an
animal, then the homeless *ñoli* wanders about, working
good or evil according to its disposition.   The good,

however, is generally confined to the family of the man in whose body it last resided, and for which, through association, it seems to have some friendly feeling. It works evil by causing sickness, by entering human bodies during the temporary absences of their *luwoo*, or sometimes even by attempting to force a way in and displace the *luwo*. When such an internal struggle is taking place in a man, he is convulsed and foams at the mouth, writhes, and gnashes his teeth. A *ñoli* who works evil is classed as an *abonsã*, " malicious spirit."

Thus far the beliefs of the Ewe-speaking peoples are in accord with those of the Tshi-speaking peoples, but the *luwo*, while it is wandering about and departing from the body, is called an *aklama*, and this division of the career of the indwelling spirit into three states or conditions is a new departure. The word *aklama* is from *kla,* " to desert, abandon, bid farewell," and is from the same root as the Tshi *kra,* and the Ga *kla.*

Another change is that the notion that a *ñoli* (Tshi, *sisa*) can enter the body of a ferocious animal and prey upon men has been more elaborated ; so that, as in the case of the crocodile, a whole species is worshipped and elevated to the dignity of a god. An example of how this belief may cause the worship of a particular animal is well shown in the case of the pet ox of Mepon, a king of Porto Novo, who died in 1872. This ox, which had been presented to him by M. Baudin, a French missionary, had been made a great favourite, and used to come every day to the palace to receive green food from the hand of the king. When Mepon died, the ox came as usual for his food, and receiving none, began to bellow. His bellowing was so persistent that the priests were asked for an explanation of it; upon which they declared that the *ñoli*, the late *luwo* of Mepon, had passed into the animal, which henceforward was allowed to go where it pleased, and was treated with the greatest respect. It died in 1883, and was buried with great honours. The carcass was wrapped in cotton cloths, sheep and fowls were sacrificed, and libations of rum and palm-wine poured out. It was then carried in procession, amid the din of drums and horns and discharges of musketry, to the grave, where the blood of fresh sacrifices was sprinkled upon it, and the earth then filled in.

The greatest change, however, is in the high importance that is attached by the Ewe-speaking peoples to a family *ñoli* as a protector. On the Gold Coast there was barely a trace of this idea, but on the Slave Coast, especially in the western districts, the *ñoli* who has been a *luwo* in one of the family, ordinarily the head of the family, often becomes the family protector, and sometimes even of small communities or villages. He sometimes has his shrine, and occasionally his image, and so really becomes a god of a sub-order, though he is believed to be subject to and required to worship the gods proper, nearly as much as man is. On the Gold Coast such tutelary deities are obtained through the priest from the local gods, the family or village protector being held to be a subordinate spirit appointed by the local god; but here, owing perhaps to the inferior position of the local gods, this manner of origin has apparently been lost sight of, and the *ñoli* origin substituted. In Whydah and its neighbourhood the friendly *ñoli* is believed to frequently take up its abode in the body of the iguana; whence these reptiles are allowed to run about the house, and are regarded almost as tutelary deities, the death of one being considered a calamity. A malicious *ñoli,* or *abonsã,* is kept out of the house by the sacrifice of a fowl, which is then hung head downwards on a light framework of poles, so planted that the path to the house-door leads between them.

The Ewe-speaking native offers worship and sacrifice to his indwelling spirit in much the same way as is done on the Gold Coast. In both cases the natal day of the man is the day kept sacred to the indwelling spirit, and is commenced by a sacrifice, either a sheep or a fowl, according to the means of the worshipper; after which the latter washes himself from head to foot, and arrays himself in a white cloth. The procedure on the Slave Coast then varies somewhat. The worshipper, having provided a fowl, some kola-nuts, water and rum, seats himself on a clean mat, and a woman, dipping her hand in the water, touches him with the fluid on the forehead, crown, nape of the neck, and breast. This process is repeated with the rum, then with chewed kola-nut, and lastly with the bleeding head of the fowl, which is torn from the living body.

Toadstools and similar fungoidal growths are termed by the western Ewe tribes *ñoli-khekhio,* " *ñoli*-shelters," a name which calls to mind the old English superstition, that still lingers in remote districts, of fairies using them for the same purpose.

The ghost-man, the shadowy being who continues the existence of the bodily man after death, and who therefore answers to the European term " soul," is called by the western Ewe tribes *edsieto,* that is, an inhabitant of *edsie* (Dead-land, or Ghost-land), and by the eastern tribes *dsi*, a word which means the interior of man, the thinking part of man, or ghost, and is probably the root of *edsie*. There is a verb *gbogbo dsi*, literally " to breathe out the ghost," meaning " to die," and another verb *dsi*, " to go out," or " extinguish." Another word sometimes used for ghost is *vovoli*, which, however, properly means " shadow."

The soul, that is the ghost-man, has so frequently been confused with the indwelling spirit (*kra*, or *luwo*), that it may not be out of place to again insist upon their existence in the native mind as absolutely distinct entities. When the indwelling spirit leaves the body of the man it inhabits, that man suffers no physical inconvenience ; it goes out, when he is asleep, without his knowledge ; and if it should leave him when he is awake, he is only made aware of its departure by a sneeze or a yawn. He suffers no pain, and to all appearances nothing has happened to him. When, however, the soul, the vehicle of individual personal existence, leaves the body, that body falls into a condition of suspended animation ; it is cold, pulseless, and apparently lifeless. Sometimes, though rarely, the soul returns after such an absence, and then the man has been in a swoon or trance ; more generally it does not return, and then the man is dead. It is in consequence of the belief that the soul does occasionally return after leaving the body, that appeals to the dead to come back are always made immediately after death ; and, generally speaking, it is only when the corpse begins to become corrupt, and the relatives thereby become certain that the soul does not intend to return, that it is buried. Swoons, trances, and death are phenomena directly caused by the soul quitting the body ; apoplectic and epileptic fits, hysteria, delirium, and mania are phenomena connected with the absence of the indwelling spirit ; but they do not directly result from its departure, and are caused by a spirit without a bodily tenement entering the body during the absence of the proper tenant, by the struggle between the two when the latter returns and finds his place usurped, or by the former trying to force a way in and displace the latter—they are in fact cases of " possession." The common belief seems to be that the indwelling spirit leaves the body and returns to it through the mouth ; hence, should it have gone out, it behoves a man to be careful about opening his mouth, lest a homeless spirit should take advantage of the opportunity and enter his body. This, it appears, is considered most likely to take place while the man is eating. The soul is also believed to leave the body through the mouth, but no other existence ever comes to usurp its place.

Amongst the eastern Ewe tribes Dead-land is called Kutome—*ku* (dead), *to* (land), *me* (interior, inside, place of)—and is believed to be situated to the west, across the river Volta, the exact reverse of the belief of the inhabitants of the Gold Coast, who place Dead-land across the same river, to the east; but by the western Ewe tribes, who live near the Volta, it is commonly believed to be situated to the north. Dead-land is like the earth, and the " continuance theory " is here in full force, every man being believed to occupy the same position and to have the same powers, avocations, and tastes in Dead-land as he had in the world. He also carries with him his bodily imperfections, the hunchback in the world becoming a ghost-hunchback in Dead-land.

Hence when a deaf man dies his relatives do not make
the usual appeals to him not to desert them, for the
ghost or soul, being also deaf, cannot hear them. In
short, at death a man does nothing more than get rid
of his corporeal body and change his place of residence;
everything else remains the same.

The notion of an absolute immortality of the dead does
not appear to be held. If left to themselves, the natives
do not inquire into such matters as to how long the
dead live in Dead-land ; but if a European asks them if
they live for ever, they nearly always reply that nothing
can live for ever, and that the dead must also die. Of
course the memory of past generations soon dies out
amongst a people who have no knowledge of writing
and no records ; so that the negroes, when thinking of
Dead-land, practically only think of it as inhabited by
the ghosts of men who lived in times approaching
their own.

Early in April of every year a general day of remembrance for the dead is held. Among the eastern tribes
this is held more specially for those who have died
during the past year, and it is believed that if the festival were not observed, the ghosts would wander on the
banks of the Volta without being able to cross over.
From this it might be inferred that these tribes do not
believe, as do the western, that the ghost-man proceeds
to Dead-land immediately after the funeral ; but if
questioned on this point, they inconsistently reply that
they do so believe. It seems probable that the notion
of the Volta being a species of purgatory, across which
the ghost must be assisted by the prayers of the surviving relatives, is a corruption of European beliefs.

Amongst the Ewe-speaking peoples priests are believed to be able to send out their souls, or ghosts, either
to visit distant places or to go to Dead-land, a departure
from the belief held on the Gold Coast, where the soul
is subject to no such control. As the absence of the
soul causes, in the views of the natives, a condition of
suspended animation, the priest who is pretending to
despatch his soul on a mission simulates a trance, or
sits motionless for hours with his head covered with a
cloth ; after which he affects to recover consciousness, and
recounts what he has seen and heard.

On the Gold Coast the dead are believed to be cognizant of what is taking place in the world, and to retain
some interest in the welfare of their descendants, hence
they are sometimes appealed to for aid ; but on the
Slave Coast this idea has been further developed, it
being held that sickness is frequently caused by some
ancestral ghost, who requires the services of his descendant in Dead-land, and so is hastening his departure from
the world. In such a case the sick man sends for a
priest, pays him a fee, and begs him to send his soul to
Dead-land, to put a stop to the importunities of the
family ghost. For this duty the priests of Dañh-gbi
and Wu are never employed ; a priest of any other god
will do, but those of Sapatan, Anyi-ewo, or Loko are
generally preferred. The priest pretends to despatch
his soul on this mission, in the manner already described,
and on recovering consciousness informs his dupe that
he has been to Dead-land, and has seen the ghost, whom
he names. If he thinks that the patient is not very ill
and in no risk of his life, he comforts him with the
assurance that the unquiet ghost has been pacified ; if,

on the contrary, the case should appear serious, he deals in ambiguities, and leaves his dupe in doubt as to whether the mission has been successful.

Captain Thomas Phillips, who made a voyage to Whydah (1693-4), informs us that a Mr. Smith, the chief factor of the English fort, having fallen sick, the king of Whydah, being positive that the sickness was due to the machinations of a ghost in Dead-land, sent a priest to his aid. The latter, bringing with him rum, brandy, oil, and other offerings, proceeded to the detached building in which the Europeans of the Royal African Company were buried, and thus addressed them—

" Oh, ye dead whites that live here ! you have a mind to have with you this factor that is sick, but he is a friend to the king, who loves him, and who will not part with him as yet."

He then proceeded to the grave of Captain Wilburne, the founder of the fort, and continued—

" Oh, thou captain of all the dead whites that lie here ! this is thy doing ; thou wouldst have this man from us to bear thee company, because he is a good man, but our king will not part with him, and thou shalt not have him yet."

He then made a hole in the earth of the grave and poured in the offerings, but the Englishmen who were present, disgusted, turned him out of the fort. Shortly after, Mr. Smith died, and the natives had no hesitation in attributing his decease to the interference with the priest.

Another change from the customs of the Gold Coast, in the direction of ancestor worship, is found in Dahomi, where, amongst what may be termed the upper classes, for the poorer families have not the facilities for their preservation, it is the custom to have the skulls of the family dead exhumed after a few years of sepulture, and placed in earthen pots, which are carefully kept in a corner of the house. The dead are appealed to for advice and assistance before these skulls. The reason of this may perhaps be found in the widespread notion that it is necessary to be in the presence of, or to have in possession something belonging to, a superhuman being, to enable that being to take cognizance of the prayers made to it; or it may be that, by a simple association of ideas, the dead are believed to keep up some connection with their remains.

As amongst the natives of the Gold Coast, where ancestor worship reaches its highest development in the royal house of Ashanti, so amongst the Ewe-speaking peoples it is most fully developed in the royal family of Dahomi; where, in fact, there are greater facilities for preserving the remains, and with them the memories, of dead rulers. At the Dahomi court there is a female official appointed to represent each deceased monarch on ceremonial occasions. These officials are termed Bassa-ji, and they walk in the processions at the Annual Customs as representatives of the former kings, in company with other women who represent their dead mothers. If a king has recently died, however, a covered screen, called *Ză-ku-ku*, " Night-dead-dead," and which contains his state umbrella, is carried in the processions to represent the place of the dead king; and, as it passes by, the spectators turn away their heads, for no one is supposed to know what is inside it. In addition to the Bassa-ji there are other female officials termed Tansi-no, whose duty it is to take care of the royal graves.

At the Sin-kwain (? Tsi-kwain), or Water-sprinkling Custom, one of the Annual Customs of Dahomi, the king repairs to the graves of the former kings, who are interred in different buildings in the palace of Agbomi; and, commencing with the first of the dynasty, sacrifices one or two victims on each grave in succession. This sacrifice is believed to induce the ghosts of the old kings to lend their aid in time of war. The number of persons sacrificed on each grave is said never to exceed two. The ceremony much resembles that performed in Ashanti when the king visits Bantama.[1] The king, accompanied by his ministers and captains, approaches each tomb on all fours, followed by officials in the same attitude, bringing the sacrifices, which consist of men, sheep, fowls, rum, palm-oil, water, &c. A Tansi-no then invokes the ghost in favour of his living descendant; water and rum are poured on the grave, and the blood of living sacrifices, who are killed on the spot, is sprinkled on it. The flesh of the non-human sacrifices is then dressed and put on a table with drink and food of other kinds, and the stool of the deceased placed before it.

As has been said, each ghost-man is believed on arrival in Dead-land to be exactly like the man of whom he is now the ghost; a child who dies becomes a ghost-child, and an aged man a ghost-aged man; also a man who is a cripple in this world will be a ghost-cripple in the next. But this reproduction of imperfections in Dead-land only applies to those which date from birth; a man, for instance, who has lost an arm in war, does not, when he dies, become a one-armed ghost; nor do the ghosts of those who are slain by decapitation appear in

[1] *Tshi-speaking Peoples*, p. 168.

Dead-land without heads ; the negro appears to recognize that these are artificially-produced imperfections, and quite different to those with which a man is born. On this point the natives seem to be agreed, but as to whether a child in Dead-land always remains a child, or grows to manhood, or whether a man infirm from extreme age always remains an equally infirm ghost, there is no agreement; though with regard to the latter case the prevailing opinion seems to be that aged and infirm people do not, on becoming ghosts, recover any of their lost powers.   However, obscurity is to be expected in such matters, and in truth our own ideas are equally obscure ; for it would puzzle any Christian parent who had lost a child, to determine whether, when he again met that child in the next world, it would be exactly as it was when it died, or be grown up.   Practically, the negroes never inquire about such things at all ; and as every person, when he thinks of the dead, thinks of them as he knew them when they were in the world, it really results that the ghosts of men are supposed to remain in Dead-land in the exact condition in which the men were when they died.

Their ideas with regard to the position and power held by the dead are more precise.   In 1878, at Quittah, I cross-examined a native of Dahomi, through an interpreter, concerning the rank and power held in Dead-land by the deceased kings of his country ; and having gained from him the admission that each king in succession had become a king in Dead-land, I thought to puzzle him by asking how there could be six or seven kings at once.   To this he replied that each son was under his father, and Dako Donun, the first king of the

I

dynasty, was the head of all. I objected that this did
not agree with the " continuance " theory, for a king of
Dahomi, during life, was " under " no one, and he said,
" That is not so.   Is not every king under his father,
who can call him to Dead-land ?   Does not the king ask
assistance and advice from the dead ones ?   Does he
not send them slaves and wives ?   And if he does these
things it is because they are before him.   At Agbomi
his dead father was before him, and in Dead-land he will
also be before him.   Dako Donun came first, and all are
under Dako Donun."

I have said that in the minds of the Ewe-speaking
natives, the indwelling spirit and the soul of man are
absolutely distinct entities; but this requires some
slight qualification in the case of the inhabitants of
Porto Novo, Ewemi, Kotonu, Whydah, and the eastern
parts of Dahomi, where the two entities are sometimes
partly confounded together. This is due to contact with
the Yoruba-speaking peoples, who are found in considerable numbers in the first three states, and who have no
belief corresponding to that of the *luwo*, but who believe
in metempsychosis.   In consequence of this foreign
influence, one frequently finds cases in the above-
mentioned districts, in which the *dsi*, or soul, is believed
to have returned to enter the body of a new-born child
instead of the *ñoli;* but the ideas of the natives are so
indefinite, that at the same time they believe that the
soul remains in Dead-land.

This obscure belief has been considered by the French
missionaries to be metempsychosis, which it is not,
though it may indicate how a belief in such a doctrine
might arise.   The notion of the *ñoli* entering a new-

born human body would have paved the way for it, and if the *ñoli* became at all confounded in men's minds with the soul, it is easy to see how, after a time, it might be the latter which was believed to return to a human body. This change would probably be accelerated by the desire to explain the reproduction of features, gestures, and mannerisms from generation to generation in families ; for the native who had preserved a vague remembrance of the *ñoli* entering new-born bodies, would find a reasonable hypothesis to account for the phenomena, in the belief that a progenitor had returned from Dead-land to animate a new-born child, and reproduce his own characteristics. This, however, is not quite the case in these eastern Ewe districts. The soul is still believed to remain in Dead-land, and yet to animate the child, so that the change of belief to metempsychosis is not yet complete. As a child can only reproduce characteristics that have been transmitted to it by heredity, it is believed that a soul in Dead-land never animates an embryo in a strange family ; it is always one in the family to which he belonged in life.

It is not uncommon in these eastern Ewe districts for a Buko-no, or diviner of the Yoruba god Ife, to be sent for a few days after a birth, to say what ancestral soul has sent the child, and he never fails to give the required information. Sometimes his decision is influenced by some mark on the body of the child. For instance, a widow of Porto Novo, whose husband had been killed in a skirmish, having given birth to a child which had a peculiar mark on its forehead, the Buko-no declared that it was animated by the soul of its own father, and that this mark indicated where

he had been struck by the musket-ball that killed
him.   According to local report at Whydah, a child that
was born with teeth at Agbomi, about 1883, was thrown
into the sea at Whydah by order of the king, because
the Buko-no declared that it was animated by the soul
of the preceding monarch.

CHAPTER VIII.

AMONGST the Ewe-speaking peoples, as amongst the Tshi-speaking peoples, and generally throughout the world, human beings are sacrificed to fulfil two ends, viz.—

1. To propitiate or mollify the gods, or as a thank-offering to the gods.

2. To provide or increase the ghostly retinues of deceased men of rank, or to convey some message to the dead from their descendants.

Human sacrifices to the gods are ordinarily only made in time of war, pestilence, or great calamity; in fact when the urgency of the need for divine clemency or assistance prompts the worshippers to offer the highest form of offering. Those made to the gods during war, after a victory, are a thank-offering for the services rendered; the gods being believed to take part in the struggle, by contending against those of the foe, and to be nearly as much interested in the result as the human combatants; a belief which ranges from these higher grades of savagery onward through the progressive stages of civilization, as exemplified by the Jews and the ancient Greeks, up to mediæval Mohammedanism, and may be found, in a modified form, even in civilized Europe at the present day.

Human sacrifices to provide attendants for the dead, take place at the decease of kings or chiefs, or whenever their living descendants think it desirable to increase their retinues, or to inform them of some occurrence which seems important. Sacrifices made with these motives are the direct outcome of the " continuance " theory, for a man who has been accustomed to be served by a number of followers and wives in this world, will equally require such attendance to enable him to support his position in Dead-land; but the slaying of victims to convey messages is a later modification, and is seemingly at variance with the accepted idea that the dead are cognizant of what is taking place in the world.

The souls, or ghosts, of persons slain at funerals, or in after years to swell the retinues of dead rulers, proceed directly to Dead-land, and fulfil the purpose for which they were released from their bodies, as do those of persons slain to bear messages, the message being given to the man, who is asked if he understands it, and then instantly decapitated. In the case of persons sacrificed to the gods, it is not quite so clear as to what becomes of their souls. On the Gold Coast the general belief seems to be that they pass into the service of the gods, who, being strictly anthropomorphic conceptions, are believed to have need of servitors as much as man ; but on the Slave Coast this belief can barely be traced. This may partly be due to the chief local gods having been generalized into types which are virtually omnipresent ; for when a god was identified with a locality, it might more easily be supposed that the souls of those sacrificed to him in that locality, remained there in his service.

Amongst the Ewe-speaking peoples the intention of sacrifice to a god seems to be three-fold :—Firstly, the sacrifice is a gift, which is designed to propitiate; secondly, it is an act of homage ; and thirdly, it is an act of self-denial, the worshipper depriving himself of something he values in order to please the god. This last motive frequently survives when every other trace of malignancy as the primary characteristic of a god has disappeared. In the case of offerings of food and drink, the gods are believed to eat and drink the spiritual part, the substance being left behind, but in the case of human victims the gods are not believed to devour the souls ; and as these souls are, by the majority of the natives, believed to proceed to Dead-land like all others, the object of human sacrifice seems to be to gratify or satiate the malignancy of the gods at the expense of chosen individuals, instead of leaving it to chance—the victims are in fact slain for the benefit of the community at large. There is also a certain amount of homage in the act, man being the highest form of offering ; but there does not seem to be any self-abnegation, for a man deprives himself of nothing by sacrificing his neighbour or his neighbour's slave.

When prisoners of war are sacrificed as a thank-offering for a victory, homage and a hope of the continuance of future favours appear the chief motives ; but these thank-offerings are not, as a rule, spontaneous; the gods demand them, as their fruits of the victory, through the priests. Of late years such thank-offerings have been reduced to very insignificant proportions, but

in the early days of the Dahomi kingdom, massacres
such as might well rival those mentioned in the Old
Testament, as taking place under similar circumstances,
used to follow every successful contest.[1]

To obtain any account of thank-offerings to the gods
made on a large scale we have to go back to the last
century, when they were frequent, 4000 Whydahs,
for instance, having been sacrificed to the gods at the
conquest of that state by Dahomi in 1727. Captain
Snelgrave, who saw the heads of these victims piled up,
was in the same year himself an eye-witness of the
sacrifice of 400 more prisoners. He says [2]—

"Of this ceremony, curiosity, getting the better of
our feelings, impelled the Dutch captain and myself to
become spectators ; and having, by our interpreter,
obtained of the priests the necessary permission, we
went with him to the place where the sacrifices were
to be performed, which was about a quarter of a mile
from the camp. Great numbers of people were assembled
on the occasion ; and our guards, making way for us
through the crowd, brought us near to four small stages,
erected about five feet from the ground ; at the side of
one of which we took our stand, in a situation whence
we could plainly see all that passed.

"The first victim was a comely old man, between
fifty and sixty years of age. His hands were tied behind
him. In his behaviour, he showed a brave and undaunted
mind without any semblance of fear. He was brought
to the side of one of the stages, and standing upright, a
Fetisher, or priest, laid his hand on his head, repeating

[1] See Joshua x. 40, 42 ; and elsewhere.
[2] Dalzel's *History of Dahomey*, p. 37.

some words of consecration, which lasted about two minutes : after which he made the sign to a man that stood behind the prisoner with a broad-sword ; who immediately, at one blow, severed his head from his body."

The rabble, on this, gave a great shout, the attendants threw the head up on to the stage, and the body, after having lain long enough to be drained of blood, was carried away by slaves, and thrown on the ground near the camp of the army. Four hundred persons in all were sacrificed in this manner, the men going to the stages bold and unconcerned, but the women and children with piteous cries. These people were Toffos, a tribe said to reside six days' journey from Whydah ; and in honour of the conquest the present town of Toffo, which lies south of the Ko, and about ten miles west of the direct road to Agbomi, was built. In the evening, when Snelgrave walked out, he saw two great heaps of bodies, the corpses of the four hundred victims. Next morning they had all disappeared ; they having been, the interpreter told him, solemnly eaten in the night by the Dahomis.

Human sacrifices to furnish attendants for the dead have, as might be expected, reached the greatest height in Dahomi ; where, besides the Grand Custom that is held after the death of a king, there is an Annual Custom, which is designed principally for the purpose of supplying the dead kings periodically with fresh servitors ; though it serves also, like the Ashanti Yam Custom, a political end ; all the officials of the kingdom being required to attend the capital and bring presents. As the Grand Custom is the first held for a deceased king, we have not many accounts of one, only ten having taken place since the institution of the Customs by

Adanzu I., who reigned between 1650 and 1680. Mr.
Hogg, governor of Appollonia Fort on the Gold Coast,
was, however, present at the Grand Custom held in
1791 for Adanzu II., at which ·500 victims are said to
have been sacrificed ; and M. Lartigue has described, in
the *Annales de la Propagation de la Foi*, that which
took place in 1860 for King Gezo, who had died in
1858 ; it being usual, after expediting a few first attendants, to delay the real funeral custom till numerous
victims can be collected, and the ceremony performed
with the greater pomp. The latter's description is given
intact, the political and religious elements being so mixed
together in these Customs, that to separate them would
be to render any account misleading.

"The 18th (July), donations of the king to his
troops. Each chief is borne on the shoulders of a
soldier. Each battalion has as a distinctive mark a
strip of cloth of different colour fastened to the hair,
so that the soldiers of each corps can recognize one
another in the wild struggle that is preparing. More,
each soldier has a bag hung round the waist, in which
must be promptly thrust the article which the king
throws down, or else any neighbour has the right to
seize it. Once in the bag, it is sacred. The gifts consisted of cowries and cotton goods. Directly a prize was
thrown to the crowd, it rushed in a mass to seize it;
the ranks were so close that the greater part of those
who could not get near to the spot where it had fallen,
climbed up upon the mob of struggling men, and made
their way on their heads and their shoulders, as if on a
platform. Others again, mounting in their turn upon
this second layer, formed a new story, and made a

human pyramid, which would fall to pieces all at once under a stronger oscillation of the crowd, to begin again elsewhere.

"The 23rd, I assist at the nomination of twenty-three chiefs and musicians, who are going to be sacrificed in order that they may enter into the service of the deceased king.

" The 28th, immolation of fourteen captives, whose heads are carried to different parts of the town, to the sound of a big bell.

"The 29th, they are preparing to offer, to the memory of King Gezo, the customary victims. The captives have a gag in the shape of a cross, which must make them suffer terribly. The pointed end is put into the mouth, and presses upon the tongue, which prevents them doubling it, and, in consequence, crying out. Almost all these unfortunates have their eyes starting out of their heads. In the coming night there will be a great massacre.

"The chants are incessant, like the butcheries. The palace square gives out a pestilential odour : forty thousand negroes station themselves there day and night in the midst of filth. Join to this the exhalations from the blood, and the putrifying corpses, whose place of deposit is only at a little distance, and one can believe without any trouble that the air one breathes here is deadly. The 30th and 31st, the principal mulattoes of Whydah offer their victims, who are paraded three times round the square, to the sound of infernal music. At the termination of the third round the king advances to the deputation, and while he is complimenting each donor, the slaughtering is accomplished.

" During these last two nights more than five hundred heads have fallen. They were carried out of the palace by basketfuls, together with large calabashes in which the blood has been collected to water the grave of the dead king. The bodies were dragged away by the feet and thrown into the town ditches, where the vultures, crows, and wolves fight for the fragments, which they scatter about almost everywhere. Many of these ditches are heaped up with human bones.

" The succeeding days, continuation of the same sacrifices.

" The grave of the late king is a great cellar, dug in the earth. Gezo is in the middle of all his wives, who, before poisoning themselves, placed themselves around him according to the rank which they held at his court. These voluntary victims may bring the total number up to six hundred.

" August 4th, exhibition of fifteen female prisoners, who are destined to take care of Gezo in the other world. They appear to divine the fate which awaits them, for they are sad and look often behind them. They will be killed to-night by a stab in the breast.

" The 5th, day reserved for the king's offerings. They form a collection of everything that is required by an African monarch : fifteen women and thirty-five men, gagged and bound, the knees bent under the chin, and the arms tied to the ankles, each one held in a basket which is carried on the head. The defile has lasted more than an hour and a half. It was a diabolical spectacle; only to see the animation, the gestures, and the contortions of all these negroes.

" Behind me were four magnificent blacks, acting as

coachmen around a little carriage, which was intended to be sent to the deceased, in company with these unfortunates. They were ignorant of their fate. When they were called, they advanced sadly, without uttering a word ; one of them had two large tears which glistened on his cheeks. They were all four killed like chickens, by the king in person.

" The sacrifices were to take place on a scaffold constructed in the middle of the square. His majesty came and sat down on it, accompanied by the minister of justice, the governor of Whydah, and all the principal personages of the kingdom, who were going to serve as executioners. After a few words the king lights his pipe and gives the signal, and then all the cutlasses are drawn, and the heads fall. The blood streamed in every direction ; the sacrifices were covered with it, and the unhappy prisoners who were waiting their turn at the foot of the scaffold, were coloured red.

" These ceremonies will continue a month and a half, after which the king will take the field in order to make fresh captives, and recommence the Customs towards the end of October. Seven or eight hundred heads will fall then also."

The continuation of the Custom in October was witnessed by a mulatto named Bernasko, a native missionary of the Wesleyan Society, whose account,[1] it is to be regretted, is nearly as incoherent as that of Mr. Lartigue. He says—

" Monday, the 15th (October), I arrived at Abomey.

" Tuesday, the 16th, we were called to the king's palace, and at the gate saw ninety human heads cut off

[1] *Wesleyan Missionary Notices*, Feb. 25th, 1861.

that morning, and the poor creatures' blood flowed on the ground like a flood. Their heads lay upon swish beds at each side of the gate, for public view. We went in to sit down, and soon after he sent out the property of his fathers, as follows :—Two chariots, one glass wheel, seven plain wheels, three solid silver dishes, two silver tea-pots, one silver sugar-pot, one silver butter-pot, one large cushion on a wheel bar[1] drawn by six Amazons, three well-dressed silk hammocks, with silk awnings.

"Three days after we went to see the same things. I saw at the same gate, sixty heads laid upon the same place ; and, on three days again, thirty-six heads laid up. He made four platforms in their large market-place, and on which he threw cowries and cloths to his people, and sacrificed there about sixty souls. I dare say he killed more than two thousand, because he kills men outside, to be seen by all, and women inside, privately. Oh, he destroyed many souls during this wicked custom."

*   *   *   *   *   *

"The pit at Abomey which was reported to have been dug deep enough to contain human blood sufficient to float a canoe, was false. There were two small pits, of two feet deep and four feet in diameter each, to contain poor human blood, but not to float a canoe."

Mr. Lartigue is seemingly in error in supposing that captives formed the greater number of those slain to serve Gezo in Dead-land, for the general rule is, and there was no reason for departing from it in this case, to despatch the immediate attendants and favourite wives of the deceased, so that he may find himself surrounded

[1] Wheelbarrow.

by those he knows. The exhibition of grief and fear that he mentions is also very unusual, and one is almost tempted to think that he was influenced by his ideas of what the victims ought to feel; for, almost invariably, those doomed to die exhibit the greatest coolness and unconcern. The natural dread of death which the instinct of self-preservation has implanted in every breast, often leads persons who are liable to be seized for immolation to endeavour to escape; but once they are seized and bound, they resign themselves to their fate with the greatest apathy. This is partly due to the less delicate nervous system of the negro; but one reason, and that not the least, is that they have nothing to fear. As has been said, they have but to undergo a surgical operation and a change of place of residence; there is no uncertain future to be faced, and above all there is an entire absence of that notion of a place of terrible punishment which makes so many Europeans cowards when face to face with death.

As a rule those sacrificed at a Grand Custom are the Joto-si (personal attendants on the king, answering to the *okra* of Ashanti, though here women as well as men can join the body), the chief eunuch, the head-wives, the birthday wives, *i. e.* those whom the king married on his natal day, the *kpo-si*, or leopard wives, usually the youngest and handsomest of the harem, and a suitable following of soldiers, Amazons, bards, drummers, &c. After the sacrifice of the victims it is usual for the new king to build a mausoleum for his predecessor, the swish of which is kneaded with rum and human blood, and interspersed with glass beads and cowries. This building is called a missanga.

In former times, as soon as the king expired, the women of the palace commenced breaking up the furniture, ornaments, and utensils, and then proceeded to destroy themselves. The reason of course was that they might at once join their lord, and he be surrounded by familiar and useful articles. This wholesale destruction used to continue until the successor to the throne was appointed; and when Bossa Ahadee (Tegbwesun) died in 1774, 285 of the women were killed before the king elect, Adanzu II., could break into the palace and put an end to the carnage. Bossa was interred in a sedan chair that had been presented to him by Mr. Norris, six of his wives being buried alive with him, and the bodies of all those who had perished in the palace were put into the same grave. This slaughter, however, was surpassed when Adanzu II. himself died in 1789, for on that occasion 595 of the palace women are said to have destroyed each other. Gezo put an end to this practice by making all his officials, men and women, take a sacred oath to prevent it by all means in their power. He also materially reduced the number of human sacrifices throughout the kingdom, by forbidding any victim to be put to death at the decease of any official, the Mingan and Mehu excepted, who were to be allowed one slave each.

Winahiu, or Agongoro, who succeeded Adanzu II., took with him from Kana, on his first visit to his father's tomb at Agbomi, forty-eight men, whom he caused to be killed at intervals along the road, saying, " He would walk in blood all the way from Kana to Agbomi, to see his father."

The Annual Custom now usually takes place in

October, November, or December, and may be considered
to be a continuation of the Grand Custom in a modified
form, the number of victims rarely exceeding seventy or
eighty, half of whom are men, sacrificed in the town, and
half women, put to death by the Amazons in the palaces,
and unseen by the outer world. The execution of the
men takes place in public, the king commencing the
sacrifice by decapitating a kneeling victim, and the chief
officials then following suit in order of rank. Usually
most of the victims are criminals who have been sentenced to death, and reserved for execution until this
period. Until the reign of Gelele (1858), the male
victims were led about the town for some days before
execution, gagged and bound; and all visitors to Agbomi,
Europeans not excepted, were compelled to witness the
sacrifices.

In 1772, Mr. Robert Norris, Governor of the English
fort at Whydah, visited the then king, Bossa Ahadee, at
Agbomi, and witnessed the Annual Custom, which that
year was held in February. At that time the king had
two palaces in the town, called respectively Dahomi
and Agringomi, and one outside called Dampogi.
Each consisted of a number of detached buildings,
standing in a court some 1700 yards square, enclosed
by a wall about 20 feet high. The town itself was
surrounded by a ditch, without a breastwork, the clay
from the former having apparently been used to build
the houses. The ditch was crossed by four wooden
bridges, and at each there was a guard-house with
soldiers. The Annual Custom then, as now, lasted
about a month, during which there was some public
exhibition every fourth, or market, day.

K

On February 5th, 1772, Norris had an interview with
the king.   He was received at the palace-gate by the
Mehu, the second officer of the kingdom.   On each side
of it was a human head, recently cut off, lying on a flat
stone, with the face down and the bloody neck towards
the entrance.   In the guard-house were about forty
women, each armed with musket and cutlass, and
twenty eunuchs with bright iron rods in their hands,
one of whom went to announce his arrival.   The Mehu
led him through the first court to a door, near which
were two more heads, where he prostrated himself and
kissed the ground.   On this it was opened by a woman,
and they entered a second court, surrounded by piazzas.
In this they met the Mingan, the first official of the
kingdom, and the Yevo-gan, or Viceroy of Whydah,
who, with the Mehu, frequently knelt down and kissed
the ground, calling aloud some of the king's "strong
names."   In this court were arranged six human heads.
Entering a third court Norris found the king, seated in
a chair of crimson velvet ornamented with gold fringe,
and placed on a carpet in a piazza.   The Mingan and
his two companions immediately prostrated themselves,
rubbed their foreheads in the dust, kissed the ground
repeatedly, and crawled towards the king on their hands
and knees, prostrating themselves, and throwing dust on
their heads with both hands.   Norris presented the king
with a sedan-chair, with which he was much pleased,
and went off in it to show himself to his women.

On February 6th, Norris saw seven human victims,
fastened by the wrists and ankles to tall posts fixed in
the ground.   They were to remain thus secured till the
eve of the next market-day, when their heads were to

be struck off. They seemed quite indifferent concerning their fate, and he saw them endeavóuring to beat time to some music that was going on. An equal number of horses, fastened to stakes, were to suffer the same fate as the men. In another part of the town were the heads of thirty-two horses and thirty-six men, who had been killed at the two preceding festivals.

At the entrance of the market-place he saw two gibbets, about 20 feet high, with a dead man hanging naked by the ankles from each ; and at the other end of the market were two other gibbets, similarly furnished. These men had been beaten to death with clubs, and "had their privities cut close off, that the delicacy of the king's women, who had to march under them in a procession, on a festival about eight days before, might not be offended."

On February 7th, there was a procession of about 700 of the king's women, who danced before the guard-house at Dahomi palace, while a number of men under arms were drawn up at a distance to prevent the populace approaching. When the women retired, the commander-in-chief advanced with about 5000 soldiers, who went through various evolutions, concluding with a general dance.

Next day there was a festival at the parade-ground at Agringomi palace. On each side of the entrance were three human heads, which had been cut off the night before. In the centre of the square was a lofty tent, or large umbrella, conical in shape, about 50 feet high, and 40 feet wide. It rested upon a circular iron railing, through which the king could see what passed. He soon made his appearance and seated

himself under his tent. After the music had played about
an hour, a buffoon danced a grotesque dance, and the
procession then began. First came a guard of 120
men, carrying blunderbusses, and marching two abreast.
Next came fifteen of the king's daughters, attended by
fifty female slaves; and then, marching in single file, 730
of his wives, bearing provisions and drink for an enter-
tainment in the market-place. These were followed by
a guard of ninety women-soldiers, with drums beating.
Next, six troops, each of seventy women, succeeded; each
headed by a favourite, walking under an umbrella. She
who led the van was considered too precious to be seen,
her attendants hiding her from sight with an umbrella,
and certain long shields of leather, covered with red and
blue taffeta, with which they surrounded her. All these
performed songs and dances as they passed, and the
favourites went into the tent to pay their respects, and
received considerable presents of cowries. The women
were succeeded by ten bands of the king's younger
children, fifteen in each, from about seven to fifteen years
of age, each band consisting of those of about the same
size. Seven troops of fifty women followed next, each
troop preceded by two English flags. These, like the
preceding ones, danced and sang when passing the king.
Four of the women had each a long leopard's tail
fastened to the loins, which by a circular movement of
the hips they caused to swing round and round with
surprising velocity.

When the women had marched out, the eunuchs
began their songs in the king's praise, enumerating his
" strong names." and proclaiming his grandeur and
gallant deeds. This continued till the women had com-

pleted the preparations in the market-place, when the king retired and a procession was formed. First came two coaches, drawn each by twelve men ; next, the sedan-chair presented by Mr. Norris ; then three hammocks screened from the sun by large umbrellas of gold and silver tissue, and covered with canopies of the same. Each of these was surrounded by a strong guard, and the king was in one of them, but whether in coach, chair, or hammock it would have been criminal for any of the bystanders to guess. Norris' hammock followed next, and then five others belonging to the principal officers of state, accompanied by an immense crowd of attendants and spectators.

In this order they proceeded to Aj-yahi market, passing under five gibbets, with a man suspended on each, as before described, and who had been slain the previous night. Norris, the principal officers, and their attendants, entered an inclosure divided off from the crowd by gay cloths upon rails, and at one end of which was a higher inclosure of finer cloth, for the king. A dinner was served inside, and food and brandy in large quantities distributed amongst the crowd.

Nothing material occurred during the three succeeding days, but on the 12th was another festival. The dances and processions were much the same as before, except that the dresses and ornaments of the women were more showy. The display of rich silks, silver bracelets, coral and other valuable beads was great ; and there was a troop of forty women with silver helmets. There was a parade of the king's property, some of the women carrying swords, others, silver-mounted guns ; more than 100 had gold or silver-headed canes; some fifty bore silver candlesticks, and others lamps, &c, Dinner was served, as before, in the market-place.

Another festival took place on the 16th. A large stage, 100 feet long and 40 broad, was built against the palace wall, on a number of posts some 10 feet high. The front and sides were protected by railings, which with the floor were covered with carpets and country cloths. At a little distance, a thorn fence kept off the crowd. On the stage were piled a great quantity of cowries, strung in bunches of 2000 each, pieces of silk, brocade, European and native cloths, coral beads, tobacco, pipes, &c. The king, with his principal officers, seated himself on this stage, where, after each official had been allowed to choose a piece of stuff for himself, the remainder were thrown over the thorn fence to the crowd ; who, stark naked, except for the bag suspended round the loins and hanging in front for the reception of the cowries, &c., scrambled and fought for the spoil. At the end, a man tied neck and heels, a muzzled crocodile, and a couple of pigeons with their wings clipped were thrown down. A great scramble to obtain the heads of these took place, for the heads are the prizes, and the winners are rewarded with a handsome present. This human sacrifice concluded the Custom, and, according to report, the body of the victim was almost entirely devoured, as all the mob below would have a taste of it.

During this century the Annual Custom seems to have taken two forms, one called the Attoh-ton-we, or Attoh year, which terminates with the distribution of the king's gifts from the platform, called Attoh ; and the other the So-sin-we, or Horse-tie-year, at which horses are sacrificed as well as human beings. Both of these ceremonies are mentioned in the above account by Mr. Norris as having taken place at the one Custom ; but now the rule seems to be that they take place on alternate years, and never together. Barbarous and semi - civilized peoples cling so tenaciously to established customs, that, with this exception, the ceremonial of the Annual Custom has scarcely altered at all since 1772 ; and it will therefore be unnecessary to give descriptions from the works of later travellers, except upon the point which is the immediate subject of this chapter.

In 1850, an Attoh year, when Commander Forbes, R.N., visited Agbomi, twelve men (eight lashed in baskets and four in small canoes), a crocodile, and a cat were thrown down from the platform. The mob cried to the king to "feed them, they were hungry." Forbes says [1]—" As we reached our seats, a fearful yell rent the air. The victims were held high above the heads of their bearers, and the naked ruffians (the mob) thus acknowledged the munificence of their prince. Silence again ruled, and the king made a speech, stating that of his prisoners he gave a portion to his soldiers, as his father and grandfather had done before. These were Attoh-pahms. Having called their names, the one nearest was divested of his clothes, the foot of the basket placed on the parapet, when the king gave the upper part an impetus, and the victim fell at once into the pit beneath. A fall of upwards of 12 feet might have stunned him, and before sense was returned the head was cut off and the body thrown to the mob, who, now armed with clubs and branches, brutally mutilated, and

[1] *Dahomey and the Dahomans,* vol. ii. p. 52.

dragged it to a distant pit, where it was left as food for the beasts and birds of prey. After the third victim had thus been sacrificed the king retired, and the chiefs and slave-dealers completed the deed which the monarch blushed to finish." According to this author, Gezo had reduced the total number of human victims sacrificed at the Annual Custom to thirty-six.

The year 1862, in which Captain Wilmot, R.N., visited Agbomi, was also an Attoh year. On that occasion a number of fowls (all cocks), tied to long poles, some goats in baskets, a bull, and seven men secured in baskets, were thrown down from the platform.

The only account of a So-sin year is the exceedingly minute and detailed one given by Captain R. F. Burton,[1] who was at Agbomi in 1863-4. He saw twenty victims in a shed in the Uhun-jro market-place, seated on stools, and secured to the posts; and nineteen in a similar structure in front of the palace. The bodies of nine from the first shed were afterwards seen on scaffolds in the market-place, and the heads of fourteen occupants of the second shed near the palace-gates; the remainder were apparently spared.

The Annual Custom, whether Attoh or So-sin, is always opened by a ceremony at Kana, to celebrate the downfall of the Yorubas, to whom, until the reign of Gezo, Dahomi used to pay tribute at Kana. The ceremony is called Gezo's Custom, and is said to have been instituted by him. About a dozen human victims are sacrificed, and their bodies placed on platforms from 30 to 40 feet high. The corpses are dressed in the Yoruba fashion, and placed in an erect position.

[1] *Mission to Gelele*, vol. i. pp. 348—386; vol. ii. pp. 1—62.

)ne usually leads a dead sheep, and the others hold in
heir hands calabashes containing maize or some other
ountry product; the idea being to show that the
'orubas are an agricultural and pastoral people.

The despatching of messages to the deceased kings
auses a far greater loss of human life than do the
Justoms, it having been estimated that 500 persons are
lain in ordinary years to convey messages to the dead.
'his number seems enormous, but it has become the
ustom to report the most trivial occurrences, such as a
hange of residence from one palace to another, and the
stimate is probably within the mark. Frequently too
t occurs to the king that he has omitted something he
vished to add to the message, and this has to be confided
o a new messenger, who at once follows the first.
Several messengers were despatched in the presence of
J. Lartigue, who says—

" A captive, carefully gagged, was presented to the
:ing by the minister of justice, who asked if he had
to message for his father to confide to the prisoner.   In
act he had something to communicate, and several
fficials took his instructions and transmitted them to
he victim, who answered in the affirmative by nodding
:is head.   It was strange to see the faith of this man,
vho was going to be killed, in order that he might carry
ut his mission.   He was decapitated, after having
eceived a piastre and a bottle of rum for the expenses
f the journey.   Two hours after, four other messengers
leparted under the same conditions, but these were
.ccompanied by a turkey-buzzard, an antelope, and a
nonkey gagged like the men."

Of these last victims, one man was to go to the

markets of Dead-land, and tell the people there what a
magnificent Custom Gelele was going to make for his
father, Gezo; another was to go to the roads of Dead-
land and tell the travellers, and a third to its waters,
and inform the fishermen and others.   The antelope
was to hasten to the forests of Dead-land and prepare
the ghost-antelopes for the great event, and the monkey
to the mangrove swamps to inform the ghost-monkeys.
These two animals were slain like the men, but the
turkey-buzzard was set free to fly up into the air and
inform the denizens of Khe-khe-me, "Free-air Region,"
what was about to take place.

Human sacrifices rarely take place amongst the
Ewe-speaking peoples, except in Dahomi, but they used
to be frequent in Porto Novo, and have not yet quite
ceased, notwithstanding the French Protectorate.   The
victims, however, criminals or prisoners of war, are now
put to death privately.   There is a shrine in the town
of Porto Novo, called by the French *Le temple de la
Mort*, where sacrifices used to be made in public up to
within thirty years ago.   It is still covered with human
skulls nailed to the walls, and cemented into the
masonry posts.

The constant spectacle of human sacrifice has in
Dahomi, as in Ashanti, produced a general callousness
to human suffering, and a want of human sympathy
that is most revolting.   Victims destined for sacrifice are
however, treated as well as can be expected; they being
well fed, and partially released from their bonds to
enable them to sleep, even when they are criminals or
war-captives, and as the general mode of execution is
by decapitation, death is almost instantaneous.

CHAPTER IX.

THE PRIESTHOOD.

On the Gold Coast the priesthood is quite un-
organized, and possesses neither discipline nor combination, but on the Slave Coast there is a marked change
in this respect, the priests of each general or tribal god
forming a distinct body or sect, which has its own rules
and distinctive practices. As might be expected, this
is the more marked in Dahomi than among the western
tribes, where the people have but little cohesion, and
the inhabitants of the towns and villages live in a state
of semi-independence, which is naturally reflected in
their hierarchy. Amongst the Ewe-speaking people
also women take a much larger part in the business of
religion than is the case on the Gold Coast, and there
are probably nearly as many women engaged in it as
men. In Dahomi, where the "wives" of the gods are
very numerous, it has even been estimated that every
fourth woman is connected with the service of the
gods.

The ordinary designation for a priest amongst the
eastern Ewe tribes is *vōdu-no*, which is applied equally
to priest or priestess. As the word *no* now means
"mother," *vōdu-no* is commonly believed to mean

" võdu-mother"; and the use of *no* in this and other titles has led some Europeans, notably Captain Burton,[1] to suppose that women take precedence of men. This is, however, a mistake. The word *no* was originally a verb, having the meaning " to sit, or stay with "; its use in the sense of " mother " is comparatively modern, and it still retains its old meaning in compound words. Hence *võdu-no* does not mean " võdu-mother," but " he who stays with the võdu "; and a priest is so styled because the priests live near the temples or shrines. Amongst the western tribes the term for a priest is *nunola*, which word is derived from the verb *no nu*, literally " to sit in the mouth," which is used almost solely with reference to priests, and means " to mediate." The termination *la* signifies " person who." Another word used by the western tribes to convey the meaning of " priest " or " priestess " is *edrõ-kosi*, though this term really covers all persons belonging to or connected with an *edrõ*, or god.

Recruits for the priesthood are obtained in two ways, viz., by the affiliation of young persons, and by the direct consecration of adults. Young people of either sex dedicated or affiliated to a god are termed *kosio*, from *kono*, " unfruitful," because a child dedicated to a god passes into his service and is practically lost to his parents, and *si*, " to run away." As the females become the " wives " of the god to whom they are dedicated, the termination *si* in *kosi*, and also in *võdu-si*, has been translated " wife " by some Europeans; but it is never used in the general acceptation of that term, being entirely restricted to persons consecrated to the gods.

[1] *Loc. cit.* note to p. 95, vol. i.

The chief business of the female *kosi* is prostitution, and in every town there is at least one institution in which the best-looking girls, between ten and twelve years of age, are received. Here they remain for three years, learning the chants and dances peculiar to the worship of the gods, and prostituting themselves to the priests and the inmates of the male seminaries; and at the termination of their novitiate they become public prostitutes. This condition, however, is not regarded as one for reproach; they are considered to be married to the god, and their excesses are supposed to be caused and directed by him. Properly speaking, their libertinage should be confined to the male worshippers at the temple of the god, but practically it is indiscriminate. Children who are born from such unions belong to the god.

Girls dedicated to a god do not necessarily serve him during the whole of their lives, for some only bear his name, and sacrifice to him on their birthdays; and in Dahomi there seems to be a marked distinction between those who actually minister to the service of the temple, and those who are merely temple prostitutes. The former are called *vōdu-sio*, and may be regarded as priestesses proper, while the latter alone are in that kingdom termed *kosio*. In Dahomi these *kosio* are obliged to confine themselves to certain localities, and have to pay an annual tax to the king; while the price of their favours is also fixed by law and is very small. Owing to these regulations, most Europeans have considered that the institution of the *kosio* is the outcome of state policy, designed to remedy the evils of polygamy and the monopolization of large numbers of women by

the chiefs, whereas it is essentially religious in it
origin, and intimately connected with phallic worship
The tax is paid by the *kosio* at the Annual Custom, an
Norris saw 252 of them dancing before the king
Captain Burton also saw some at Agbomi in 1863-4
They played the *addugba* drum during the day at th
palace, and at night retired to their own quarters, nea
the Agbomi gate and Bwekon village. They wore blu
cloths and white fillets, and had their bosoms covered
an unusual distinction amongst the women of DaLomi.

Vōdu-sio and female *kosio* must not be confounded
with the *vōdu-vio* (*vōdu*, and *vi*, a child), the latte
being children who are claimed by a god, and who only
wear the priestly raiment on ceremonial occasions ; or
in Dahomi, during the Annual Custom, when they dance
in the public squares of Agbomi. A *vōdu-si* or *kos*
may not marry, since she is already the spouse of a god
but a *vōdu-vi* may. The husband of a *vōdu-vi* must
however, treat her with great respect, and he may not
reprove or punish her for any excesses, sexual or other
which she may commit when the god inspires her.

Male *kosio* undergo, like the females, a three years
novitiate in their seminaries, which it may be observed
are much less common than those for female *kosio*
learning the chants, dances, and general ceremonial of
religion ; and at the termination of that period, each
candidate has to show, as on the Gold Coast, that the
god whom he has elected to serve, accepts him and
finds him worthy of inspiration.

The ceremony is very similar to that described at
length in Chapter X. of the Tshi-speaking peoples—
pages 131—138. The would-be priest, accompanied by

relatives and friends, is taken by a party of priests
to a shrine of the god in question, to whom sacrifices
are offered forthwith. His head is then shaved, his
cloth removed, and his body lubricated with a decoction
of herbs, the exact number required for its preparation
being, according to the priests, 101. He is next girded
round the loins with a girdle of palm-leaves, and then
led in procession round and round the shrine, the priests
chanting invocations, and the relatives and friends
prostrating themselves. This lasts for some time, after
which he is attired in a new cloth, usually white in
colour, and the crucial test is made. The aspirant to
holy orders is seated on the stool that appertains to
the god, and the priests anoint his head with the
mystic decoction, invoking the while the god to declare
whether he accepts him as his priest or not. The invocation takes the form of a wild chorus, which lasts
for some ten minutes, and is repeated three times;
after which, if the god has not entered the body of the
candidate, it is understood that he rejects him. It is
rare for a person to be thus rejected, for it is very
exceptional for a youth to be affiliated against his will;
consequently it nearly always happens that, as the
chorus is raised for the third time, he begins to tremble
violently, simulates convulsions, foams at the mouth,
then dances as if frenzied, and at last, after the most
violent exertions which sometimes last more than an
hour, suddenly returns to his senses. The god having
thus accepted him, a feast is held, after which the new
priest is conducted by his fellows to a temple, where he
has to remain for seven days and nights without speaking a word. At the end of this time he is brought out,

a priest opens his mouth to show that he may now use his tongue, a new name is given him, and he is fully ordained. A man who becomes a priest in this way is considered to belong to the family of the chief priest who initiated him, and, if the latter should die childless, he becomes his heir. As a consequence of this adoption he cannot marry one of the priest's children.

In the direct ordination ceremony the aspirant, an adult, is surrounded by images set in a ring, or by symbols of the different gods. Then, if a god thinks him worthy, he is possessed ; and during the possession falls down as if in a fit before the image or symbol of the god who has accepted him. After this he is removed to a temple of the god in question, where he undergoes a three years' novitiate, learning the business of religion and the priestly language, a secret tongue, unintelligible to the laity. As will be seen, the main difference between this and the other mode of ordination is that the three years' training follows, instead of preceding, the test of being found worthy by the gods for the office. It is, however, more expensive, as the family have to pay heavy fees at the termination of the novitiate.

In the kingdoms of Dahomi and Porto Novo the king is regarded as the head of the priesthood; he convokes councils of the priests on extraordinary occasions, and in the first-named every new priest has to be taken before the king in Agbomi, where he is invested in a new cloth, given a new name, and advised as to his future duties. The union between despotism and priestcraft is not, however, very close, and if the king were to disregard religious customs he would soon suffer.

As an example—when Mesi was king of Porto Novo
(1872-5), a young man, who had been sentenced by the
priests of Dañh-gbi to be burned alive for accidentally
killing a python, contrived to escape from the hut in
which he was confined, and flying to the king placed
himself under his protection by offering him his head,
a native formula by which a person makes himself the
slave of another. As soon as the priests discovered his
place of refuge, they went in a body to the palace and
demanded his surrender. The king proposed that a
heavy fine should be imposed instead, but the priests
insisted that nothing but the death of the offender
would satisfy the outraged god; and when Mesi finally
declined to surrender him to them, the whole body,
priests and priestesses, rushed about the town as if
demented, some with their faces painted red and white,
others covered with blood or mud, and all crying for
vengeance. The whole town was in a tumult, and the
ordinary market could not be held, as the infuriated
priests molested the market people and upset their
wares. Mesi, upon this, caused the priests to be informed
that if they would assemble in the large market-place
next morning he would give them satisfaction; in the
meantime he had the Zangbeto, or secret police, quietly
gathered together in the palace during the night, and
when the priests and priestesses were assembled, he let
the police out on them. Most of the priesthood escaped,
but a great number were seized by the Zangbeto and sold
for slaves. After this, Mesi's authority in ecclesiastical
matters was not openly disputed, but the priests did
not forgive him, and before long he died from the
effects of poison administered by them.

L

Priests and priestesses may usually be distinguished by their having half the head shaved, while the hair is allowed to grow long on the other half; priests always conform to this custom, and so do the great majority of the priestesses, though it is only imperatively required to be observed by those of Sapatan. Priests generally wear white caps, and priestesses decorate the head with beads, cowries, or the red feathers of parrots. In Dahomi the latter wear a broad-brimmed, steeple-crowned hat, called the *ta-bla*, the crown of which is very narrow, while the brim is enormous; they have gay-coloured cloths wrapped round the waist and falling to the feet, and handkerchiefs covering the bosom.

Besides the ordinary tribal tattoo marks borne by all natives, the priesthood in Dahomi bear a variety of such marks, some very elaborate, and an expert can tell by the marks on a priest to what god he is vowed, and what rank he holds in the order. These hierarchal marks consist of lines, scrolls, diamonds, and other patterns, with sometimes a figure, such as that of the croco-dile or chameleon. The shoulders are frequently seen covered with an infinite number of small marks, like dots, set close together. All these marks are considered sacred, and the laity are forbidden to touch them.

Priests frequently carry a long stick, peculiar to the craft, terminating in a fork, to which one or two shreds of calico are attached. They are restricted in diet according to the god they serve, some being forbidden to eat mutton, others fowls, &c. Most of them live upon the fees paid by worshippers and the offerings made at the temples; but many who do not realize enough by their profession follow other avocations as well. They learn a number of medicinal receipts, and are proficient in the knowledge of poisons and their antidotes, which is a secret of the craft, and they derive a considerable income from this source.

The priesthood have many privileges. In Dahomi they may wear dresses forbidden by the sumptuary laws to the commonalty, and in former times no priest was liable to capital punishment. Any crime a priest might commit while possessed by a god also bore no consequences to him ; but this was so abused by members of the priesthood, who took advantage of it to gratify their hatred or their lust, that, under Gezo, the law was altered ; and though, while posssssed, the criminal is still safe, yet as soon as the god leaves him he is now liable to punishment. Amongst the Eẃe-speaking peoples as a whole, the person of a priest or priestess is sacred. Not only must a layman not lay hands on or insult one ; he must be careful not even to knock one by accident, or jostle against one in the street. The Abbé Bouche relates [1] that once when he was paying a visit to the chief of Agweh, one of the wives of the chief was brought into the house by four priestesses, her face bloody, and her body covered with stripes. She had been savagely flogged for having accidentally trodden upon the foot of one of them ; and the chief not only dared not give vent to his anger, but had to give them a bottle of rum as a peace-offering.

A priest or priestess who is struck on the head, a crime which entails very serious consequences to the assailant, is considered thereby to lose favour with the god he serves ; to use the English expression in vogue

[1] *La Côte des Esclaves,* pp. 127, 128.

on the Slave Coast, he "loses the fetish." A member
of the priesthood who has been thus assaulted, disappears for about forty days, during which time the
other members of the fraternity hold daily ceremonies,
at the expense of the person who has committed the
sacrilege, to induce the god to take their brother again
into favour. At the end of this period the god usually
signifies his compliance, and then the outraged priest
appears in public, clothed from head to foot in a mantle
of palm-leaves, and wearing, slung across the breast, a
bag containing seven or eight short bludgeons. He
carries another of these weapons in his hand, and, simulating possession, with rolling eyes, uncertain step, and
strange gestures, he promenades the streets, threatening
passers-by with the bludgeon, and hurling one at any-
body who does not seem to exhibit sufficient respect.
This performance lasts for some hours, at the end of
which the priest assumes his ordinary demeanour. The
leaves of the palm-leaf costume are sold, and eagerly
purchased, for they are believed to be a powerful charm
against sickness.

The female *kosio* of Dañh-gbi, or *Dañh-sio*, that is,
the wives, priestesses, and temple prostitutes of Dañh-
gbi, the python-god, have their own organization.
Generally they live together in a group of houses or
huts inclosed by a fence, and in these inclosures the
novices undergo their three years of initiation. Most
new members are obtained by the affiliation of young
girls; but any woman whatever, married or single,
slave or free, by publicly simulating possession, and
uttering the conventional cries recognized as indicative
of possession by the god, can at once join the body, and

be admitted to the habitations of the order. The person of a woman who has joined in this manner is inviolable, and during the period of her novitiate she is forbidden, if single, to enter the house of her parents, and, if married, that of her husband. This inviolability, while it gives women opportunities of gratifying an illicit passion, at the same time serves occasionally to save the persecuted slave, or neglected wife, from the ill-treatment of the lord and master; for she has only to go through the conventional form of possession and an asylum is assured. The accounts of the older writers on the Slave Coast, in Astley's and Churchill's collections, abound with instances of this, with full descriptions of the procedure observed at that time.

Dañh-sio usually appear in public with the bosom smeared with palm-oil; but their distinguishing mark is a necklace, called *adunka*, made of a very fine string twisted from the filaments of a palm-leaf. On ceremonial occasions they wear a fillet of the same material, with anklets, bracelets, and neck-strings of cowries. Their ordinary clothing consists of a strip of cotton-print, hanging from the waist and barely reaching to the knee. They are most licentious, and have not the slightest regard for public decency. Should a *Dañh-si* meet a man alone in the street, she unfastens her waist-cloth, and, holding it back, exposes herself naked without the least shame; sometimes even she goes so far as to importune or seize the man. Whenever it rains they strip off their cloths, fold them up, hold them under the arm-pit, and proceed about their business stark naked.

At Agweh and the two Popos custom forbids the

Dañh-sio to use the ordinary salutations *ndo nao*, or *ndo na mi*, "Good-day"; and when they meet a superior whom they wish to salute, they turn the back, kneel down, and strike the palms of the hands together several times, only rising after the salutation *ndo nao* has been returned.

When a *Dañh-si* is insulted, as sometimes happens, she raises a loud cry, which is at once taken up by all her fellows, who run to her assistance, armed with sticks and whips; and proceeding to the house of the offending person, they throw themselves on the ground, and howl and yell and behave like Furies. If compensation be not then offered, they enter the house, tear down the fences, and commence to pillage; but this can always be checked by placing palm-leaves in their path. They are bound to respect this frail barrier and retire to the street; for, used in this manner, the palm-leaf signifies that the house is placed under the protection of the python-god.

It is difficult to arrive at an exact conclusion as to what the priests themselves believe of the gods whose worship they inculcate; but I think that, as a rule, they are convinced of their existence as superhuman beings; and if sometimes a priest may be found who does not believe in the god in whose service he is himself enrolled, he believes none the less in the other gods. In regard to possession, the priests seem to be fully aware of the fact that an empty stomach is productive of hallucinations and mental aberrations; hence persons who wish to consult the gods are enjoined to fast, while drugs are sometimes administered as well. The honest priest, in a condition of morbid mental exaltation produced by these means, firmly believes, I think, that he is inspired by a god, when, wound up to a great pitch of religious enthusiasm, he makes those utterances which are regarded by the bystanders as the words of the god. He imposes on himself first, and afterwards upon others, while the impostors who pretend to be possessed conform to the procedure established by honest visionaries. Moreover, mental exaltation, like all other forms of mania, often becomes contagious; so that, when acting in concert, one ecstatic priest sometimes makes many.

Amongst these people ecstasy or ecstatic rapture does not reach such extremes as were common with female fanatics in the early days of Christianity; principally, it seems, because, as continence is not regarded as a virtue by the natives, the laws of nature are not thereby violated, and the element of hysteria is lacking. Hence there are never instances of women who imagine themselves in contact with a material and anthropomorphous deity, who fires them with an ardent love; and, perhaps as a consequence of this, myths of unions between the gods and women are unheard of, except to the extent of erotic dreams being ascribed to Legba.

In many of the minor practices of religion, most, if not all, of the priests must be conscious of their fraud; but this does not affect their belief in the truth of their religion as a whole. Many believe that in cases of trial by ordeal, it is really the god who decides the guilt or innocence of the accused; but those who are "behind the scenes" must know well that the result of the ordeal is determined upon beforehand. All seem to believe firmly in divination as a means of drawing inferences concerning the course of future events. Without reasoning how it is done, they think that coming events are somehow foreshadowed by it; just as I have seen English ladies telling fortunes by cards, and deducing vague generalities from the succession in which the cards fall, more than half persuaded that there is something in it.

Fasting, amongst the Ewe-speaking peoples, means absolute abstention from food of all kinds; but not from drink, and intoxicants are freely indulged in. There is no food that can be taken without violating the fast, as is the case on the Gold Coast, where in Ashanti fruit can be so eaten. The modification which there obtains may perhaps be regarded as a commencement of that exercise of priestly ingenuity, which in more civilized communities now enables the letter of ecclesiastical enactments with regard to fasting to be observed, while the spirit is eluded.

CHAPTER X.

CEREMONIES AT BIRTH, MARRIAGE, AND DEATH.

I.—AT BIRTH.

THE customs of peoples upon the same plane of
civilization so nearly resemble one another, that the
account I have given of the ceremonies observed at
birth by the Tshi-speaking peoples applies generally to
the Ewe-speaking peoples. As on the Gold Coast the
woman, as soon as she finds herself pregnant, offers
sacrifice to the gods, more especially to the protecting
ñoli of the family ; and as soon as the child is born,
both mother and infant are taken charge of by a priestess,
who offers sacrifice to Legba, to prevent his interfering
with or doing harm to them. The mother and child
are considered unclean, and it is not until forty days
have elapsed that the former may return to her usual
avocation, though she is usually purified with lustral
water seven days after the birth.

This is all much the same as on the Gold Coast,
and there is little to add except with regard to those
easterly Ewe tribes, who have acquired a hazy notion of
metempsychosis from their Yoruba-speaking neighbours.
Amongst these the Bukono, as the priest of Ife, God of

Divination, is termed by them, is sent for soon after the birth, to announce what ancestor has sent the child, and eight days after birth it is given a name. This, which is the proper or birth-name, is called *nyi*, in contra-distinction to the *nyi-sese*, or "strong names," that are adopted in later life. The choice of the *nyi* is governed by certain rules. Usually it is the *nyi* of the ancestor whom the Bukono alleges to have sent the child into the world, but Atsu is the name given to the first-born of twin-brothers, Tse to the second, and Dosu to a male child born after twins; while children who have been sent by their great-grandmothers are called Degen-no. If a man adopts the worship and divination of Ife before the births of his children, the first boy is called Amoso and the first girl Alugba; the second boy Mocho, and the second girl Alugba-we. In Dahomi, the *nyi* is not retained long by male children, being usually dropped when the boy reaches manhood, after which he takes his name from the position he holds, changing it as he changes his position.

It is worthy of note that it is the priest who here names the child; not the father, as is the case on the Gold Coast; a new departure which marks the increased power of the priesthood and their disposition to control and interfere in all the principal events of life. The name-giving is also combined with the purification of the new-born child, the priest bathing its forehead with water, and repeating three times the name it is to bear, while on the Gold Coast there is no connection between these two ceremonies.

A child does not here take a name from the day of the week on which it is born, for it is only the western

Ewe tribes who have names for the days of the week, and these they seem to have borrowed from their Ga-speaking neighbours.

II.—AT MARRIAGE.

As on the Gold Coast, a young girl advertises her arrival at the age of puberty by visiting her relatives and friends, attired in her best cloths, and bedecked with the family jewelry; after which, should she not already be betrothed, a suitor soon declares himself. This he does by sending a man and a woman to her father's house with two large flasks of rum, which they deposit on the floor, with the remark—"Our uncle wants to marry one of your girls;" and the father, having learned from them the name of the suitor, the emissaries retire. If the proposal be acceptable the family is informed of the offer, and the two rum-flasks are returned empty to the suitor as a sign that he is accepted. He then sends two more full flasks, with two heads of cowries and two pieces of cotton cloth for the girl; after which he enters into negotiations with the parents as to the price he will be required to pay for her. The gift of cowries and cotton cloth constitutes betrothal, after which the suitor can claim compensation for any liberties that other men may take with his *fiancée;* on the other hand, the suitor, during the period between the betrothal and the marriage, and which, if he be poor and the girl's price high, may be long, is expected to perform all the religious duties that may be incumbent on her.

On the day of the marriage ceremony, which in

Dahomi is usually celebrated on a Sunday, the bridegroom sends a messenger with rum to the parents of the
bride soon after daybreak, and asks for his wife.   The
parents affect reluctance, and delay the messenger with
various excuses till about noon, when the bridegroom
despatches a second messenger on the same errand.
This messenger also fails, and it is not until the arrival
of a third one, who comes about sunset, that the parents
overcome their hesitation.   The bride, scented with
civet (*atiki*), and her skin given a reddish hue with a
preparation of the bark of a tree called *to*, is then
escorted by her family to the house of the bridegroom,
where a feast has been prepared.

The feasting continues till about midnight, when the
bridegroom retires to his bedroom and sits on his couch.
The bride is then brought in to him by four matrons,
who place her hands in those of her husband, saying—
"This is your wife—we give her to you.   Take her.
If she pleases you and behaves well, treat her kindly.
If she behaves ill, correct her."   They then drink rum
with the young couple and retire.

Should the girl prove to be a virgin the bridegroom
soon reappears amongst the revellers with the "tokens
of virginity" on the cloth that covered the couch, and
exhibits them to his friends ; while on the part of the
bride, a young girl who has been purposely left concealed when the matrons retired, so as to prevent the
possibility of false accusation on the part of the husband,
bears to her friends the under cloth which all native
women wear passed through the girdle of beads.   Should
the girl prove to have been unchaste, the husband has
the right to send her back to her parents, and recover

from them both the money he paid for her and the value of all presents he has made.

The next morning, supposing all to have gone well, the husband sends presents to the parents of the bride, and the latter, after a week's cohabitation with him, returns to her old home. Seven days later she cooks food and sends it to her husband, who next morning sends a present in return, and in the evening the wife returns to the husband and permanently takes up her abode with him. This postponement of regular cohabitation with the husband after the marriage has been consummated, is also found amongst the Turcomans and other peoples, and is perhaps a survival in a disintegrated shape of the form of marriage by capture. The final return to the husband is celebrated by a feast given on the day following it.

III.—AT DEATH.

A death in a family is announced by an outbreak of shrieks and lamentations on the part of the women, who throw themselves on the ground, strike their heads against the walls, and commit a variety of extravagances ; calling upon the deceased the meanwhile not to desert them, and endeavouring, by all kinds of supplications, to induce the soul to return and reanimate the body. The neighbours and friends come in and seek to console them, and at last, after a time, they recover their composure, narrate the circumstances of the melancholy event, eulogize the deceased, and finally set about preparing for the death ceremony.

The corpse is washed, attired in the best cloths, bedecked with ornaments and placed in a chair, before which a small table with food and drink is set out, while another piece of cloth is placed beside it as a change of raiment for Dead-land. The deceased is implored to eat, and portions of food are put to his lips. During this part of the ceremony the relatives must fast and not wash. They indulge largely, however, in intoxicants, and dance and sing in honour of the deceased, amid the beating of drums and the firing of guns. The friends of the family visit the mourners, and bring presents to assist towards the expenses, while the wealthy send their slaves with powder and guns, to fire salvos in honour of the dead. The ceremony usually lasts three days, a sufficiently long time to keep a corpse unburied in a tropical country, and it usually becomes offensive some thirty-six hours after death. The reason of this practice has already been given. At the beginning of the "wake" the widows and daughters of the deceased are obliged by custom to remain in a room by themselves, whence their cries and shrieks are heard mingling with the outside din; but after eight or ten hours they usually join the company.

The dead are always buried in the earthen floor of the house, which, after the interment, is always smoothed down with water. In wealthy families the room in which a person has been buried is always kept locked, and is not used. Amongst the eastern Ewe tribes the grave is so dug that the head of the deceased may project beyond the foundations of the outer wall. The poor are wrapped in grass mats, the wealthy enclosed in coffins, the sizes of which are proportionate to their riches and the quantity of goods to be buried with them. The body is always laid on one side, in an attitude as if asleep. Usually a flat-topped iron is planted on the grave, on which water, rum, or blood are poured as libations to the deceased.

When a person dies abroad, the family try to obtain something that appertained to him, such as pieces of his hair or nail-cuttings, over which the funeral ceremonies are then performed ; for the general belief is that the ghost or soul lingers near the remains until these ceremonies are carried out, and either cannot or will not depart to Dead-land before them. Hence, to declare to a criminal that, after his execution, no funeral rites will be held over his body, is to him more terrifying than death itself ; for the latter merely transmits him to another sphere, where he continues his ordinary avocations, while the former opens up to his imagination all kinds of ill-defined terrors. This rule with regard to the ill-effects of the non-performance of funeral rites, does not apply to those who are sacrificed to the gods, or to the manes of kings or chiefs, for whom such rites are rarely, if ever, held. The idea seems to be that as such persons are deprived of life for a specific religious purpose, they are not liable to the vicissitudes of ordinary ghosts.

When a Dahomi is buried abroad, some earth from his grave is always brought home, and the bodies of all Dahomi chiefs who die abroad are, whenever it is possible, sent to Agbomi for interment. The probable reason of this town being specially chosen is that nearly all the officials of the kingdom are natives of Agbomi, so that their family houses are there.

It is considered most disgraceful for a family to be unable to make some show of wealth in connection with the funeral ceremonies, and people frequently reduce themselves to poverty, or even enslave themselves or their children, in order to conduct the rites with sufficient pomp.

A widow is by custom supposed to remain in the house for forty days after the death of her husband; but, if affairs oblige her to go out, she adopts a conventional attitude of mourning, with drooping head, downcast eyes, and the arms crossed on the breast. At the termination of the forty days, her relations come to console her, her head is shaved, and she resumes her ordinary avocations.

In Agweh a widow is supposed to remain shut up for six months in the room in which her husband is buried, during which time she may not wash or change her clothes. Food is carried to her by the family. According to report, in bygone days widows underwent a kind of fumigation in these burial chambers, a fire being lighted on the floor and strewn with red peppers, till they were nearly suffocated by the fumes. At the end of the period of mourning the widows wash, shave the head, pare the nails, and put on clean cloths, the old cloths, the hair and the nail-parings being burned. At Agweh men who have lost their head wives do this also, after having remained shut up in a room of the house for eight days. Dark blue baft is usually worn in sign of mourning, but sometimes a blue thread worn round the left arm is considered sufficient.

Contact with a corpse renders a person unclean, and he must purify himself by washing in water from head to foot.

CHAPTER XI.

SYSTEM OF GOVERNMENT.

As on the Gold Coast, the government of a tribe is in the hands of the chiefs and the king, to whom the former owe allegiance as their suzerain lord. It is that of an aristocracy, for the king is controlled by the chiefs, and can make neither peace nor war, nor enter into any engagements or negotiations which affect the interests of the tribe, without their consent, and such matters are always deliberated upon by the king and chiefs in council. The populace have no voice in the government at all.

The king usually deals only with the chiefs of districts, each of whom is, as it were, a petty king in his own domain; for the sub-chiefs and head-men of his district owe direct allegiance to him. These district chiefs have their own local courts for the investigation and settlement of disputes and the punishment of crime; but any person who may be dissatisfied with the decision arrived at by a local court, has the right of appeal to the court of the king. The chiefs of minor towns, and the head-men of villages, in the district, similarly exercise jurisdiction in minor matters in their own spheres, subject to the right of appeal to the court

M

of the district chief. For the purposes of the district
in which he himself resides, the king, besides being the
paramount head of the tribe, exercises the functions of
a district chief. There is no taxation and no state
revenue, properly speaking. The sub-chiefs and head-
men subsist on the fees, bribes, and presents they
receive from those under their control, and in their
turn contribute to the wants of the district chiefs, who,
finally, subscribe to those of the king. The expenses of
war fall upon the king and chiefs, who have to supply
their followers with powder and lead; but every man
is expected to provide for his own commissariat and
transport.

The foregoing applies to the Ewe-speaking tribes
generally, but the government of Dahomi differs from
these, in that the king of Dahomi is absolute, his will
being law, and he subject to no control whatever. All
kinds of property, including the land of the kingdom,
which, in the case of other tribes, is the property of the
tribe, and only attached to the "stool" of the king, is
by law the property of the King of Dahomi; and he
can, when he pleases, confiscate the property and goods
of any individual. Of course this right is, from motives
of prudence, not exercised very frequently; but, in
theory at least, everything in Dahomi belongs to the
king, and if any man has anything in his possession, it
is only because the king tolerates it for the time being.
This theory is pushed so far that parents are held to
have no right or claim to their children, who, like everything else, belong to the king, and are only retained by
the parents at the king's pleasure.

The person of the king is sacred, and if he drink in

public, every one must turn the head so as not to see him, while some of the court women hold up a cloth before him as a screen. He never eats in public, and the people affect to believe that he neither eats nor sleeps. It is criminal to say the contrary. In the royal presence chiefs even of the highest rank are obliged to prostrate themselves like the meanest subject. There is no distinction of personages ; before the king all are slaves alike, hence it is not etiquette for him to visit even his highest officers. Persons who prostrate themselves grovel face downward on the earth, and throw handfuls of dust over their heads, shoulders, and arms. The officials of the kingdom of Dahomi are as follows :—

The Megan, or Mingan, who is the principal adviser and first civil officer of the kingdom. He is the only person in the realm whose head the king may not have struck off at will. He is the first of the Bonugan, or civilian captains, and is head of the police. As it is his duty to see death sentences carried into execution, and, in the case of distinguished criminals, to execute them himself, he is also entitled *Ame-wu-to*, " The man-killer."

Next is the Mehu, who is master of the ceremonies and a counsellor. He directs and superintends the public festivals, and has charge of all strangers, both European and native, who visit Agbomi. He speaks to the people from the king, collects revenue, and receives tribute. According to some natives, he appoints the Gau and the Posu.

The Megan and the Mehu appoint a successor to the throne from amongst the king's sons. The eldest son is considered the next heir, succession in this kingdom being, contrary to the usual practice, traced through the male line and primogenitive ; but these two officers have the power of rejecting him, and selecting one of the other children. They are judges in criminal cases, and one or the other of them is constantly with the king, informing him of everything that takes place. It may be here noted that, in the interregnum between the death of a king and the appointment of his successor, all law and order is suspended. It is a relapse into anarchy ; the greatest license prevails, and persons can plunder, or even murder, without being called to account.

Next to the Mehu is the Yevo-gan, or Governor of Whydah, the literal meaning of whose title is "Captain of the White-men." *Yevo*, or more properly *yofu*, "white," hence "white-man"; and *gan*, "captain." He never goes to war, his chief duty being to watch over Whydah, but his lieutenant, the Akho-vi, attends all campaigns.

The fourth official in the kingdom is the To-no-nun, or chief of the royal attendants, an office always held by a eunuch. He is chief of the palace interior, attends on the king, and on state occasions acts as interpreter between the Amazons and strangers. His authority is limited to the palaces, and he is put to death when the king dies.

The fifth officer is the Gau, or chief military commander ; and the sixth, his assistant, the Posu. Both of these are required by law to live near the principal gate of Agbomi.

Next comes the Ajyaho, or Jahu, who has the superintendence of the plantations which supply the king's household with provisions. He also has charge of all criminals, and in the matter of executions acts as an assistant to the Megan.

These seven are the principal personages of the kingdom. The offices are not hereditary, and the king appoints any one he thinks fit. Inferiors must salute them with bent knees and the clapping of hands. Even the king's sons are not exempted from this, for, during their father's life, they have no rank; but usually these officials, out of respect for the blood royal, take them by the hand and raise them from their deferential attitude.

The Bonugan, or civilian captains, rank next after these chief officials ; then come the royal attendants ; then the military officers; then the provincial officials and chiefs; and, lastly, the traders, who pay the duties to the king. Agriculturists, artisans, labourers, &c., have no rank. The nation in the mass are the slaves of the king, and the lower classes the slaves of the officials as well.

The officialdom of the interior of the palaces is almost an exact copy of that of the outside, nearly every male officer of the kingdom having a corresponding female official in the palace ; and this system is carried so far that, although the inmates of the palaces are all women or eunuchs, there are even female *kosio* for the "inside." The Gundeme is the female Megan, the Akpadumi the female Mehu, and the Yavedo and the Khetungan correspond to the To-no-nun and the Gau, the last being a commander of Amazons. The authority of all these palace officials does not extend beyond the palaces, but at the court they take precedence of the corresponding male officials; apparently in consequence of the state fiction that all the women of the court, including the Amazons, are the wives of the king. The female officials are called the "mothers" of the corresponding male officials, and everybody of note must have a "mother" in the palace to represent him or his interests. There is thus an "English mother" for English visitors, and every European nation that frequents or used to frequent Whydah is similarly represented. "Mother," it may be mentioned, is the official designation of an Amazon.

The provincial chiefs or officials are, like the high personages of the kingdom, appointed by the king, and are removable at will. Each village, town, or quarter of a town has its own chief, who exercises certain functions in what are called "King's Courts." The chief of a village, or quarter of a town, exercises magisterial duties in his own area, and gives decisions in ordinary disputes; matters of higher importance are referred to the chief of the town to which the quarter belongs or the village depends; and still graver matters are reserved for the judgment of the priests, or, finally, of the king. Any provincial chief can proclaim a "King's Court," by prostrating himself and kissing the ground, and at the termination of the investigation the court is closed by the same ceremony.

Officers of state and chiefs are recognizable by certain insignia, which are—

(1) The umbrella canopy, without which no high officer or chief can appear on public occasions. It is similar to that used on the Gold Coast, being large enough to shelter several persons, with a flounce, or

vallance, scalloped or cut in curves. The umbrella, when presented to a newly-made chief, is white, and he is expected to ornament it in illustration of his feats. This is done by sewing on to the vallance rude representations of knives, human heads, etc., cut out of coloured stuffs, usually red or blue. These conventional emblems have a recognized meaning, and may be regarded as a species of symbol writing.

(2) The stool, made out of a solid block of the wood of the silk-cotton tree. The more important the chief, the taller his stool. These stools are only made in Agbomi.

(3) The long pipe, enclosed in a wooden case, and the large tobacco-pouch of leather. The manufacture of the pipes is a monopoly of the palace-women. (1) and (2) are commonly only used on ceremonial occasions, but no chief may leave his house without wearing the leather tobacco-pouch, with the pipe thrust under the flap.

Chiefs may also usually be distinguished by their silver bracelets, and necklaces of coral or Popo beads. The officers of state carry, as badges of office, ivory clubs, carved out of an elephant's tusk, and the five principal dignitaries of the kingdom have, in addition, each a pair of silver horns. When the king appoints a chief, he furnishes him with the various insignia, which must be returned at his death, or upon his being degraded from his office. The royal stool of Dahomi is said to have been in the possession of the royal family since the days of Adanzu I., who died in 1680. Each leg is supported by the skull of a once formidable foe, and every third or fourth year they have, by custom, to be renewed.

The king alone has the right to take human life, and all offences which appear worthy of punishment by death are reserved for his judgment. The chiefs have the power of fine, imprisonment, or subjection to ordeal; they can also indirectly sentence a man to death by ordering him to be "given to the king," in which case he is sent to the capital and reserved for sacrifice at the Customs. The right to take human life is practically only denied to the chiefs so far as direct execution is concerned; for any chief may throw an accused into prison and there allow him to die of starvation, without being called to account. Men who die from the effects of the poisonous draughts they are compelled to drink in trials by ordeal, are, of course, believed to be slain by the deity invoked; and in this way the chiefs have open to them a safe and easy method for the removal of obnoxious persons.

Affairs of state and political matters are discussed at the capital during the Annual Custom, and inquiry into minor offences is often deferred to that time, when the meanest slave has the right of access to the king for the purpose of seeking redress. Serious offences that have not been discovered or dealt with by the provincial chiefs, and which have come to the king's knowledge, are always inquired into at once. The state executioners, called by Europeans "half-heads," from their custom of shaving one half of the head and allowing the hair to grow long on the other half, and who combine police duties with their other office, are sent to arrest the offender, whom they then bring before his immediate chief. If he be proved guilty, his head is struck off and brought to the king by the "half-heads," to show that the sentence has been carried out, or—and this is the more frequent practice—he is carried to the capital and there executed. In past times these " half-heads " used to wear round the neck and over the right shoulder strings of the teeth of the persons they had put to death ; and it was a capital offence for them to string a tooth of a man who had not fallen by their hands.

The king's time is occupied throughout the year in a routine prescribed by custom. In January or February he marches with the army on the annual marauding expedition, to return in March or April to the capital. About May he moves to Kana, and there performs the customs in memory of the defeat of the Yorubas and the cessation of tribute. In October or November he summons his officers and chiefs, leaves Kana, sleeps one night at a palace some three miles out of Kana, said to have been built by Tegbwesun, and then makes a state entry to the capital. He then holds the Annual Custom, and remains in Agbomi till the time for the annual expedition has once more arrived.

As the king is the state, the revenue belongs to him, and with it he defrays all his expenses, both public and private. It is derived from a variety of sources. First, there is that produced by a direct taxation on local productions and on all imports. This impost is called by the natives " Cowries of the Street," and the collectors are termed " Masters of the Street." The latter are posted on the most frequented roads, at certain places on the lagoons, where, to facilitate the collection of dues, the channel is closed by a fence of stakes, and at the doors of the European trading establishments. A rope stretched across a road shows that it is a spot where dues are to be paid, and no one can pass till the collectors are satisfied ; while at the entrance of every town there is a *De-nun*, or Custom-House, where traders must pay duty before they can offer their goods for sale. Vessels which anchor in the Whydah roadstead also pay a percentage of their cargo to the king. These dues are generally levied in kind. Another source of revenue is found in the gifts made by the chiefs and others at the time of the Annual Custom, when all the provincial chiefs, the head-men of villages, the heads of families, and traders, must attend the capital and bring presents proportionate to their condition. Prisoners of war, again, can only be sold on the king's account ; but as he pays his troops a fixed sum for every prisoner and every head brought in, and the majority of the captives are put to death, this source does not produce much. The property of persons sentenced to death or slavery at once reverts to the king.

These are the ostensible sources of revenue, but the greater portion is really extorted from the people by means of "palavers," brought against them for real or imaginary offences. The provincial chiefs, who receive no pay, make use of this machinery to supply their own requirements, and from the sums wrung from the people of their districts they make their presents to the king— in the phraseology of the country, they "give the king something to eat." This is, in the eyes of the king, one of their principal duties, and a chief who neglected to make a suitable present would soon be removed. While the provincial chiefs thus plunder the masses for their own and the king's advantage, the latter plunders the wealthier and more influential classes. It is in Dahomi dangerous to make any show of affluence, for before long some pretext for a palaver will surely be found, and the injudicious individual who has paraded his wealth will find his property confiscated and himself reduced to poverty, if indeed he should escape being sold as a slave.

In order to facilitate extortion, arbitrary regulations are suddenly made and published in the capital or in Whydah, and officers despatched to all parts of the kingdom to seize and fine people for breaches of them. In vain a man might urge that he had heard nothing of the new regulations, and that they had never been proclaimed in his district, for ignorance of the law is no defence. One favourite mode is for the king to send a messenger to one of the trading establishments at Whydah, to buy for him a particular kind of cotton goods. According to law, that is, the king's will, by the very fact of this purchase having been made for the king, an embargo is laid upon all cotton goods of the same pattern or kind, and no one may buy or wear such. Usually a kind much in vogue is selected, and as the establishment of the embargo is never proclaimed, numbers of people render themselves liable to fine or confiscation by continuing to wear cloths of that description. L'Abbé Bouche mentions the case of a native of Whydah who, returning from Porto Novo wearing a cotton cloth of a kind that had been purchased for the king in Whydah during his absence, was seized as soon as he appeared in the street, dragged before a chief, thrown into prison, and compelled to pay a heavy fine. The same author tells us that a brother missionary once asked the Yevogan why he did not have the native laws and customs

reduced to writing, so that the Europeans residing in
Whydah might learn them, and be able to conform to
them. The reply of the Yevogan was characteristic.
" That is fine advice you are giving," he said, ironically.
" If the whites knew our customs and conformed to
them, there would be no more palavers ; and if there
were no more palavers, ' what should we eat ' ? "

For purposes of plunder the king also largely avails
himself of the services of his " wives," under which
designation are included not only his actual wives, but
all the women of the palaces, and even the eunuchs.
Acting under secret instructions, these palace-women
soon contrive to compromise any one whom the king
may have marked for his prey ; with the usual result of
confiscation and perhaps death.

The European traders residing in Whydah are
exempted from the more direct methods of plunder, but
as their wealth cannot fail to arouse the cupidity of the
king, there is a mode provided for bringing pressure to
bear upon them. This is done by " closing the roads,"
which means that trade is not allowed to flow in a certain
direction. When a European trader has refused to submit to some exaction, or has offended in some way, the
roads to his shop are closed ; whereupon no produce of
any kind can be taken to him, and no goods can be
purchased of him. His business is thus brought to a
complete standstill, and he must either submit to the
conditions the king imposes, or run the risk of far
greater loss through this species of quarantine, which
may be prolonged indefinitely, and most certainly rigidly,
for no native would dare to enter into any business
relations with him.

As another way of making Europeans contribute to his requirements, the king has in his pay a number of professional burglars, whose business it is to break into and steal from the European factories. It is not openly avowed that these housebreakers are in the king's service, but it is no secret, and they are everywhere known as " The King's Thieves." These men are obliged to perform their duties secretly and without violence, and, even if they are caught red-handed, they are always acquitted by the chiefs before whom they are brought, provided that they have not kept back any of the plunder for their own use. To rob for the king is their duty, and as long as they confine themselves to that they are guiltless ; but directly they exercise their talents on their own account, their action is criminal. This monopoly of theft on the part of the king possesses certain advantages, for the traders are constantly on the alert, and ordinary individuals dare not attempt to rob, because it would be dangerous to compete with the king.

As theoretically everything in the kingdom belongs to the king, and no man can call anything his own, his life even not excepted, it would seem at first sight as if the king had no need to resort to these circuitous methods of plunder, since he has an acknowledged right to take anything he wishes openly, without assigning any reason. But this right exists really in theory only, for though it may occasionally be exercised, it is not so often, as even the servile negro of Dahomi would resent such depredations if they were at all systematic. It is therefore for reasons of policy that pretexts for plunder are brought forward, and the right to plunder kept in abeyance. It was the wholesale pillage practised by

Adandosan (1812—1818), who sent out gangs of men to plunder in his name in all directions, that caused the Dahomis for once to forget their abject submission to the royal will, and led to the tyrant's downfall. Upon the rare occasions when the right to plunder is now exercised, the houses of the chiefs and more influential natives are generally exempted from search.

It may be wondered how any people can be found sufficiently slavish to submit to such a *régime*, where neither life nor property is secure from one day to another ; but the king's power is supported in many ways. Firstly, he has at his command a large standing army, whose interests he is careful to make identical with his own, and which blindly obeys all his commands ; then he has the power to take life at any moment, with or without reason, and is thus able to terrorize the populace. The prostration and apparent abject humiliation of the ministers of state and chiefs when in presence of the king, also serves to keep the masses in subjection. If these tyrants, so terrible to them, are as nothing when before the king, how great then must his power be ! Thus a rule of terror prevails, and the most oppressive mandates are submitted to without a murmur. Robert Norris gives an example of the blind obedience of the Dahomis to their king, which applies equally well to the present day. A man, to whom he had expressed a hope that he would escape injury in an impending battle, replied—" It is not material. My head belongs to the king, not to myself. If he please to send for it, I am ready to resign it ; or if it be shot through in battle, I am satisfied ; it is in his service." [1] The people are

---

[1] Dalzel's *History of Dahomey*, p. 69.

utterly crushed and demoralized. In their own proper localities the masses are terrorized by their local chiefs, whom they know to be backed by the king, and the chiefs in their turn are overawed by the king. The chiefs and priesthood combined, however, are too strong for the king, and if he were to violate popular prejudices and offend these two classes collectively, he would soon be removed. Hence, though individual chiefs and officers of state are often degraded and punished by the king, he is careful not to act counter to the interests and prejudices of the classes as a body.

As the interests of the chiefs and the king are commonly identical, and both are entirely in accord as to what they consider the great end of government, namely, the subjection and plunder of the masses, there is rarely any friction between them ; but in order to prevent conspiracies against him, the king has established a system of espionage which is so far-reaching that no man dare breathe to his dearest friend anything which might be twisted to his injury. Every chief has, as it were, his duplicate, his man-in-waiting, who in theory is supposed to be destined to be his successor, and to be learning the methods of government ; but who is in reality a spy, constantly on the watch to catch his principal tripping, and who reports with the greatest minuteness every occurrence that takes place, and even every suspicion he may entertain. The king has spies who watch over the officers of state and principal chiefs, the latter have theirs over the secondary chiefs, and these last theirs over the subordinate chiefs. The system is pushed so far that agents and labourers are imposed upon the Europeans, whom the latter cannot get rid of, although they well know that they are there for the purpose of watching their actions and reporting their words. To further this process the king sometimes presents some of his palace-women to his chiefs, as wives. These palace-women are nominally the king's wives, and such a gift is regarded as an honour, which cannot be declined ; and the chiefs are therefore obliged to admit these women to their families, although they well know they are sent for the purpose of observing and reporting upon their most secret actions and conversations. Nothing then is secret in Dahomi. Nobody dares to murmur at any oppression or injustice, lest his words should be reported and he called to account ; as a consequence universal distrust prevails, and any plot or secret combination is rendered almost impossible.

The spy-system reaches its height in Whydah, where, besides the king's spies, the Megan and Mehu have their own secret agents. It is not too much to say that everybody in Whydah, from the Yevogan down to the most insignificant native trader, is watched by three or four spies, who are in their turn secretly watched and reported upon by others. This is because Whydah is still considered a conquered territory, rather than an integral portion of the kingdom. To this day its inhabitants speak of Dahomi as if its territory only extended as far south as the Ko, and consisted merely of the tract originally occupied by Takudonu and his adherents ; a fiction which is kept alive by the fact that every new king of Dahomi has to go through a sort of coronation ceremony at Allada, where he is invested in a coat of honour, in token of his sovereignty over the Whydah district.

The government of the kingdom of Porto Novo resembles in many respects that of Dahomi, the officers of state and chiefs being appointed by the king, and removable at pleasure ; but though the king is theoretically an absolute monarch, he is really controlled by the aristocracy. There, as in Dahomi, the dues collected on produce and on imports form the revenue of the king, but the chiefs also have a share. There is no female precedence at court, and the ministers of state are not represented by female duplicates in the palaces. Succession, too, is traced through females, the heirs to the throne being the king's brothers in order of seniority, or failing these, a sister's son. The Megan and Mehu of Porto Novo can, like their prototypes in Dahomi, set aside the heir-apparent and select a successor to the throne from among the other members of the royal family. After such an election all the unsuccessful candidates are by law compelled to leave the capital and settle in the country districts ; where they usually become petty tyrants, who are known to the inhabitants of the capital by the derisive title of " Bush Kings." The insignia of Porto Novo chiefs are virtually the same as those in use in Dahomi, except that in place of the umbrella canopy, umbrellas of the ordinary European kind, but of brilliant hues, are used.

Porto Novo has a kind of police, certain servants of the king, who are distinguished from the general public by having the sides of the head shaved, and the hair in the middle of the crown dressed in a sort of crest ; and whose duty it is to regulate and preserve order in the markets, and receive custom dues at the gate of the town. The persons of these men are inviolable, by law.

N

At night the public safety is watched over by a society called Zan-gbeto—according to most authorities _zăme_, "night," and _gbeto_, "people" (?) — "People of the night;" but, more properly, it seems, _zăme_, "in the night," _gbe_, "voice," and _to_, "person who does"—"He whose voice is heard in the night." It is composed of the young men of the upper class, and is an organization something akin to the Egungun of the Yorubas, but without its political power. This society works as follows :—One of the number, covered from head to foot with a long robe of grass, to which Achatina shells are attached so as to rattle when the robe is agitated, goes to one of the principal quarters of the town and dances about, uttering plaintive and weird cries ; while five or six of his companions, undisguised, accompany his performance with a charivari of drums, iron pots, calabash-rattles, &c., from the concealment of a wall or a clump of bushes. The credulous lower orders believe, or profess to believe, that this apparition is a demon who comes out of the sea by night to watch over the town. The Zan-gbeto have the right to arrest any persons who may be found abroad in the town after nine o'clock at night, and they thus serve to check nocturnal robberies and incendiary fires.

Amongst the whole of the Ewe-speaking tribes, the stick of office, usually silver-headed, is regarded as the sign of authority, and the same honours and respect are paid to the stick as to the person to whom it belongs. It has an almost sacred character, and it is an unheard-of crime for an ambassador, furnished with this emblem, to be molested. This, in a country where communication is difficult and hazardous, and life insecure, guarantees the safe transmission of important messages. As a rule, there are three kinds of sticks employed— the official stick, used for ceremonial occasions and affairs of importance ; the semi-official stick, used for ordinary communications between local authorities ; and the private stick, used for private and friendly communications. No message is ever despatched by a chief without one of these sticks, borne by a *mosi*, or stick-bearer.

The person to whom the stick is sent receives it from the *mosi*, holding it in his hand while the latter delivers the message, and he retains it in his possession till he is ready with his reply, even though that may not be for some weeks. When Europeans visit a chief, the slave or dependant who admits them, takes their sticks and carries them to his master ; and the latter, if he does not wish to receive the visitors, sends their sticks back to them. If the contrary, he keeps the sticks and hands them to his visitors as they are ushered in.

When the stick of the King of Dahomi is carried in public the people prostrate before it with demonstrations of respect. It is always wrapped up in several pieces of cloth, and is carried by a chief of the royal household, escorted by a party of palace-guards. It is received in the following manner by the person to whom it is sent :—On the first appearance of the stick, he and his followers rise and uncover the head and shoulders ; the wrappers are then removed, the chief to whom it is addressed places his hand upon it, then prostrates himself with his followers, and in that attitude listens to the royal message. This stick, like all others, is retained till the reply is ready.

European traders have very generally adopted this native custom, and send their messages or letters accompanied by a stick, which represents the firm or house. Although these "trade" sticks are not considered by natives so inviolable as those used by chiefs, still they are regarded with respect, and the bearers and their companions are not usually molested. Bouche relates an incident which shows the native feeling with regard to them.[1] A European trading agent at Grand Popo despatched a canoe-load of goods to Whydah, by way of the lagoons, accompanied by the stick of the firm. The canoe was stopped by some people of a small lagoon-side community, the goods plundered and the canoe-men beaten. When the news reached the agent he applied for redress to a neighbouring chief, who summoned the plunderers before him. These stated, in their defence, that one of their number had been maltreated by a former agent of the same trading house, that they were unaware that there had been a change of agents, and that in seizing the goods of the firm as a set-off for the said ill-treatment they had only exercised their rights. This plea was held to be valid, and the case was virtually settled in favour of the defendants, when one of the agent's canoe-men stated that in the struggle for the merchandise the stick had been broken in pieces. This changed the aspect of affairs entirely ; the former decision was reversed, the plunderers condemned to restore the goods, and to collect the pieces of the stick and return them to the agent. Should there be any delay about this, the agent was empowered to seize, and detain as a

[1] *La Côte des Esclaves*, pp. 85, 86.

hostage, any member of the wrong-doing community,
whom he might happen to meet within a period of
six months. It was no offence to have pillaged the
canoe, but to have broken the stick, even accidentally,
was a serious crime.

CHAPTER XII.

MILITARY SYSTEM OF DAHOMI.

EXCEPT in the case of the kingdom of Dahomi, the military system of the Ewe-speaking peoples calls for little remark, the military force of any particular tribe consisting, as is the case amongst most uncivilized people, of the whole effective male population. When war has been decided upon, the head-men of hamlets and villages, accompanied by the able-bodied men of their communities, join the contingents of the towns to which their hamlets belong, and all join the general rendezvous. Many of them are accompanied by their wives and female slaves, who look after the commissariat and carry the baggage; and when a native army takes the field the towns and villages are deserted by all save women, children, and old men. This system is also in vogue in Dahomi, but, in addition, there is there a standing army, which is maintained by the king, and is always ready for active service.

The standing army of Dahomi consists of two bodies —(1) A female corps, called "The Amazons" by Europeans, and known in Dahomi by the titles of "The King's Wives" and "Our Mothers." (2) A male corps, composed of the palace-guards, court-criers, and other officials, and the men of Agbomi. Behind these two corps is the male population of the kingdom, which is liable to be called out, in part or as a whole, to take part in any expedition, and thus forms a sort of reserve.

The female corps, to use the common expression, the Amazons, was raised about the year 1729,[1] when a body of women who had been armed and furnished with banners, merely as a stratagem to make the attacking force appear larger, behaved with such unexpected gallantry as to lead to a permanent corps of women being embodied. Up to the reign of Gezo, who came to the stool in 1818, the Amazon force was composed chiefly of criminals, that is criminals in the Dahomi sense of the word. Wives detected in adultery, and termagants and scolds were drafted into its ranks; and the great majority of the women " given to the king " by the provincial chiefs, that is, sent to him as being worthy of death for misdemeanours or crimes, were, instead of being sacrificed at the Annual Custom, made women soldiers. Gezo, who largely made use of the Amazons to keep his own subjects in check and to promote military rivalry, increased and improved the force. He directed every head of a family to send his daughters to Agbomi for inspection; the most suitable were enlisted, and the corps thus placed on a new footing. This course was also followed by Gelele, his successor, who had every girl brought to him before marriage, and enrolled those who pleased him. The women of Dahomi, having for many generations past endured all the toil and performed all the hard labour

---

[1] See the chapter on History.

of the country, have, for the weaker sex, an exceptional physique, which enables them to bear hardships and privations as well as, if not better than, the men ; and this fact no doubt was an important factor in the causes which led to the formation of the corps. As Captain Burton noted, the women are generally tall, muscular, and broad, and the men " smooth, full-breasted, round-limbed, and effeminate-looking."

By state policy the Amazons are considered the king's wives, and cannot be touched without danger of death. They are sworn to celibacy, a necessary restriction in the case of a female corps, but the king has the privilege of taking any of their number to wife. A peculiar *vō-sesa*, placed over the palace-gate, is supposed to cause certain pregnancy in the Amazon who has been frail ; and it is said that the dread of impending discovery has often led the woman to confess, and doom herself and her paramour to a dreadful death. Nature, however, will assert itself, and when Captain Burton visited Agbomi, 150 Amazons were found to be pregnant, and were brought to trial. Such offenders are always put to death in secret within the palace, with cruelties that are only whispered of outside.

In peace time one of the duties of the Amazons is to escort the palace-women when they go to the wells outside Agbomi to fetch water. They, in common with the real wives of the king, never leave their quarters without being preceded by a bell, which is the signal for men to leave the road. The Amazons only meet the opposite sex when on the march or in the field ; for when the two corps of the standing army parade at the palace, the sexes are kept apart by pieces of bamboo laid along the ground, which barrier no one may pass.

The Amazon corps is divided into three bodies, called the Right Wing, the Left Wing, and the King's Body-guards. The male corps is divided into Right and Left Wings only, except when the male population, or reserve, is called out, when it also, with the latter, is divided into three bodies like the Amazons. The wings are named right and left, from the positions they take up before the king on ceremonial occasions. The right wing is that of the Megan, and the left that of the Mehu. In war the Megan's soldiers are joined by the Amazons of the Gundeme, or female Megan, and those of the Mehu by the Amazons of the female Mehu.

In war each wing consists of four bodies, which may, for convenience' sake, be termed battalions. The organization is as follows :—

RIGHT WING.

1st Male Battalion—led by the Megan, who commands the Right Wing.

1st Amazon Battalion—led by the Gundeme, or female Megan.

2nd Male Battalion—led by the Gau, or military premier.

2nd Amazon Battalion—led by the Khetungan, or female Gau.

LEFT WING.

1st Male Battalion—led by the Mehu, who commands the Left Wing.

1st Amazon Battalion—led by the Akpadumi, or female Mehu.

2nd Male Battalion—led by the Posu, or second
military chief.
2nd Amazon Battalion—led by the female Posu.

Other military officers are the Ajyaho, who has charge
of the king's supplies; the So-gan, or Captain of the
Horses; the Go-gan, or Captain of the Bottles; and the
Cakawo, who has jurisdiction over the war-captains of
the sea-board district, and is military premier of Whydah.
War-captain (*Awá-gan*) is a title bestowed upon every
chief or head-man who can bring twenty or more
followers into the field.

The male and Amazon battalions are subdivided
into further bodies, which may be called companies,
and whose strength varies from thirty to 300, or more.
The Male Companies are—(1) The Bayoneteers. This
Company is composed of picked men, and was formed
during the reign of Gezo. (2) The Eunuch Company.
(3) The Hunters, styled "Conquerors of all Animals,"
and composed also of picked men. (4) The Bards' or
Drummers' Company, a *corps d'élite*, distinguished by
a horse-tail, to the handle of which a human jawbone is
attached. (5) The "Fire to the Front" Company. (6)
The Blunderbuss Company. (7) The Blue Company, so
called because the men wear blue caps or fillets. The
Amazon Companies are—(1) The Blunderbuss Company,
composed of the biggest and strongest women. (2) The
Elephant Hunters. (3) The Razor Company, armed with
razor-shaped weapons, with a blade about eighteen
inches long, shutting into a wooden handle. They were
invented during the reign of Gezo, to inspire terror. (4)
The Musket Company—which forms the bulk of the

Amazons. It may be remarked that the number of companies is constantly varying, new ones being formed and old ones broken up, according to the caprice of the king. There used to be an Amazon company armed with bows and arrows, but this seems to have been extinct for some time. Each company, both of the Male and Amazon Corps, has its band, consisting of drums, horns, and the *chinfugu*, or native cymbals. Each also has its tutelary deity, whose shrine is in or near the capital. The third division of the Amazons, called the King's Body-guards, which is commanded by the Akutu, is similarly divided into companies. Women-soldiers of this division wear white fillets round the head, upon which rude images of crocodiles, cut out of blue cloth, are sewn. On active service the arms of the entire standing army are flint muskets and long knives or swords. The powder is carried in cylindrical wooden cases, worn in bandoleers round the waist, and the lead in pouches of antelope, or goat, skin.

When the male population is called out, each chief takes the field with the men of his own district, who are under his orders. The women accompany them to transport ammunition and supplies; and, armed with clubs, frequently take part in the combat, and aid in securing the wounded. This reserve force is also armed with flint muskets and knives, but it is but poor material. The whole military force of the kingdom may be set down at between 16,000 and 20,000 combatants, of whom perhaps less than 3000 are Amazons, while the male corps of the standing army does not exceed 5000. At a review held at Agbomi in 1850, Commander Forbes counted 6785 soldiers, 4377 men and 2408 women, apparently all belonging to the standing army ; yet, in the different attacks upon Abeokuta, where the full strength of Dahomi was said to have been put out, the attacking force scarcely at any time exceeded 12,000.

When the king has decided upon a military expedition, he sends for the Megan, and says, in open court—" My house wants thatch," or " My house is uncovered." This is the official announcement of war, and these expressions, which originally meant that the human skulls which adorned the walls enclosing the palaces required renewing, are still preserved through custom ; though the fashion of having the walls always surmounted with skulls in a good state of preservation has of late years fallen into disuse. To perpetuate the traditional practice, however, the heads of fallen foes are still placed on the roofs of the guard-houses, and on the palace-gates.

As soon as this declaration is made, messengers depart to all parts of the kingdom, to give orders for the concentration of the provincial levies at Agbomi ; but as the primary object of every campaign is to obtain plunder and secure prisoners, the destination of the army is kept a profound secret, known only to the Megan and Mehu, lest the inhabitants of the territory it is proposed to ravage should take alarm and have time to escape.

Gezo established a custom of swearing before his assembled soldiery what he would do in the coming campaign, and receiving in his turn their *braggadocio* oaths. This ceremony took place in a small circular hut, with a conical roof of thatch, near the south gate of Agbomi, but later kings do not seem to have kept it up. Captain Burton (1863-4) says, that when war was declared against Abeokuta, the king, Gelele, sent a small knapsack-shaped leathern case, containing rum, to the Megan, who forwarded it to the Gau. The latter received it with a great show of enthusiasm, and, after a warlike speech, ran to the palace-gate, crying to those outside that war-rum had been given.[1]

The levies from the various districts having arrived at the capital, the army sets forth; marching by night as silently as possible, and lying hid during the day in the forests. Scouts are pushed far ahead, who seize and make prisoners of the unsuspecting agriculturists at work in their provision-grounds, who otherwise might give the alarm; and thus, undiscovered, the army arrives at the territory which is the objective of the campaign. If it be a district in which the inhabitants live in a number of scattered hamlets, the army pours at once over the whole country like a flood; dispersing in bands in every direction; pillaging, destroying the villages, and sweeping off men, women, and children as captives. If, however, there be some central point, such as a considerable town, or group of large villages, the usual plan is for the army to divide into two bodies; one of which lies ambushed till the other has gained the rear of the position, when they both advance to the assault. If they receive no check, the Amazons and Male Corps of the standing army carry the place with a rush, while the levies cut off fugitives and plunder. If they are checked, they carry on a desultory fight for an hour or so; when, if the enemy still obstinately declines

[1] *Mission to Gelele.* vol. ii. p. 263.

to give in, they retreat with so little order that it resembles a rout. The great object of Dahomi strategy is to surprise the foe, and when they fail in this they rarely succeed in capturing any place of note.

In both of the corps of the standing army, but more especially in the corps of Amazons, the military spirit is strongly cultivated, and they are taught to disregard obstacles, dangers, wounds, and death itself. Hence they often display a ferocious courage which carries all before it. Their chief aim in battle is to carry off a large number of trophies of their prowess, in the shape of prisoners, human heads and jawbones ; and they care little for plunder. The men of the general levy, however, have none of this ambition. Unskilled, and untrained to arms, they are chiefly of use in following a defeated enemy, or in ravaging the country ; and their object is to take as many captives and as much spoil as they and their women can carry. The standing army fights with the ferocity and cruelty of savages, who have been intoxicated with a craving for military glory ; it fights to conquer and to kill. The general levy fights after the ordinary manner of untrained savages ; that is, it avoids direct combats and unnecessary risks, and its object is plunder and profit. Gelele held the cultivation of the warlike spirit to be of the first importance. The chief objection he raised to a request made by the British Government in 1864, that the boys of English-town, Whydah, might be allowed to attend the Wesleyan Mission school, was that " when black men learned to read and write, they could not be taken to war."

Both the regular army and the levies show an equal

callousness to human suffering. Wounded prisoners are denied all assistance, and all prisoners who are not destined to slavery are kept in a condition of semi-starvation that speedily reduces them to mere skeletons. The lower jawbone is much prized as a trophy for the ornamentation of horns, drums, sword-handles, &c., and it is very frequently torn from the wounded and living foe.

Amazons, or soldiers of the male corps, who lose their weapons, or expend their ammunition without bringing back either a prisoner or a human head, are punished.

Reviews, or rather manœuvres of the Amazons, seem to be held frequently during the Annual Customs. Commander Forbes witnessed one at Agbomi in 1850. On the south side of the parade-ground there was a stockade of palm-branches to represent a town, the inhabitants of which were represented by slaves confined in three large enclosures inside the stockade. The Amazons were formed up on the north side of the parade-ground, and were to attack and carry the supposed town. He says [1]—

" First came an advanced guard in single file, reconnoitring and placing sentinels along the road ; then came the main army in two battalions. As each passed, the sentries were relieved and sent on with the report of the advance. All carried their muskets over their shoulders, with the muzzles in front. Next came the fetish gear, the war-stools and equipage of the monarch, guarded by a reserve, and in the rear the commissariat (all females). A second time they marched past in the

[1] *Dahomey and the Dahomans*, vol. ii. p. 123 *et seq.*

same order; this time giving a silent salute, *en passant*, by dropping on one knee, their muskets over the shoulder, but reversed. A third time they marched past, but now in close column, and with constant attention and arms shouldered. This, we were told, represents a night march.

"During this scene the heralds were continually crying, 'Oh, King of kings! war is coming, let all come to see it.'

"After the third round, the army collected in the centre of the parade-ground. Pioneers then advanced, and, settling down in front of the tent (attended by the Amazon chiefs), held a council of war. After which scouts were sent out, and soon returned with a spy covered from head to heel with a country cloth. He was placed in the centre of the council, and an examination took place; whilst aides-de-amps were constantly running between the council and the army. Again scouts were sent out, and this time returned with six prisoners, who were examined before the council and marched into the rear. Then a body of officers advanced, to report the state of the country and position of the enemy to the king, who told them that, as this was a mere skirmish, the young troops were to take the lead.

"The king now left his stool and inspected the stockade; while we took up positions on the right. There was a method of keeping time which I failed in understanding: it was measured by paces, the measurer having a thread, which, at a slow pace, he passed round two sticks, at a certain distance apart. After the manœuvre these threads were measured.

" At noon a musket was fired, and a portion of the army attacked the stockade, made an *entrée*, and speedily reappeared, some with prisoners, some with tufts of grass to imitate heads.

" Several regiments now advanced, and again made an *entrée*. The slaves this time broke out of their inclosure, and a slave-hunt followed with much spirit, until all were caught.

" All the army now assembled in front, except a reserve which guarded the prisoners, and at a signal advanced at double-quick time, and by force of weight threw down the stockade. The slaves from the third inclosure escaping, a similar hunt ensued as in the case of the previous stockade.

" The regiments now divided, and, as we were informed, surrounded the country. All the slaves were again let loose (about 2000), and again hunted until all were recaptured, tied, and dragged before the royal canopy, whither the king and ourselves had returned."

Another account of Amazon manœuvres is that given by M. Borghéro, who visited Agbomi in 1861, and from which it will be seen that a sham-fight in Dahomi is not altogether the make-believe that it is in civilized countries. He says—

" In a space used as a drill-ground there had been raised a bank, not of earth, but of bundles of very thorny bushes, about 400 metres long, six broad, and two high. Forty paces beyond, and parallel with this heap, rose the framework of a house of the same length, but about five metres broad and high. The two slopes of the roof were covered with a thick bed of the same thorns. Fifteen metres beyond this curious house

o

was a row of huts. The whole represented a fortified town, the assault of which would have cost heavy loss. According to the programme, the bare-footed female warriors were to surmount three times the heap of thorns which represented the curtain of the works, descend into the clear space which took the place of the ditch, escalade the house, which represented a citadel bristling with defences, and go and take the town simulated by the row of huts. They were to be twice repulsed by the enemy, but at the third assault they were to be victorious, and drag the prisoners to the king's feet in token of success. The first to surmount all the obstacles would receive from his hand the reward of bravery; for, said the king to me—' We reckon military valour as the first of virtues.'

"The king gives the order to attack. Then the expedition enters on its first phase. The whole army reconnoitres the position of the town to be taken; it advances crouching, almost crawling, so as not to be seen by the enemy; weapons are lowered, and there is strict silence.

" In a second reconnaissance our Amazons march erect, with heads high. Out of the 3000 women, 200 have, instead of muskets, large cutlasses shaped like razors, which are used with both hands, and a single blow of which would cut a man in two. These female warriors have their cutlasses still sheathed.

" At the third act all are in position and in battle array, with weapons raised and the cutlasses opened. In defiling before the king, some give him assurances of their devotion, and promises of victory. Finally, they are drawn up in line of battle before the point of attack. The king rises, places himself at the head of the columns, harangues them, inflames them, and at a given signal, they throw themselves with indescribable fury upon the bank of thorns, cross it, leap upon the thorny house, retire from it as if driven back, and return three times to the charge—all this with such rapidity that the eye can scarcely follow them. They clamber over the thorny obstacles as lightly as a dancer vaults upon a floor, and that though their naked feet are pierced in all directions with the sharp thorns of the cactus.

"At the first assault, when the most intrepid had already gained the summit of the house, a woman-soldier, who was at one of the ends, fell to the ground from a height of five metres. She was wringing her hands and remaining seated, though her comrades were striving to reanimate her courage, when the king himself came up, and threw at her a glance and cry of indignation. She sprang up then as if electrified, continued the manœuvres, and carried off the first prize. It is impossible to give any idea of the scene."

The military supremacy of Dahomi at the present time is no doubt chiefly due to its standing army. In the early days of the kingdom its conquests were the old story of hordes of barbarians, in the full possession of courage and vigour, overrunning the territories of other barbarians; who had lost much of their original hardihood, through having been engaged for many years in the peaceable pursuit of commerce. Such were the victories over the kingdoms of Ardra and Whydah in 1724 and 1727; but even in those days, before the Dahomi character itself began to lose its asperities,

Dahomi was often unsuccessful when pitted against people who had not been exposed to softening agencies. Fifty years of desultory fighting took place before the Mahis, or Makkis, on the western frontier of Dahomi, were finally driven from their territories; and although expedition after expedition was despatched against the Popos, that warlike people, protected by their network of lagoons, was never conquered.

In more recent times Gezo despatched an expedition against the Attakpamis, a tribe of mountaineers situated about 7° 20′ N. latitude; but they offered so determined a resistance, that no subsequent king has ventured to molest them, notwithstanding many provocations and insulting messages. During the reign of Gelele, the Attakpamis sent a message to ask why he did not come to attack them, and how he could rest under the disgrace of his father's defeat. The messenger, a young girl, offered to show the Dahomi army the way, but Gelele did not think proper to accept the invitation.

Practically, in modern times the arms of Dahomi have been almost exclusively directed against the western Yoruba tribes, who, peaceful and devoted to trade, offer at the best but a passive resistance. Thus time after time the army has appeared before Abeokuta, a town whose population is nearly equal to that of the whole of Dahomi; and though the Dahomis have suffered several reverses under its walls, the Egbas have never ventured to follow up their successes, much less to take the initiative and carry the war into the enemy's country. Again, Ketu is invaded almost every year without the inhabitants attempting any reprisals; and this is at least as much due to the character of the people, who have no taste for war, as to the intestine struggles and jealousies which have weakened all western Yoruba. Every year the Dahomi army makes an irruption into the territories adjoining the eastern frontier of the kingdom; and, as a consequence, the inhabitants have concentrated for mutual security into towns, which are separated from each other by large tracts of country that are almost depopulated. In Ewemi, or Wemi, the houses are all fortified and built in groups; while, on the south side of the No-we Lagoon (Lake Denham Waters) there are several villages of moderate size built on piles in the middle of the water. The two principal of these are Afatonu and Awansoli, and the inhabitants have been driven to build in this manner in order to be secure from the hordes of Dahomi.

Like most uncivilized powers, Dahomi can conquer, but cannot assimilate the conquered peoples, or retain their territories. The conquests of the old kingdoms of Ardra and Whydah are notable exceptions, but in these cases there was the pressing necessity of gaining access to the sea and the European trade. The other territories were, and are, periodically over-run and then abandoned; and the chief end of the annual expeditions is plunder, not conquest. Dahomi may be likened to a vast association of banditti, who at fixed periods, generally in March or April, make raids upon their eastern neighbours, and return on the approach of the rains, laden with spoil. Originally no doubt these raids were designed for dominion and power; later on they were useful as furnishing slaves for the trade, and victims for the Annual Custom; and, in the later days of the slave-trade, that was their avowed object. The export slave-trade came to an end in 1864, when a steamer which had successfully run several cargoes of slaves to Brazil was captured ; but the annual slave-hunts still continue, for a ready market for slaves is easily found amongst the Mohammedan tribes about the Niger.

The population of Dahomi is estimated at about 200,000, out of which number the towns of Whydah, Agbomi, and Kana contain about 25,000 each. There is practically no Dahomi nation. The original stock disappeared through the great loss of life incurred in the incessant wars, and the waste of reproduction represented by the enforced celibacy of some 3000 Amazons and 2000 palace women, and has been replaced long since by slaves, mongrels, and Yorubas. It is really a political organization, and if the monarchy were overthrown, Dahomi would cease to exist.

CHAPTER XIII.

LAWS AND CUSTOMS.

I.—RELATING TO MARRIAGE AND THE RELATIONS OF THE SEXES.

MARRIAGE contracts are made by the payment of certain sums to the family of the bride, which vary according to the rank of the girl. The amount to be paid is fixed by the family of the girl, and the marriage is arranged without, as a rule, any reference being made to her wishes, though she cannot be forced into a union that is absolutely repugnant to her. The payment of "head-money," as the sum paid for a wife is termed, constitutes a marriage; and the head-money may be paid in actual coin or cowries, or, as is more commonly the case, in merchandise and rum. Amongst the poorest people the sum paid may be merely nominal; but something, even if it be only a bottle of rum, must be paid as head-money, in order to give a union the dignity of marriage.

This is the custom at the present day amongst all the Ewe-speaking tribes; but, according to Norris, a different rule was in force in Dahomi towards the latter end of the eighteenth century. At that time, he says,[1] every young man in Dahomi who wanted a wife had to

[1] Dalzel's *History of Dahomey*, 1793.

present himself at the capital at the Annual Customs with five "heads" of cowries (20,000 cowries, then worth a dollar a head), which he laid before the king's gate, prostrating himself and asking for a wife. The women were handed out of the palace to these applicants, and the cowries received in return. Each man was obliged to take the woman assigned to him, whether young or old, handsome or deformed. Sometimes the king's wives, who managed this business, gave a man out of malice his own mother, whom he was thenceforth obliged to maintain. In explanation of this custom, Norris says, that it was in accordance with the Dahomi state principle, that parents had no sort of right or claim to their children, which belonged to the king ; that children were taken from their mothers at an early age and sent to villages at a distance ; and that the idea was to destroy the possibility of family combinations, that might be prejudicial to the king's absolute power.

Although native laws and customs have undoubtedly been occasionally changed by the exercise of arbitrary power in Dahomi, yet it seems probable that in this case Norris was misinformed, at all events with regard to the general application of the rule. It is inconceivable that a whole nation, and Dahomi was a nation at that time, should submit to have their children taken away from them, and sent to strangers at a distance. It might be the case with the children of captured women, who would be held to be of the tribes of their mothers, and women-captives might have been assigned to applicants for wives in the manner described ; but it is unlikely that the rule was general. In any case it must soon have lapsed, for no other writer refers to it, and there is not now a trace of any such a custom to be discovered.

Betrothals are made by the payment on account, by an intending husband, of a portion of the head-money demanded for a girl ; or, between children, by a present made by the parents of the male child to those of the female child. In the first case the girl need not be of a marriageable age ; she may be a mere child, and sometimes even she may not yet be born. In any case, whether the girl be marriageable or not, she is regarded as contracted to the man to whom she is betrothed ; the contract cannot be annulled without his consent, and he can claim compensation for liberties, no matter how innocent, which men may take with her, just as if she were his wife in fact. Betrothal seems to confer all the rights of marriage upon the male-contracting party, except that of consummating the union, and of deriving benefit from the girl's services. Should a betrothed girl die, her family are bound to substitute another, who then stands in the same position to the man as did the first.

If, after a bride has been conveyed to the house of her husband, the *primitiæ* are found to be wanting, the husband may repudiate her, and recover from the family the amount both of the head-money he has paid, and of all expenses he has incurred upon her account. To insure fair play, a young girl is, on the part of the bride, always concealed in the bridal chamber. If a husband make a false accusation of this nature, he is summoned before the chief or head-man of the community, and the "tokens of virginity" being produced, he is fined for defamation of character. In such a case the bride has the right to leave her husband without making restitution.

The penalty for seduction is the payment of the amount of the head-money that would have been demanded, and marriage; or a heavy fine without marriage, with the alternative of enslavement. If the woman seduced be a slave, the seducer must pay a fine to her owner. If the seducer be a slave, and the girl belong to a family of rank, the slave is ordinarily put to death; and in any case in which a slave seduces a girl, the owner of the slave has to pay compensation to the girl's family.

Adultery can only be committed with a married woman. It may be defined as "intercourse with a married woman without the consent of her husband"; for men can and do lend their wives, and the latter do not seem to have the right to refuse compliance. In Dahomi adultery is, in theory, punished by death or slavery. Amongst the other tribes it is, except in extreme cases, punished by fine. A chief has the right to put to death an adulterous wife, but it is a privilege rarely exercised; and he, like his humbler fellow-men, castigates her instead, and recovers damages from the paramour. If the latter should be a slave, the fine is recovered from his owner; and if the adulteress be a woman of rank, the slave is put to death. The fine imposed for adultery is always relatively large, and varies according to the rank of the injured husband. If it be paid there is an end of the matter; but if the adulterer cannot pay, the plaintiff has the right to reduce him to slavery.

If the husband agree, the paramour can take the adulterous wife, and in this case he refunds the head-money originally paid, and the amount of all expenses incurred on her behalf, but pays no fine. Any children she may have go with her. The wife then becomes responsible to her new man for the sum he has paid for her, and she cannot quit him without payment in full. Moreover, if she should die without having repaid the sum, her family are obliged to replace her by another girl of the family, upon whom the debt then devolves, or pay the debt themselves. If, on the other hand, the man should die first, she passes to his heir, unless she can pay him the debt. An adulterous wife who has in this manner passed into the keeping of the paramour, seems to occupy a position in which the liabilities of a pawn are superadded to those of a wife.

In the different royal palaces in Dahomi, more than 5000 women are immured, and any frailty on their part is punished by death, while their lovers are also liable to death, though they are sometimes sold as slaves. Dalzel tells us that during the reign of Adanzu II. some of the king's women were found to be pregnant, and on being questioned, accused over 150 young men belonging to some villages in the neighbourhood of Kana, all of whom were sold as slaves, but most of whom were afterwards found to have been innocent. Another instance, mentioned by Captain Burton, has already been quoted.

In Dahomi it is unlawful for a man to look at the king's wives and women of the palace. The latter, when they leave the palace in the morning to fetch water, are preceded by one of their number wearing a bell round the neck, which she shakes vigorously at the sight of a man. At the sound of the bell every man must run off the road into the bush, and wait with averted face till the women have passed. If any accident happened, even if a water-pot chanced to be broken, the nearest male would be blamed and punished. Europeans are expected to comply with this custom, which perhaps has its origin in the Mohammedan practice of secluding women.

In former times the women of the blood-royal of Dahomi were permitted to intrigue with any man they pleased, as is still the case in Ashanti; but this custom was put to an end by Gelele, on account of the scandals it caused. Since his reign women of the blood-royal marry like other women, but the husband of a princess must confine his attentions to her, even if he has other wives.

It is an offence, punishable by fine, to praise the beauty of another man's wife, it being considered adultery by implication.

Polygamy prevails, but is only pushed to excess in Dahomi, where a man's rank and position is estimated by the number of his wives. Each wife has her own separate dwelling in the inclosure in which her husband's house stands, and her children and slaves reside with her. When the boys are big enough to be of use to the father, they leave the mother's house and live in that of the father; but the girls remain under the maternal roof until they are married. The first wife is termed the " head-wife "; she supervises the internal arrangements of the entire household, is consulted by her husband, and sometimes her opinion has weight. The second wife acts as the assistant of the head-wife; those married later are all classed together. It is unusual, except amongst chiefs, for a man to have more than four or five wives.

The concubines live in the same inclosure with the wives. Usually these concubines are slave-girls, who are presented to the wives on their marriage by their families, to lighten their labours, and give them a personal attendant in their new home. As the girl is the slave of the wife, *i. e.* her property, and as the property of the wife is always distinct from that of the husband, the latter cannot demand to use her as a concubine as a matter of right, but the wife ordinarily encourages him to take her. The child belongs to the mother and not to the father, except in the case in which the mother is a slave, in which case the child of the slave belongs to the slave's owner. Hence the children born of a concubinous union belong to the wife to whom the concubine is a slave ; and if the wife has no children of her own, these are regarded as hers. Where a slave-girl is purchased by a man and made his concubine, the children born of the union are his property. The condition of a concubine is but little inferior to that of the third, fourth, and later wives. If she should bear a child, she cannot under any circumstances be sold ; the title of " wife " is, however, denied her.

When a man dies, his widows devolve upon his heir, whose wives they become, in name at all events, for it is not incumbent upon him to consummate the union. When a brother succeeds a brother it is more usual for the union to be consummated than when a nephew succeeds an uncle. Whether the second union be consummated or not, the widows of a deceased man are regarded in every respect as the wives of the successor to the property, and damages can be recovered from any man who may take liberties with them.

A wife can, with her husband's consent, leave him at any time by refunding the head-money, and the amount of all the expenditure he has ever incurred on her behalf; but, if she has been grossly neglected or ill-treated by him, she can, on proving the facts before the head-men of the community, leave him without making any payment. In all cases of separation the children accompany the wife, who pays to the husband a sum to reimburse him for what he has paid for their maintenance. The general custom of regarding children as related to the mother and not to the father, does not apply, it must be observed, to the upper classes of Dahomi, in which the father is regarded as having the greater claim; an exception to the usual rule which will be discussed under the head of kinship.

Women may not, by country custom, admit the male during pregnancy, while suckling, or during menstruation. At the latter periods they are considered impure, and have to retire to a quarter set apart in each town or village for their reception. Children are ordinarily suckled for two or three years, a practice which, combined with the restriction during pregnancy, renders polygamy a necessity, and also tends to limit population.

According to Des Marchais,[1] a girl at Whydah was in more request for marriage if she had had many lovers. At the present time, however, virginity in a bride is as highly prized there as elsewhere; the absence of the *primitiæ* is *ipso facto* a reason for repudiation,

---

[1] *Voyage en Guinée*, 1731.

and as Des Marchais' statement is not supported by any other writer, the probability is that he was in error.

Kissing, here as elsewhere amongst negro tribes, is absolutely unknown as a mode of showing affection. The people of the sea-board, however, who have heard of the practice from Europeans, have invented a verb, *du do nu,* to express it, which literally means—" To lick the mouth." *Few ahnu,* the verb invented by the Tshi-speaking peoples under similar circumstances, means, it may be remembered—" To suck the mouth."

As is usual with people who are divided into totem-clans, the Ewe tribes are exogamous ; marriage between members of the same clan being forbidden. This restriction is, however, not now always scrupulously observed by the sea-board tribes.

II.—RELATING TO KINSHIP, SUCCESSION, AND PROPERTY.

Kinship is traced through females, and the order of succession to property, &c. is brother, sister's son. The eldest brother is the head of the family, and his heir is the brother next in age to himself ; if he has no brother, his heir is the eldest son of his eldest sister. The following table will serve to show who are comprised in an Ewe family, the capital letters representing females and the others males.

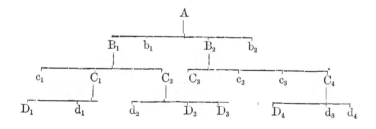

B_1, B_2, b_1, b_2, are sisters and brothers, the children of one mother A.   All the C's and c's, the children of B_1 and B_2, are related to each other, to all the B's and b's, and to A.   The children of b_1, however, are not related to those of b_2, and neither are related to A, to B_1, or B_2, or to any of the younger generations; because they belong to the stocks of their mothers, the wives of b_1 and b_2.   If we suppose A to have had two sisters, then there would be three such families, in which all the descendants through females would be related to each other.   It is rare for representatives of more than four generations to be alive at one time, and kinship does not appear to be traced beyond fourth cousins.   This system of kinship may doubtless be attributed to an early social condition in which the paternity of children was necessarily doubtful.   If b_1 be the head of the family in the above table, b_2 is the heir first in order of succession, then c_1, and then d_1.   Similarly c_3 is the heir of c_2, and, failing c_3, d_3 inherits.

Members of a family have a right to be fed and clothed by the family head, and the latter has in his turn a right to pawn, and in some cases to sell, them. The family collectively is responsible for all crimes and injuries to person or property committed by any one of its members, and each member is assessible for a share of the compensation to be paid.   On the other hand, each member of the family receives a share of the compensation paid to it for any crime or injury committed against the person or property of any one of its members. Compensation is always demanded from the family instead of from the individual wrong-doer, and is paid to the family instead of to the individual wronged.   In respect to this custom of collective responsibility and indemnification, the Eẃe family resembles the old Welsh "kindred" : the practice in Wales, however, has generally been regarded as being connected with the tenure of the family lands, whilst, amongst the Eẃe-speaking peoples there is no private property in land, which all belongs to the tribe.

It seems that this system of family responsibility was, amongst the Eẃe and Tshi-speaking peoples, preceded by one of community responsibility; under which each member of a village, or other community, was assessible for a share of the fine to be paid in compensation of injuries committed by one of the community upon others not belonging to it. This wider responsibility only now survives amongst the Eẃe tribes in the liability of any member of a village or town to be seized and held as a hostage for the payment of a debt owing by another member of the same community; and amongst the Tshi-speaking peoples in the right which every creditor has to seize, in payment of a debt, the goods or person of any third party who belongs to the same community as the debtor. This custom seems to show that the community preceded the family, which one would certainly expect to be the case, when it is remembered that men must have dwelt together in groups, long before any such notion as that of kinship had been formed.

Amongst the upper classes of Dahomi we find, as has already been stated, a different system of kinship existing, it being there traced through males. This, which carries with it a proprietorship of a father in his children not recognized elsewhere, has very probably

P

been brought about by the exercise of arbitrary power. Owing to the manner in which the actual wives of the king are immured in palaces, hedged in by various restrictions, and guarded by women soldiers who are the king's wives in name, the paternity of the children borne by the king's wives would no longer be doubtful; and an autocratic ruler might well set aside custom and declare that his son should be his heir and successor, instead of his brother or nephew. The upper classes might follow his example, but, unless the new system were imposed by law, the masses would hardly do so; and in Dahomi we find that this system is confined to the upper classes, the masses still reckoning kinship through females only. That universally in Dahomi descent used formerly to be traced through females, the existence of such words as *no-vi-nutsu*, "brother," literally "mother's son," and *no-vi-nyonu*, "sister," literally "mother's daughter," seems to show. The fact that the king's sons have no rank during the lifetime of their father may also be a survival of such a system.

Several of the laws and customs of the Ewe-speaking peoples seem to support the general correctness of the views of the late Mr. McLennan regarding primitive marriage and kinship, which I regret to find I somewhat mis-stated in my former work. Shortly summarized, his theory is as follows :—

1st Stage. Promiscuity. Paternity uncertain, which leads to a system of kinship through women only.

2nd Stage. A rude polyandry, in which the husbands are not related by blood. Kinship through women only still in force.

3rd Stage. A less rude polyandry, in which the

husbands are brothers. Paternity still uncertain, but paternal blood not uncertain. This leads to a system of kinship through males.

During the first stage women were seized and carried off, to be used as wives by the men of the group who had seized them. After this custom of taking women from other groups for wives, which McLennan holds was caused by the prevalence of female infanticide, had been in force for a long time, it would come to be considered improper, because unusual, for a man to marry a woman of his own group. Each group would become exoga-mous; that is, each man in a group would have to seek a wife outside his own blood stock. But as the only system of kinship in force would be that through women, the children born of captured women would be held to be of the stocks of their mothers; that is of a stock alien to the men of the group. Hence in each group there would be females who could be taken to wife by the men of the group without violating the law of exogamy; and the rite of capture, or some symbol of it, would, through custom, still be preserved in these marriages, although these wives might be acquired by purchase, or in other modes.[1]

Now the Ewe system of tracing relationship through females only, seems to point to a period of promiscuity, when paternity was uncertain; as does, perhaps, the custom of husbands lending wives. Perhaps also the custom, which used to allow women of the blood-royal of Dahomi to intrigue with any men they pleased, is a survival of the first stage; for, in the gradual loss of

[1] See McLennan's *Studies in Ancient History*, Macmillan & Co. London, 1886.

independence and power by woman, the highest in rank
would be likely to preserve their freedom from male
control longest. The custom still exists in Ashanti, and
though it is there now explained on the grounds that
it insures handsome men for the succession, yet this
explanation looks very much as if it were invented to
account for a practice whose real origin and meaning
has long been lost sight of.

The fact of a younger brother inheriting the widows
of an elder brother is perhaps a survival of McLennan's
third stage ; for under that system of polyandry, which
he has called the Tibetan, the eldest brother is the head
of the house ; the wife, children, and property are called
his ; and at his death the brother next in age succeeds
to them all. The custom which requires a bride to
return to the house of her parents after a short period
of cohabitation with her husband, may, as has already
been pointed out, be a survival of the form of marriage
by capture. Marriage by capture *de facto* still exists,
for the great majority of the women captured in the
annual raids are used as wives ; and as the race is
exogamous, we must conclude that in earlier times all
wives were obtained by capture, for McLennan has
clearly established the invariable coincidence of the law
of exogamy with the rite of capture.

If McLennan's theory be correct, and if the Ewe
peoples have passed through these three stages to polygamy, without however, except in Dahomi, as referred
to, arriving at a system of kinship through males, we
should expect to find some indication of it in the words
now in use expressing relationships. The word expressing " father," for instance, would probably be applied to

relations who were not actual fathers; for under stages two and three there would be several fathers, and though, under existing conditions, there is, in theory at all events, only one father, yet we should expect to find some trace of the former condition of affairs still existing.

The word now most commonly used to express "father" is *to*, which, it seems, first existed as a verb with the meaning "to belong to"; then came to be a noun meaning "property, share, something owned"; and finally came to mean "father," because the father was the owner or master of the household. After having been used to mean "father," it acquired an adjectival meaning "male." Suffixed to a word, *to* still means "he who owns," as in *afiafi-to* (*afiafi*—theft), "he who owns theft," *i. e.* "he who thieves," hence "thief"; and in *awe-to* (*awe*—house), "he who owns the house," *i. e.* house-master, a title given to the head of a family. An older term for "father" is *fofo*, which is derived from the verb *fo*, "to support, maintain, raise up"; hence *fofo* means "he who maintains." The same word *fofo* means also "foot," because the foot supports the whole body.

Neither of the words now used to express "father" has then any relation to the act of begetting. They do not mean "he who begets," but "he who owns," and "he who maintains." During McLennan's third stage, if the wife lived in the house of the brothers who were her husbands, the eldest of the brothers, the head of the family would be *fofo* or *to*, the "maintainer," or "owner," and the other brothers something akin, if not the same. Well, at the present day the word *to* is used as a salutation, "Father," when the brothers of a father

are addressed ; and the word *to-dia*, which is used to
mean " uncle," seems to be compounded of *to* and *di*,
v. " to be equal to," or of *to* and *di*, v. " to stay in one
place with." Uncle, *to-dia*, is therefore literally, " he
who is equal to the father," or, " he who stays in the
same place with the father." If, on the contrary, during
the third stage, the wife lived in the house of her own
family, with her brothers, and was visited by or paid
visits to her husbands, as is the case in the Nair polyandry, which McLennan holds to have preceded the
Tibetan polyandry ; then, there being no begetting
father in the house with the children, the mother's
brothers would be *fofo* or *to*, maintainers or owners ;
and *to*, as well as *to-dia*, is a title given at the present
day to uncles on the female side. Under the existing
system of kinship, a mother's brothers are relations, but
a father's brothers are not ; and it is therefore strange
that both should be expressed by the same words. The
above may be the explanation, or it may be that *to* and
to-dia are general terms, applicable to all the males of
the generation next above the speaker, and not specific
ones denoting degrees of relationship.

The word now used for " mother " is *no*, which seems
to be derived from a verb *no*, " to sit, stay, or dwell " ;
and came to be used as " mother," because the mother
stayed in the house to look after the domestic affairs,
and take care of the children. Having come to mean
" mother," it then acquired the further meanings,
" bosom, breast, udder," and an adjectival one, " female."
The head-wife is termed *awe-no*, " she who stays in the
house," or " house-mother." An older word for " mother "
is *da* or *dada*, which appears to be derived from the

verb *da*, " to cook " ; it being the mother who prepared
the food for the family. The terms for " mother," then,
like those for " father," have no relation to the act of
begetting or of birth ; but mean " she who stays in the
house," or " she who cooks."

As maternity can never be doubtful, we cannot
expect to find the words *da* and *no* applied to other
female relatives, but it is somewhat strange that *da-dia*
is the word for a younger sister of the mother, and
da-gã for an elder. *Da-dia* would mean, " she who is
equal to the mother," or " she who stays in the same
place with the mother," and *da-gã* means literally,
" great mother." These terms might be survivals from
the Nair system of polyandry, where all the sisters live
in the same household, their several husbands living
elsewhere ; but can hardly be reconciled with the Tibetan
system, under which each sister would be living by
herself in the house of her husbands.

The Ewe language has no specific word for " son " or
" daughter." *Vi* signifies " child," and is derived from
vi (weak, weakly, delicate, little) ; and to express the
meaning of " son " or " daughter," the words *nutsu*
(*nu*—appearance, outside, shape : *tsu*—hard, strong),
" male," and *nyonu* (*nyo*—to be pleasant or beautiful :
nu—appearance, etc.), " female," have to be added. *No-
vi-nutsu* (mother's-child-male) = brother, and *no-vi-
nyonu* (mother's-child-female) = sister ; but it is to be
noted that there is no term meaning " father's child."
Other words denoting relationships are *mã-ma*, " grandmother," perhaps from *mã* (to divide, share) ; *to-gbe* (*to*—
and, *agbe*—life), " grandfather," and *togbe-togbe*, great-
grandfather." There is a great deal more to be learned

with regard to words expressing relationships, but when I collected these notes I was not aware of the importance of the subject.

A wife's property is always separate from that of her husband, and at her death passes to her children. If a wife should become involved in any litigation she involves her family, that is, the Ewe family bound together by uterine ties, but not her husband.

Succession to property carries with it the obligation to defray the debts of the deceased. If a family bury a deceased member, they become, *ipso facto*, responsible for his debts ; and no man who dies in debt can be buried without the consent of the creditors, unless the family liquidates or becomes responsible for the amount of the indebtedness. If the family declines to do so, and the creditors refuse permission to bury, the corpse is placed on a platform of sticks outside the town, and is there left ; but this is considered a very disgraceful evasion of family responsibility, and is very rarely resorted to. Amongst the Popos a family may acquit all its debts, no matter what the amount may be, by one of its members voluntarily enslaving himself. The deathbed declaration of a man concerning sums due to him by others, if made in the presence of responsible witnesses, is considered presumptive proof of the amounts being due.

III.—RELATING TO LAND.

Since by Dahomi law no individual save the king can possess property of any kind except by pure tolerance, the land of the kingdom as a whole is the property of the king, who allows his subjects to cultivate or otherwise use portions for themselves. When a man

has received a grant of land from the king, he can cultivate it and make use of its products, secure from the
interference of any third party; but he holds the land
only during the king's pleasure, and the latter can at
any moment revoke his former grant, and give the same
piece of land to another. The king, in short, yields
only the usufruct of the land; but the right to oust the
man in occupation is, like the right to plunder, only
rarely exercised. Waste land which has not been
granted to any one by the king may be cultivated by
any one; but a man who takes advantage of this privilege runs the risk of having the land, which he has
made fruitful by his labour, granted by the king to
some other person, without his having the right even to
take for himself the standing crops.

Amongst the other tribes, the land of the tribe belongs
to the tribe collectively, and is attached to the stool of
the king. He allots land to the different districts, which
is attached to the stools of the district chiefs, and the
latter allot portions to the villages and towns in their
districts; the chiefs or head-men of the towns or villages
apportioning it amongst the various families of which
the communities are composed.

By native law and custom there is no private
property in land, but a family in occupation of land cannot be disturbed; and land so occupied only practically
reverts to the community when it is abandoned or
thrown out of cultivation. When once land has been
allotted to a family, the usufruct belongs to that family
for as long as it chooses to cultivate it; but the land
cannot be sold by the occupiers or assigned to any third
party. Amongst the inhabitants of the sea-board towns,

however, the decisions of the colonial law-courts have fostered the notion of individual property in land, in so far as the land on which houses are built is concerned, and there are indications of its extending still further.

Members of a tribe who migrate and occupy a tract of uninhabited land not claimed by any tribe, do not become an independent community. They still owe allegiance to the chief or king of the tribe from whose territories they emigrated, and the land they occupy becomes attached to his stool by the very fact of their occupying it. Thus the people of Agotine, a Ga-speaking community who fled from Accra about 1680, and settled among the Ewe tribes to the east of Krepe, owe allegiance to the King of Accra, to whose stool the land they occupy is also attached.

IV.—RELATING TO SLAVERY AND PAWNING.

Slaves are of two kinds, namely, native-born and imported. The first are slaves by birth, persons who have voluntarily enslaved themselves, or have been enslaved by the head of the family in settlement of debts, and those who have been condemned to slavery for crimes or misdemeanours. The second are foreigners purchased as slaves, prisoners of war, and persons who have been " pan-yarred," that is, kidnapped, from surrounding tribes and carried off as slaves. Kidnapping is extremely common ; for, man being a marketable commodity, it is as profitable to steal him as to steal merchandise. It cannot, however, be carried on in Dahomi, on account of the impossibility of leaving the kingdom undetected.

As is the case on the Gold Coast, the owner of a

slave is responsible for all the actions of his slave, just
the same as if he had performed those actions himself.
He is responsible for his slave's crimes, misdemeanours,
and debts, and has to make compensation for them.
On the other hand, the slave must efface his own identity
and be the blind implement of his owner, obeying him
implicitly in all things, even to the extent of committing
murder, if he should order it.

Here, as in West Africa generally, the condition of
slavery is not regarded as degrading, and a slave is not
considered an inferior being. This is a necessary consequence of the conditions of enslavement. If a man be a
slave it may be because he has been sold by the head of
his family to liquidate some debt with which he, the
slave, had nothing to do, or because he or his mother
were so unfortunate as to have been kidnapped or made
prisoners in war. Hence the condition of slavery is
attributed to misfortune or accident, and not to any
innate inferiority on the part of those enslaved.

A slave is regarded in every sense as a member of
his owner's family ; he calls his owner " father," and is
called by him " son " or " daughter," as the case may
be. Slaves have the right to acquire and inherit wealth,
and even to own slaves themselves. It is not at all
unusual for a slave to earn sufficient to purchase his
freedom, though he cannot demand his liberty on payment of a fixed sum, and sometimes they attain to
wealth and power. Ordinarily their lot is not a hard
one. The great majority of slaves are domestic servants,
whose duties are very light, and who can employ their
leisure hours in any way they please. Those who are
employed in cultivation have rather a harder life, but

their toil is not in any way comparable with that of an
agricultural labourer in England.   A slave who is hired
out to a third person can only be employed by the latter
on the work for which he was specifically engaged.

Idle, vicious, and mutinous slaves are punished by
floggings and by imprisonment, but no slave-owner may
take the life of a slave.   A runaway slave who has been
recaptured is, as a rule, either sold into Dahomi as a
punishment, with the prospect of his being given to the
king for sacrifice at the Annual Customs, or flogged and
condemned to wear a heavy iron collar, to which a long
chain is attached.   It is but seldom, however, that a
slave, even when ill-treated, runs away, for, if native
born, he thereby expatriates himself for life, since he can
never venture to return ;   and if he be imported, his
native land is usually at such a distance that he cannot
hope to regain it.   Both, moreover, run the risk of
falling into the hands of the bands who haunt the roads,
and make a business of carrying off and selling solitary
wayfarers.   According to custom, any slave who takes
refuge in a temple and dedicates himself to the service
of the god, cannot be reclaimed by his owner ; but as
by paying a fee to the priests the owner can close the
doors of all the temples in the neighbourhood to his
fugitive slaves, this provision of an asylum for an
ill-treated slave is more apparent than real.

By the law of Dahomi all men are slaves to the
king.   Hence, in cases of unlawful wounding, a man is
punished, not for injuring an individual, but for damaging
the property of the king.

A pawn is a person placed in temporary bondage to
a third party by the head of the family, as security for

payment of a debt, or to obtain a loan. A slave can similarly be pawned by his owner. The pawn remains in the service of the creditor till the debt, with interest, is paid by the pawner, his services to the creditor counting nothing towards the liquidation of the debt. If a pawn should die, the person who pawned him is bound to replace him by another, or else pay the debt. A pawn, like a slave, is utterly irresponsible, but in this case it is the person who pawned him who is responsible for his behaviour, and not the person in whose service he is.

A father cannot sell or pawn his children without the consent of the mother, if she be a free woman. If the mother be a slave, she and her offspring are equally the property of her owner, and he can dispose of the latter without any reference to her. A mother, on the contrary, who is a free woman, can sell or pawn her children without the consent of the father, if the latter refuses to give her what she requires. If, for instance, a woman were condemned to pay a fine, and her husband refused to give her the amount required, she would have a right to sell or pawn her children in order to raise the money. In such cases it is not unusual for a mother to sell or pawn the children to their father, and men often refuse to assist their wives in such cases, in order that they may thus acquire entire control of their children.

A man who has a woman placed in his hands as a pawn, has the right to use her as a concubine, and any children she may bear become pawns to him as well.

The custom of slavery, of men acquiring and holding property in their fellows, is so universal amongst uncivilized peoples, that its origin must be looked for in some cause that operated generally in prehistoric times.

homicide be lower in rank than the person killed, his life may be, and sometimes is, demanded. Injuries to the person are dealt with in the same way.

In Dahomi it is criminal to attempt to commit suicide, because every man is the property of the king. The bodies of suicides are exposed to public execration, and the head is always struck off and sent to Agbomi; at the expense of the family if the suicide were a free man, at that of his master if he were a slave.

In Dahomi any person whose house takes fire, even accidentally, is punished with death.

The ordinary mode of carrying out a capital sentence is by decapitation; but in Agweh and Grand Popo criminals are sometimes, in aggravated cases, impaled, burned alive, or disembowelled, and at Porto Seguro there have been one or two well-known instances in which the criminal was first impaled, and then roasted to death at a slow fire. As the royal blood of Dahomi may not be shed, offenders of the royal family are drowned or strangled. Usually they are bound hand and foot, carried out to sea in a canoe, and thrown overboard.

Criminals who are doomed to death are always gagged, because if a man should speak to the king he must be pardoned. This somewhat resembles the custom in Ashanti, where if a criminal should succeed in swearing on the king's life he also must be pardoned, because such an oath is believed to involve danger to the king. In Ashanti knives are driven through the cheeks from opposite sides, over the tongue, to prevent a criminal speaking; but the Dahomis, somewhat less brutal, use as a gag a Y-shaped stick, the fork of which holds the tongue, while the opposite end presses against the roof of the mouth.

A person found guilty of having procured, or endeavoured to procure, the death of another through the agency of the gods Huntin and Loko, is put to death, and his family is generally enslaved as well. The test of innocence or guilt in such a case is the odum-wood ordeal; but an accused is often slain without any trial whatever, the very accusation being considered presumptive proof.

Theft is punished by a fine levied upon the family of the thief, and by the restoration of the stolen goods. When a theft is committed in a household the women and the slaves are held collectively responsible until the thief is discovered. The reason of this is of course to make all personally interested in the detection of the guilty one; but it also enables a malicious slave to bring punishment, usually castigation, on his or her fellow-inmates, in revenge of real or fancied injuries.

In Dahomi thefts and minor offences committed in the king's houses, under which designation are included the so-called forts of Whydah, are punished with extra severity, and any native detected in stealing from one is put to death.

In Dahomi, and amongst the eastern Ewe tribes generally, non-influential men charged with or suspected of an offence are thrown into prison. This prison is almost invariably a dungeon, sunk below the level of the earth, from six to ten feet square, and without windows or any other opening for light and air. The condemned and those waiting trial are here equally huddled together, each secured by an iron collar,

Q

fastened to a long chain which passes through a hole in
the wall, and is secured outside. A chief who wishes
to get rid of some person who is obnoxious to him, does
so without risk by throwing him into a prison by himself, and then sending one or two confidential servants
or slaves at night, to drag the chain violently till the
man inside is jerked up close to the aperture through
which the chain passes, and strangled by the iron collar.
The man is murdered without even having seen his
assassins ; and in the morning when his corpse is found
in the prison, it is easy to attribute his death to suicide
or accident.   Prisoners are invariably half-starved, and
as the prisons are never cleaned out, they are pestilential
to the last degree.

VI.—ARBITRARY LAWS OF DAHOMI.

The following laws, which resemble in many respects
the laws of Coomassie, apply only to the kingdom of
Dahomi, and are not based upon any laws or customs
common to the Ewe-speaking peoples.   Those referring
to natives are punishable by death, but slavery or fine
is usually substituted.

1. It is criminal to say that the king eats, or that he
is so like other men as to require sleep.

2. No subject may wear sandals, or use a European
umbrella.

3. No subject may wear the *Imali fo-kpa* (slippers
made by the Mohammedan negroes) without royal
permission.

4. No subject may use anything but palm-thatch for
roofing his house. (This is perhaps devised in order to

facilitate the operations of the "king's thieves," palm-thatch being easily removed.)

5. No subject may wear a hat.

6. No leopard-skin may be exposed to view. (This is because the leopard is a sacred animal.)

7. No subject may eat with a knife and fork.

8. In Agbomi only men of rank may whitewash the interior of their houses, and have plank-doors to them.

9. None but persons of royal blood may spread counterpanes over their beds.

10. No stranger may establish himself in the kingdom without the permission of the king.

11. No stranger may travel in the kingdom until he has obtained permission.

12. No stranger may leave the kingdom without the permission of the king.

Strangers, especially Europeans, are always regarded with suspicion, and these last three laws are devised to prevent them resorting to or circulating in the kingdom, until their intentions and objects have been clearly ascertained, and to prevent them leaving it to escape the consequences of breaches of law.

In addition to the above laws there are various regulations governing commercial procedure, all made, as has been stated in the chapter on government, in order to furnish pretexts for making exactions from traders. The restriction placed on the sale of goods of a kind that have been purchased for the king has already been mentioned, and there are many others. No trader, for instance, may alter the current price paid for native produce, no matter what the quotations of European markets may be; and any increase or decrease of the trade rate renders the person who makes the change liable to a heavy fine. Traders are not permitted to purchase native produce unless the exportation has been approved by the king, and they may not import goods of a new description without permission. Some kinds of goods are not allowed to be sold by European traders except in large quantities, the privilege of retailing them being reserved to the people of the locality. No trader who has received permission to establish himself in the kingdom can commence to trade till he has " opened the road " by paying a sum to the king.

Certain restrictions are also imposed upon the people, for the benefit of the chiefs ; and the masses generally are forbidden to deal with Europeans except through the chiefs and their agents, who thus act as middlemen to both sides, and take a profit from each party. Of late years, however, this restriction has fallen into disuse.

CHAPTER XIV.

LANGUAGE.

THE Ewe language, as far as it is yet known, comprises five dialects, which are—

1. Mahi, spoken by the Mahi tribes and in the interior generally.
2. Dahomi, or Effon, spoken in Dahomi and Ewemi.
3. Anfueh, spoken in Anfueh, Krepe, Ewe-awo, &c.
4. Awuña, or Añlo, spoken by the western tribes of the sea-board.
5. Whydah, or Weta, spoken by the eastern tribes of the sea-board.

The Mahi dialect appears to be the purest. The Whydah dialect differs but little from the Dahomi.

VERBS.

There are five kinds of verbs.

1. In Ewe, as in the kindred languages Tshi and Ga, each simple root, formed of a consonant followed by a vowel, is a verb. These may be called simple-root verbs, and are undoubtedly the oldest in the language.

Examples—

du, to eat.	mi, to swallow.	so, to walk.
fa, to come.	ku, to die.	to, to own.
yi, to go.	nu, to drink.	no, to sit.

2. The second class of verbs is formed from the first, either—

    (*a*) By adding a vowel, or—

    (*b*) By interposing a consonant.

    Examples—

(*a*) *due*, to taste, experiment upon,	From	*du*, to eat.
mie, to wither, dry up,	,,	*mi*, to swallow.
biã, to be red,	,,	*bi*, to cook, boil.
tui, to spit out,	,,	*tu*, to fling, thrust, rub.
sia, to spread, extend,	,,	*si*, to flee, escape.
vie, to itch, smart,	,,	*ve*, to be bitter.
(*b*) *wlo*, to scrape, grate,	,,	*wo*, to place together.
dsi, to finish,	,,	*di*, to level, make equal.
ble, to deceive,	,,	*be*, to hide, conceal.
kla, to separate,	,,	*ka*, to break.
kle, to blaze, crackle (of a fire),	,,	*ke*, to light, shine.

3. The third class of verbs is formed from the two preceding—

    (*a*) By a simple reduplication.

    (*b*) By an irregular reduplication, in which the first syllable is altered, probably for the sake of euphony.

    Examples—

(*a*) *fafa*, to happen, be accomplished,	From	*fa*, to come.
didi, to be distant,	,,	*di*, to stay in a place.

dòdò, to mix, mingle,	From *dò,* to join, unite.
haha, to yawn,	,, *ha,* to breathe.
keke, to scatter,	,, *ke,* to separate.
tutu, to rub out, efface,	,, *tu,* to rub.
(b) *wawu,* to collect, assemble,	,, *wu,* to apportion.
gbugbo, to come back, return,	,, *gbo,* to come.
dedi, to lie, be situated,	,, *di,* to stay in a place.
khekhle, to pick out, gather,	,, *khle,* to count.
totro, to delay, wait,	,, *tro,* to turn.

The reduplication seems to strengthen the notion of the simple verb, either by intensifying it, as in *haha,* or by giving the idea of completed action, as in *tutu* and *totro.*

4. The fourth class of verbs is formed by joining two separate verbs. These verbs may be termed compound. In some cases the two verbs forming the compound are inseparable; in others they are separated by their objective noun.

Examples—

(a) Inseparable.

yidsi, to go on,	From *yi,* to go, and *dsi,* to come out.
tufe, to satisfy,	,, *tu,* to loosen, and *fe,* to be pleased.
trogbo, to come back,	,, *tro,* to turn, and *gbo,* to come.
subo, to serve,	,, *su,* to be, become, and *bo,* to stoop, bend.

kplĕdi, to abandon, de- From *kple*, to leave behind,
 sert,   and *di*, to stay in
            a place.

(*b*) Separable.
 dé gbli, to begin,   ,, *dé*, to touch, and *gbli*,
           to take.

 do di, to dip, immerse, ,, *do*, to go, and *di*, to
           stay in a place.

 dse na, to bear fruit,   ,, *dse*, to sprout, and
           na, to give.

 ke khle, to disperse,   ,, *ke*, to separate, and
           khle, to scatter.

 tso u̇u, to throw away, ,, *tso*, to take, and *u̇u*,
           to throw.

5. The fifth class of verbs is formed by using one or two verbs with a noun or an adverb.

 Examples—
 sé nu, to defame,   From *sé*, to be hard, and
           nu, mouth.

 no dsi, to overcome, van- ,, *no*, to sit, and *dsi*,
  quish,   above.

 le si, to have, hold,   ,, *le*, to seize, and *asi*,
           hand.

 ke nu, to gape,   ,, *ke*, to separate, and
           nu, mouth.

 do me, to enter,   ,, *do*, to go, and *me*,
           inner part.

 dé tsi nu, to soak,   ,, *dé*, to take, *tsi*, water,
           and *nu*, to drink.

 dé mo na, to allow,   ,, *dé*, to take, *mo*, road,
           and *na*, to give.

tro de dsi, to heap on,　　From *tro*, to turn, *de*, to go, and *dsi*, above

Verbs in Ewe, as in Tshi and Ga, possess only the indicative and the imperative moods. There are no passive verbs.

The ordinary rules for forming tenses in the indicative appear to be—

1. For the present tense—the verb in its simple form.
2. For the imperfect tense—a suffix *a*.
3. For the future tense—a prefix *a*.
4. For the past tense—a prefix *e*.

Example—

du, to eat.

Present Tense.

me du, I eat.	*mi du*, we eat.
wo du, thou eatest.	*mi du*, you eat.
e du, he eats.	*o du*, they eat.

Imperfect Tense.

me dua, I was eating.	*mi dua*, we were eating.
wo dua, thou wast eating.	*mi dua*, you were eating.
e dua, he was eating.	*o dua*, they were eating.

Future Tense.

me adu, I will eat.	*mi adu*, we will eat.
wo adu, thou wilt eat.	*mi adu*, you will eat.
e adu, he will eat.	*o adu*, they will eat.

Past Tense.

me edu, I ate.	*mi edu*, we ate.
wo edu, thou atest.	*mi edu*, you ate.
e edu, he ate.	*o edu*, they ate.

In the first and second person singular of the future tense, the vowel of the pronoun is commonly elided before the prefix *a* of the verb. Thus, *m'adu, w'adu.*

As in Tshi and Ga, verbs are also conjugated negatively. In the negative conjugation, three of the pronouns are used in their independent form,[1] instead of as above ; *nye*, I, being substituted for *me ; miao*, we, for *mi;* and *mia*, you, for *mi.* Tenses are formed as when the verb is conjugated positively, and the negative is indicated by a prefix *me*, and a suffix *o.* Thus the negative conjugation of *du*, to eat, is—

me-du-o, not to eat.

Present Tense.

nye me-du-o, I do not eat. *miao me-du-o*, we do not eat.

wo me-du-o, thou dost not eat. *mia me-du-o*, you do not eat.

e me-du-o, he does not eat. *o me-du-o*, they do not eat.

Imperfect Tense.

nye me-dua-o, I was not eating.
wo me-dua-o, thou wast not eating.
&c. &c.

Future Tense.

nye me-adu-o, I will not eat.
wo me-adu-o, thou wilt eat.
&c. &c.

[1] *See* Pronouns.

Past Tense.

nye me-edu-o, I did not eat.
wo me-edu-o, thou didst not eat.
&c.   &c.

The foregoing are the simple modes of conjugation, but, curiously enough, verbs are in Ewe conjugated also in four other different ways, viz.—

1. With the prefixes *wá* or *fa.* These give the notion of immediate or consecutive action. *Wá* is the verb *wá,* to set forth, move ; and *fa,* the verb, to come.
2. With the prefix *ga.* This gives the notion of repeated action, the prefix being the verb *ga,* to repeat.
3. With the prefix *le* and the suffix *ge.* These give the notion of intended action. *Le* is the verb *le,* to stay in a place, and *ge* the verb, to intend.
4. With the prefix *le* and the suffix *me.* These give the notion of continued action. *Le* is the same as in 3, and *me* the verb *me,* to form, shape. The *e* in *me* is generally elided.

If we like to regard these different forms as moods, then in Ewe the verb has, in addition to the indicative and imperative moods, consecutive, iterative, intentative, and continuative moods; but as all the above prefixes and suffixes are without exception verbs of the simple-root form, it seems rather that they should be regarded as auxiliary verbs, used in connection with all other verbs, to form verbs, of the fourth, or compound, class.

1. When the verb is conjugated with the prefixes, or auxiliary verbs, *wá* and *fa,* it has no imperfect tense. The formation of the other tenses is the same as in the

indicative mood, the prefixes *a* and *e*, denoting the future and past tenses, being placed before the *wá*, or *fa*. This seems to show that the latter, used with another verb, form an inseparable compound verb.

Example—
wá-du, to eat at once (literally, to set forth—to eat).

Present Tense.	Future Tense.	Past Tense.
me wá-du	*me awá-du*	*me ewá-du*
wo wá-du	*wo awá-du*	*wo ewá-du*
&c.	&c.	&c.

This form has no negative conjugation.

2. Conjugation with *ga*. This form has all four tenses, which are formed in the same way as in (1).

Example—
ga-du, to eat again (literally, to repeat—to eat).

Present Tense.	Imperfect Tense.
me ga-du	*me ga-dua*
wo ga-du	*wo ga-dua*
&c.	&c.

Future Tense.	Past Tense.
me aga-du	*me ega-du*
wo aga-du	*wo ega-du*
&c.	&c.

This form has no negative conjugation.

3. Conjugation with *le* and *ge*. This form has no imperfect and no future tense.

Example—
le-du-ge, to intend to eat (literally, to be in a place—to eat—to intend).

Present Tense.	Past Tense.
me le-du-ge	*me ele-du-ge*
wo le-du-ge	*wo ele-du-ge*
&c.	&c.

This form has a negative conjugation, as under—

> *nye me-le-du-ge-o*, not to intend to eat.

Present Tense.	Past Tense.
nye me-le-du-ge-o	*nye me-ele-du-ge-o*
wo me-le-du-ge-o	*wo mɛ-ele-du-ge-o*
&c.	&c.

4. Conjugation with *le* and *me*. This form has no imperfect and no future tense.

> Example—
>
> *le-du-m'*, to continue to eat.

Present Tense.	Past Tense.
me le-du-m'	*me ele-du-m'*
wo le-du-m'	*wo ele-du-m'*
&c.	&c.

This is also conjugated negatively.

> *me-le-du-m'-o*, not to continue to eat.

Present Tense.	Past Tense.
nye me-le-du-m'-o	*nye me-ele-du-m'-o*
wo me-le-du-m'-o	*wo me-ele-du-m'-o*
&c.	&c.

In conjugations (3) and (4), where the verb is already a compound one, the words forming it are transposed. Thus—

> *dia nu*, to challenge.
>
> *le-nu-dia-ge*, to intend to challenge.

And where the verb is one of strengthened or reduplicated root-form, it is usual to place the simple root before it. As—

I taste,	*me due* (from *du,* to eat).
I intend to taste,	*me le-du-due-ge.*

In Ewe, some verbs are both objective and subjective, thus—

> *yi,* to go, means also, to go to.

Some denote a quality, as—

> *fu,* to be white.
> *sé,* to be hard.
> *vé,* to be bitter.

Others are both transitive and intransitive, as—

> *kpā,* to break, or to be broken.
> *kla,* to separate, or to be separated.
> *bu,* to lose, or to be lost.

There are not many objective verbs. This is remedied by verbs being both transitive and intransitive, and by the use of compound verbs.

ARTICLES.

There is no indefinite article in Ewe. The definite article is *la.* It is derived from *le,* to be in a place, and its original form was *lea,* which by use has become *la,* or *a.*

In the form *la* it is suffixed to verbs, which then become nouns expressing quality or office. In the form *a* it is suffixed to nouns to give the meaning "the". Thus—

nyonu, wife.	*nyonua,* the wife.
awe, house.	*awea,* or *awa,* the house.
ge, root.	*gea,* the root.

Sometimes it is suffixed to nouns as *la*, as—

  devi, boy.   *devila,* the boy.

In such cases the *l* seems to be retained for the sake of euphony.

La should always terminate a sentence commencing with "if", or "when". Such sentences commence in Ewe with *ne.*

PRONOUNS.

1. Personal Pronouns.

In conjunction with a verb, these are—

  me, I.   *mi,* we.

  wo, thou.   *mi,* you.

  e, he, she, or it.   *o,* they.

These seem to be the original forms of the independent personal pronouns. At first they were used perhaps as personal augments to the verb, and subsequently came to be used independently, some without any change, and some changed. In their independent form they now are—

  nye, I.   *miao,* we.

  wo, thou.   *mia,* you.

  e, he, she, or it.   *o,* they.

And in this form they are used with the negative conjugation of the verb. *Nye*, I, is very probably the verb *nye*, to be.

The possessive personal pronouns are—

  nye, ye, si or *he,* mine. *miao,* our.

  wo, or *o,* thine.   *mi,* your.

  e, or *ye,* his.   *o,* their.

Ye, si, and *he,* mine, and *wo,* thine, are always placed before the noun, as—

    ye-fofo, my father.

Nye, mine, and *o,* thine, always after the noun, as—
> *fofo-nye,* my father.

The objective personal pronouns are the same as those used in conjunction with the verb.

The article *la* suffixed to a pronoun emphasizes its particularizing power, as *ara* does in *Tshi,* and may be rendered in English by " even ".

The suffix *ñuto* (*ñu,* 'shape, form, and *to,* to own) increases the particularizing power by denoting the exclusion of any other person, and is equivalent to " myself ", " himself ", &c. Thus—
> *nye-ñuto,* I myself.

The suffix *dokui* makes the personal pronouns reflective, as—
> *wo-dokui,* thyself.

Dokui seems to be derived from the verb *doko,* to go alone.

2. Relative Pronouns.

These in the simple form are *he* and *ke.* *He* seems to be the verb *he,* to have or hold, and *ke* the verb *ke,* to separate. They are suffixed to *ame,* man or person, when a person is referred to, and to *nu,* thing, when a thing is referred to. Thus—

> *ameke,* who, *i. e.* the person who (literally, the person separated).

> *nuke,* which, *i. e.* the thing which.

The adverbial relative pronouns of place, time, and manner are similarly formed by adding *he* and *ke* to certain other words, as follows—

fihe, or *fike,* where (*Afi,* place).

gbe-ke-gbe, or *gbe-he-gbe,* when (*Gbe,* to-day, the day).

aleke, how. *Ale* is here the future of the verb *le,* to be in a place.

3. Demonstrative Pronouns.
These are—

    ameke, when a person is referred to.
    nuke, when a thing is referred to.

. *la* is sometimes added to give additional emphasis.
The adverbial demonstrative pronouns of place, time, and manner are—

    fihe, fike, fi, or *gahe,* here, in this place.
    he, or *game,*   there, in that place.

ga, in both *gahe* and *game,* appears to be a contraction of *goa,* the place (*go,* place, and *a,* the) ; the *me* in the latter is the noun *me,* interior.

    azo, azoto, or *azola,*   then, at that time.
    nene, nenem, nenenko, thus, in this manner.

4. Interrogative Pronouns.
These are—

    ameka, when a person is referred to.
    nuka,   when a thing is referred to.

The adverbial interrogative pronouns are formed like the adverbial relative pronouns ; *ka,* what, being substituted for *ke.* *Ka* appears to be from the verb *kha,* to select.

5. Indefinite Pronouns.
These are—

    ame-deke, somebody, anybody.
    nu-deke, something, anything.

Used with the negative form of the verb they mean,

R

"nobody" and "nothing". *De* is the numeral, one, and *ke* means "to separate". The adverbial forms are—

  afi-deke, somewhere, anywhere.

  gbea-deke, some time, any time.

NOUNS.

Nouns are formed in the following ways :—

1. Direct from the verb, without change, as—

ku, death,	From *ku*, to die.
nyi, child,	,, *nyi*, to suckle.
gbo, place,	,, *gbo*, to come to.
kpê, stone,	,, *kpê*, to be heavy.

2. From the verb, with a prefix *a* or *e*, as—

aive, house,	From *ive*, to own.
avu, dog,	,, *vu*, to rend.
abe, speech,	,, *be*, to say.
ame, man,	,, *me*, to form, shape.
aivu, sea,	,, *ivu*, to fluctuate.
ebia, question,	,, *bia*, to ask.
eso, horse,	,, *so*, to go.
evõ, evil,	,, *võ*, to be afraid.
edà, bow,	,, *dà*, to throw.
edá, snake,	,, *dá*, to creep.

3. From the verb by reduplication, as—

(*a*) Regular reduplication.

baba, white ant,	From *ba*, to dig.
gbogbo, breath,	,, *gbo*, to breathe.
lõlõ, love,	,, *lõ*, to like.
nana, gift,	,, *na*, to give.
tãtã, foe,	,, *tã*, to hate.

(*b*) Irregular reduplication.

susui, thought,	From *su*, to compare.
gbogblo, talk,	,, *gblo*, to talk.
dedie, fatigue,	,, *de*, to walk.

4. By joining a verb and a noun, as—

dàti, arrow,	From *dà*, to throw, and *ati*, stick.
didiẁe, distance,	,, *didi*, to be broad, and *ẁe*, place.
yodo, grave,	,, *yo*, to fill up, and *do*, hole.
adétutu, dumbness,	,, *adé*, tongue, and *tutu*, to stop.

5. By transposing the component parts of a verb compounded of a verb and a noun, as—

aviedi, lamentation,	From *di avi*, to weep.
dsibi, anger,	,, *bi dsi*, to be angry.
ñubia, desire,	,, *bia ñu*, to desire.

6. From the verb by suffixing the definite article *la*. Such nouns always express quality or employment, as—

fiala, teacher,	From *fia*, to show.
kókóla, stammerer,	,, *kókó*, to stammer.
kpola, watcher,	,, *kpo*, to see.
sróla, scholar,	,, *sró*, to learn.
subola, servant,	,, *subo*, to serve.

7. By suffixing *la* to compound words, as—

mofiala, guide,	From *mo*, road, and *fia*, to show.
nutsola, carrier,	,, *nu*, thing, and *tso*, to carry.

awa-sila, fugitive,	From *awa*, war, and *si*, to escape.
mosola, traveller,	,, *mo*, road, and *so*, to go.
nunyala, wise man,	,, *nu*, thing, and *nya*, to know.

8. By suffixing *to* to other nouns. This suffix, originally a verb with the meaning " to own ", gives the meaning of " owner, he who possesses ", and thence " he who does ". Thus—

gato, captive; literally, possessor of iron,	From *ga*, iron.
hotsuito, rich man, possessor of cowries,	,, *hotsui*, cowries.
adétutu-to, mute,	,, *adétutu*, dumbness.
awe-to, house-master,	,, *awe*, house.
hasito, harlot,	,, *hasi*, copulation.

9. By suffixing *no* to other nouns. This suffix, originally a verb, " to sit ", gives primarily the meaning of " remaining, staying ", and secondarily that of " female ", or " mother ". Thus—

tokuno, deaf person,	From *toku*, deafness (*to*, ear, and *ku*, to die). " Remaining with the ear dead ".
tsukuno, idiot,	,, *tsuku*, idiocy (*tsu*, manliness, and *ku*, to die). " Remaining with the manliness dead ".
vino, mother,	,, *vi*, child.

funo, pregnant woman,   From *fu*, conception.
aive-no, house-mistress,   ,, *aive*, house.
doku-no, hen-turkey,   ,, *doku*, turkey.

10. By suffixing *ko* to other nouns. This suffix is the
    verb *kó*, to be high, or raised. It is generally
    reduplicated, as—
ñuti-kókó, greatness,   From *ñuti*, form, shape.
tsi-ko, thirst,   ,, *tsi*, water.

11. By joining two nouns, as—
aivu-ta, seashore,   From *aivu*, sea, and *ta*, top.
abo-ta, shoulder,   ,, *abo*, arm, and *ta*, top.
so-kpé, thunderbolt,   ,, *so*, fire, and *kpé*,
    stone.
koklovi, chicken,   ,, *koklo*, hen, and *vi*,
    child.
dsoti, torch,   ,, *dso*, fire, and *ati*,
    stick.
anyitsi, honey,   ,, *anyi*, bee, and *tsi*,
    water.

12. By joining a noun and an adjective, as—
ñuti-sésé, strength,   From *ñuti*, shape, and *sésé*,
    strong.
ñutiveve, pain,   ,, *ñuti*, shape, and *veve*,
    bitter.
vidzi, infant,   ,, *vi*, child, and *dzi*,
    delicate, tender.

13. By adding the definite article *a* to an adjective
    formed by reduplication from a verb, as—
kokoa, height,   From *koko*, high.
kekea, distance,   ,, *keke*, broad.

In 4, 11, and 12, that is where a verb and a noun, two nouns, or a noun and an adjective are joined, the word that stands second gives the general notion, while that which stands first particularizes, as—

dàti, arrow.　　ati, a stick (general notion) ; dà, to shoot.

Nouns are not declined. The nominative case is shown by the noun preceding the verb, and the accusative by it following it. The genitive is also shown by position, as edá ta, " snake-head ", i. e. " the head of the snake ". The dative is expressed by the verb na, to give, and the ablative by the verb gbli, to take, except when the noun is used with a verb implying direction.

The plural is formed by the suffix o, which is doubtless the personal pronoun o, they. Thus—

ame, man.　　　　ameo, men.
mo, road.　　　　moo, roads,
susui, thought.　　susuio, thoughts.

When the noun is qualified by an adjective, the suffix o is joined to the adjective, as—

kpé sésé, hard stone.　　kpé séséo, hard stones.

This is also the case when the noun is used with one of those pronouns that are always placed after the noun, as—

ati nye, my stick.　　　ati nyeo, my sticks.

When a noun is used with a cardinal number it does not take the plural form, the plural number being sufficiently indicated by the numeral. Thus—

ame alafa, a hundred men (literally, " man, a hundred ").

There is, properly speaking, no gender in Ewe. In the case of living creatures other than man the sex is indicated by the words *tsu* or *nutsu*, " male ", and *no*, " female ", as—

  so-tsu, stallion.   *so-no*, mare.

And in the case of men by *nutsu*, " male ", and *nyonu*, " female ", as—

  vi-nutsu, son.   *vi-nyonu*, daughter.

ADJECTIVES.

Adjectives are formed—

1. Directly from the verb without change, as—

 võ, bad,   From *võ*, to be afraid.
 gã, great,   ,, *ga*, to repeat.
 This form is not common.

2. From the verb by reduplication, as—

(*a*) Regular reduplication.

 bobo, bent,   From *bo*, to bend.
 fáfá, cool,   ,, *fá*, to be cool.
 kaka, broken,   ,, *ka*, to break.
 keke, broad,   ,, *ke*, to separate.
 kókó, high,   ,, *kó*, to be raised.
 kuku, dead,   ,, *ku*, to die.

(*b*) Irregular reduplication.

 beble, deceived,   From *ble*, to deceive.
 sosrõ, clever,   ,, *srõ*, to learn.
 babla, bound,   ,, *bla*, to bind.
 gõglõ, crooked,   ,, *glo*, to be crooked.
 vevie, bitter,   ,, *ve*, to be bitter.

3. By the reduplication of a noun, as—

 agbagbe, living,   From *agbe*, life.

4. By joining a verb and a noun, as—

dami, fat,	From *da*, to place, and *ami*, fat.
gbolō, empty,	,, *gbo*, place, and *lō*, to shear, shave.
wome, hollow,	,, *wo*, to sound, and *me*, interior.

The ordinary mode is by reduplication from the verb, and the others are rare.

The adjective takes no plural form except when in conjunction with a noun, as already described, and the terminal augment *o* then really belongs to the noun; the latter, with its qualifying adjective, seeming to form, in the ideas of the people, a compound word.

Adjectives do not form a comparative and superlative as in English. The comparative is expressed by the verb *wu*, to surpass, excel, as—

le võ, to be bad.   *le võ wu*, to be worse; literally, to be bad, to surpass.

And the superlative by the same verb *wu*, in conjunction with *kata*, "all", as—

le võ wu kata, to be bad, to surpass all, *i. e.* to be worst.

ADVERBS.

There are, properly speaking, no adverbs, their place being filled by verbs, nouns, pronouns, adjectives, or compounds of these, used adverbially.

Examples—

1. Adverbs of place.

Out, by *go*, place, edge.

Up, by *ta*, head, summit.

Far, by *didiŭe*, distance.

Above, by *dsi-ŭo : dsi*, upper part, and *ŭo*, contraction of *ŭeo*, plural of *ŭe*, place.

Here, by *afi*, place.

There, by *afi-ma ; afi*, place, and *me*, interior ; or by the verb *de*, to be in a place.

2. Adverbs of time.

Long ago, by *hoho*, old.

Late and long, by *dikadika ;* from *di*, to stay in a place, and *ka*, to be scattered.

Early, by *ndi*, morning, or by *foñoli ;* from *fo*, to get up, and *ñoli*, time.

Immediately and directly, by *dédé*, or *dédéla ;* from *dé*, to move, and *la*, the definite article.

When, by *ne*, give.

3. Adverbs of manner.

These, which in English are generally formed by adding *ly* to an adjective, are in Ewe expressed by the corresponding adjective.

4. Adverbs of intensity.

Much and very, by *ñuto*, real, positive, or by *kpã*, to break.

Quite, by *kpò*, to be accomplished. This when used with the negative conjugation of the verb, means "never".

5. Adverbs of frequency.

Again, by *ga*, to repeat, or *gbo*, to come to, arrive at.

No is expressed by *o* with the negative form of the verb, or by *dabi.* The latter is derived from the Tshi *dà*, day, and *bi*, some ; which, after being used with the negative form of the verb to express " never ", came to be used as " no ".

Yes is expressed by *e*. It is used differently to the English " yes ", and when said in reply to a negative question corroborates the negation. Thus the proper reply in Ewe to " You are not asleep " ? would be *e*, " yes ", while in English we should say " no ".

CONJUNCTIONS.

There are no conjunctions, properly speaking, their place being supplied by verbs, either alone or joined to nouns or pronouns.

Examples—

And, and with, by the verb *gbli*, to take, receive.

Then, by *eyia* ; from *yi*, to go, and *a*, the definite article ; literally, " the going ".

Therefore, by *eyia-ta* ; *eyia*, and *ta*, head.   Literally, " the head of the going ".   This is frequently contracted to *eata*.   Or by *eyia-nuti* ; *nuti*, thing. " The thing of the going ", *i. e.* " the cause of the going".

But, and also, by *na*, to give.

Yet, and nevertheless, by *gake* ; *ga*, to repeat and *ke*, rel. prn.

On, by *mãhã* ; *mã*, to divide, share, and *ha*, part.   This is often contracted to *hã*, and *ã*.

Because, and that, by *be*, to say, or *be-na*, to say, to give.

PREPOSITIONS.

There are also no prepositions, properly speaking, their place being supplied by verbs or nouns, or by the two combined, as—

From, by the verb *tso*, to come from.

To, by the verbs *yi*, or *de*, to go to.

For, by the verb *na*, to give.

In, into, by the verb *le*, to be in a place ; or by the nouns *me*, or *titina*, interior, or middle part.

Among,
Amid, } by the noun, *dome*, interval, interstice.
Between,

Above,
Over, } by the noun, *dsi*, upper part.
Upon,

Beneath, } by the nouns *anyi*, or *de*, lower part,
Under, } ground.

Beyond, by *godo; go*, place, edge ; and *do*, to go.

At, by *ñu*, outside, form ; or by *gbo*, place.

Before, by *mo*, face, *ñkume*, sight, or *ñgo*, the front.

Behind, by *mekpe*, the back.

NUMERALS.

The primary numerals are—

de, or *deka*, one.	*dadre*, seven.
eve, two.	*nyi*, eight.
eto, three.	*nyide*, or *asieke*, nine.
ene, four.	*ewo*, or *bla*, ten.
atõ, five.	*alafa*, hundred.
ade, six.	*akpe*, thousand.

COMPOUND NUMERALS.

The numerals from eleven to nineteen are formed by prefixing *wui*, probably a corruption of *ewo*, " ten ", to the primary numerals. Thus—

wui-deka, eleven ; *wui-ade*, sixteen.

The tens, from twenty to ninety, by prefixing *bla;* as—

bla-ve, twenty; *bla-to,* thirty; *bla-nyi,* eighty.

The intermediate numbers, between the tens, by a particle *vo;* as—

blave-vo-deka, twenty-one; *blave-vo-eve,* twenty-two.

The hundreds by placing *alafa* before the units, as—

alafa eve, two hundred.

And the thousands by placing *akpe* before them.

The ordinal numbers, with the exception of "first" and "second", are formed by suffixing *lea* to the cardinal numbers; as—

dadre-lea, seventh.

Lea is here the definite article *la,* from the verb *le,* in its original form.

First is expressed by *kpãkpiãkpã-to,* or *ñgogbea.* The former seems to be derived from *kpã,* to break, or burst, which verb also has the meaning of coming first,, as in *kpã-le,* firstling. It seems to mean "beginning", and the addition of *to* gives it the meaning of "that which has the beginning". *Ngogbea* is from *ñgogbe,* first-born.

Second is expressed by *mekpeto, eyiometo,* or *dometo.* The first is from *mekpe,* the back,· which is also used as "that which follows"; the second from *yi,* to go, and *me,* interior; and the third from *dome,* interval. The addition of *to* gives them respectively the meanings of "that which has the back", "that which has the going in", and "that which has the interval".

The original literal meaning of the units is obscure, but there is some trace of the practice of counting on the fingers. For instance, *de,* one, seems to be from

the verb *de*, to go, and to mean " a going ", or " a commencing"; and *ade*, six, that is, the first number
counted on the other hand, to mean " the other going ".
Eto, three, appears to be from *to*, father, and was
perhaps so named because the middle finger is the
longest. In Tshi the middle finger is named " Chief
of the hand ". *Asieke*, nine, is from *asi*, hand and *ke*,
to part ; and *ewo*, ten, from *wo*, to do, meaning " done ".
Bla, is the verb *bla*, to bind. In the formation of the
adverbial numerals the word *asi*, hand, is still preserved.
Thus—

> *si deka*, once, literally, one hand.
> *si eve*, twice,   ,,   two hands.

The foregoing are the numerals proper, but numbers
are frequently expressed in cowry nomenclature. Thus
hoka, a string of cowries, consisting of forty shells, is
often used for " forty" ; *homeli*, two-thirds of a string,
for " thirty", and *hoto*, a head of cowries, that is, fifty
strings, for " two thousand ". Large numbers are nearly
always expressed in this way.

From the preceding it will have been seen that all
the words in the language are derived from the simple
monosyllabic roots, consisting of a consonant followed
by a vowel, each of which is in Ewe a verb. The same
holds good for Tshi and Ga, and as these verbs mostly
express general and common notions, such as would be
the first to suggest themselves to man, they are probably
the primitive roots of the language. In Ewe, these
verbs are—

1. *ba*, to dig up.
2. *be*, to say, tell.
3. *bé*, to hide, conceal.

4. *bi*, to cook, boil.
5. *bo*, to bend, stoop.
6. *bu*, to lose, be lost.

7. *bu*, to think.
8. *da*, to place, lie down.
9. *dà*, to throw.
10. *dá*, to creep, crawl.
11. *dé*, to touch, seize.
12. *dé*, to move.
13. *de*, to go.
14. *de*, to be in a place.
15. *dè*, to be base.
16. *di*, to be willing.
17. *di*, to come down.
18. *di*, to bury.
19. *di*, to stay in a place.
20. *di*, to be clean.
21. *di*, to make equal.
22. *do*, to put, place.
23. *do*, to allow to go.
24. *dó*, to say, tell.
25. *dó*, to stamp, kick.
26. *dò*, to be sad.
27. *dò*, to join.
28. *do*, to change.
29. *dò*, to become big.
30. *do*, to sleep.
31. *dò*, to prick (of thorns).
32. *dò*, to grind, gnaw.
33. *du*, to eat.
34. *fa*, to come.
35. *fá*, to be cool.
36. *fe*, to be pleased.
37. *fi*, to steal.
38. *fo*, to rise, get up.
39. *fu*, to be white.
40. *ga*, to repeat.
41. *ge*, to lend.
42. *ge*, to intend.
43. *ha*, to breathe.
44. *he*, to have, hold.
45. *ho*, to stretch.
46. *ka*, to tear, rend.
47. *ke*, to split, cleave.
48. *ke*, to forgive.
49. *ko*, to be alone.
50. *ko*, to be cut in pieces.
51. *kó*, to be high.
52. *kó*, to be clean (of water).
53. *kó*, to be light, or bright.
54. *ku*, to die.
55. *ku*, to reach, contain.
56. *ku*, to scratch, scrape.
57. *ku*, to sound (a horn).
58. *lã*, to cut.
59. *le*, to be in a place.
60. *lé*, to seize, hold.
61. *lõ*, to shave, shear.
62. *lõ*, to love, like.
63. *lõ*, to twist, plait.
64. *mã*, to divide, share.
65. *me*, to divide in two.
66. *me*, to form, shape.
67. *mi*, to swallow.
68. *mu*, to shake, waver.

69. *mu,* to be green.
70. *mu,* to lean upon.
71. *na,* to give.
72. *nĕ,* to snap, break off.
73. *no,* to sit, remain.
74. *no,* to form, shape.
75. *ño,* to bore, perforate.
76. *nu,* to drink.
77. *sa,* to bind.
78. *se,* to be hard.
79. *se,* to hear.
80. *sĕ,* to cut, carve.
81. *se,* to reach, arrive at.
82. *si,* to flee, escape.
83. *si,* to cut, scratch.
84. *so,* to walk, go.
85. *so,* to be assembled.
86. *su,* to compare, become.
87. *tã,* to hate, pursue.
88. *tá,* to cut away.
89. *to,* to own.
90. *tu,* to thrust, kick, push.
91. *tu,* to ascend (of smoke).
92. *tu,* to be lame.
93. *tu,* to loosen.
94. *tu,* to build.
95. *va,* to weep.
96. *vé,* to be bitter or sour.
97. *ve,* to be warm.
98. *vò,* to be ready.
99. *võ,* to be afraid.
100. *vu,* to tear, rend.
101. *wã,* to sow.
102. *wa,* to grow.
103. *wã,* to be sour.
104. *wá,* to move.
105. *we,* to own.
106. *wĕ,* to stink.
107. *wo,* to do, act.
108. *wo,* to blow, sound.
109. *wó,* to strike, beat.
110. *wo,* to place together.
111. *wu,* to surpass, excel.
112. *wu,* to sow.
113. *wu,* to kill.
114. *wu,* to divide, part.
115. *wu,* to thrust, throw.
116. *yi,* to go.
117. *yo,* to call.
118. *yo,* to fill up.

All of these are not equally primitive, and some have originated from others by a change of inflection. Thus, *dá,* to creep, crawl, is probably from *da,* to lie down; *dé,* to move, push, from *de,* to go; and *dé,* to stay in a place, from *de,* to be in a place. *Mu,* to be green, is from *mu,* to shake, waver.

A comparison with verbs of similar form in Tshi and Ga assists in determining those which are derived from others. For instance, the connection between *lõ*, to love, like, and *lõ*, to twist, plait, is not at all apparent ; but on finding that there is in Ga a verb *lo*, to twist, plait, which, when used with the adverb *atu*, means " to embrace ", it becomes clear.

The letter *b*, in Tshi and Ga, frequently becomes *f*, or *v*, in Ewe ; thus—

	Tshi.	Ga.	Ewe.
To come ...	*ba*	*ba*	*fa*
Child	*ba*	*bi*	*vi*

The verb *so*, to go, walk, run, &c., seems to be the radical of *so*, or *dso*, fire. It occurs in *dudso*, to burn ; *dso-ade*, flame ; *dsuie*, hot, seething ; *dsudso*, smoke ; *so-fia*, lightning ; *dze*, to set on fire ; *dze*, to shine ; *dze-dso*, to be warm ; *dzie*, red, yellow ; *dza-dze*, to burn ; *kho-dso*, to be hot. *Fia*, to be burned, from which are derived *afi*, ashes, and *afifia*, heat, may possibly be from the root-verb *bi*, to boil, cook (in Ga, *be*, to be boiled), *b* and *f* being frequently interchanged.

In *si*, to flee, avoid, escape, shun, &c., we find the radical of *si*, or *tsi*, water, " the escaper ", that which slips through the fingers and cannot be held. It occurs in *tsi-sisi*, stream ; *detsi*, soup ; *lé-tsi*, to wash ; *ivu-tsu*, to swim ; *tsio*, to filter ; *tsiko*, thirst ; *dsa*, to splash ; *dsakpo*, to flow ; *dsidze*, to fathom ; *dsidsim*, spring of water ; *no-tsi*, milk, &c.

In Ewe, inflection of voice is used in a manner quite different from that in which it is used in English ; the modulation of tone here not merely affecting the relative force and expression of words in a sentence, but actually altering the meaning. Thus *to*, with the faintest sound of a terminal *r*, means "father"; *tó*, with the vowel slightly aspirated, means "mountain"; *to*, with a depression of tone, "lagoon"; and *to*, "ear".

There are a few words which are undoubtedly onomatopœic, such as *gba-gba*, duck; *koklo*, hen; and *kra-kra*, a rattle. *Mimi*, a mute, may be from the *m-m* sound made by mutes, or from *mi*, to swallow.

The language is very deficient in terms denoting colours. *Dzie* is used for both red and yellow; *yibo*, for black, brown, purple, dark blue, or any dark colour; and *gi*, for white. *Mu*, green, really means "the shaker", *i. e.* the foliage of a tree. Gray is denoted by *ñota*, gloomy.

Towns and villages are named from their situation, from some local peculiarity, or after their founder. Thus *Keta*, "sand-summit", because the town stands upon the sand-ridge between the lagoon and the sea; *Agbomi*, "in the gates", because surrounded by a fortification; *Togo*, "place of the lagoon"; &c.

s

CHAPTER XV.

PROVERBS AND FOLK-LORE.

THE Ewe-speaking peoples, like most races of West Africa, have a large collection of proverbs, one, at least, being provided for almost every circumstance in life; a peculiarity which is common to most peoples who have made but little progress in civilization, and amongst whom these trite aphorisms have great weight. The following are given as specimens :—

1. Stone in the water-hole does not feel the cold.
   (Answers to our " Habit is second nature.")
2. He who has to carry does not walk bent.
3. The hunchback does not sleep on his back.
4. He whose hand can meet no chair, sits on the ground.
5. If the short mat is not in a man's hand, he sleeps standing.
   (These are used to mean, " Accommodate yourself to circumstances.")
6. A poor man can never become a priest.
7. Nobody sits by a fire and cries.
   (This refers to the smoke from a wood fire getting into the eyes and giving the appearance of tears. It is used in the sense of, " Do not judge by appearances.")

8. Two eyes one has, but two things one does not see.

9. Two ears you have, but two things you do not hear.

10. Two arms you have, but two kinds of work you do not do at once.

11. No one chases two birds.

(These mean, "You cannot do two things at once.")

12. Two men are not blockheads.

(Answers to, "Two heads are better than one.")

13. One man cannot serve two masters.

14. A child and water are not together.

15. Poor and rich do not go together.

16. Water and fire are not together.

17. If a pregnant woman falls, the child in the womb answers.

(Means that nothing can be so carefully concealed that it will not be discovered, and is equivalent to "Murder will out.")

18. Whoever goes abroad does not hear family news.

19. As the child has not seen what happened before his birth, let him be satisfied with having it told him.

20. The stick you have in your hand is that with which you strike the snake.

(Means, "Make the most of your opportunities.)

21. Two kings do not rule in one town.

22. A lurking dog does not lie in the hyena's lair.

23. The goat does not pass the leopard's door.

24. If the mouse be ever so drunk, he does not go to sleep in the cat's bed.

25. Clothes are men.

    (Equivalent to, "The tailor makes the man.")

26. If the cloth be greasy, it is not burnt.

    (Means, "Things might be worse.")

27. Riches buy slaves, but not life.

28. If the boy says he wants to tie water with a string, ask him if he means the water in the pot or in the lagoon.

    (Means, "Answer a fool according to his folly.")

29. No child of man knows the day of his death.

30. The fowl in the coop does not know the day of his death.

    (These refer to the uncertainty of life, but the second is used to remind slaves that they are liable to be sold at any time.)

31. A poor man's son does not brag.

32. Cowries are men.

    (Equivalent to, "Money makes the man.")

33. The dog does not look in the room and say—"Is that your father's property, or your mother's?"

34. Have you ever buried a hunchback, and gone home?

    (These two are used to inquisitive persons, and the second means that they might be curious to know in what position a hunchback would be laid in the grave.)

35. The guest does not surpass the host.

36. If water falls on a stone it does not trickle through it.

37. Fire devours the grass, but not the roots.

38. When the leopard sleeps you might think him dead.

{ 39. The shepherd's staff does not kill the sheep.
{ 40. The lash that drives the herd does not kill them.

41. The plantation owner takes away the wood, but not the rope.

   (The cut brushwood belongs to the man who clears the ground, and this proverb supposes the case of such a person finding some of the wood tied up in a bundle by somebody else, ready for removal. It is used in the sense of, " Take only what is your own," and also in that of, " Do not act in hot haste.")

42. The death of the suicide cannot be avenged.

43. A crab cannot become a bird.

   (Equivalent to, " You cannot make a silk purse out of a sow's ear.")

44. The elephant's tail is short, but with it he drives off the flies.

45. A cask of rum cannot roll itself.

46. A large shell (of the cowry species) cannot buy goods to the value of even two cowries.

   (The large cowry shells are not circulated as money. Equivalent to " Little and good.")

47. Nobody takes a trinket and hangs it round the neck of a wild bird.

48. What hangs in the hand goes not to the well.

   (Baskets with handles are carried in the hand, while other articles, such as water-pots, are carried on the head. The proverb means, " No one fetches water in a basket.")

49. Nobody unroofs the house in the town to roof the house in the plantation.

   (The town house is the ordinary abode, that in

the plantation being only a temporary shelter, used by the family during the intervals of rest from work.)

50. To despise one's equal is to despise oneself.

51. The hater is the murderer.

52. One tree does not make a forest.
(Answers to our, " One swallow does not make a summer.")

{ 53. Fire burns property, but not iron.

{ 54. The white ant devours everything except stones.

55. The crocodile's child does not die by drowning.
(Equivalent to, " What is one man's meat is another man's poison.")

56. The bird with a long bill eats things that are far off.

57. Nobody takes a tortoise or a crab to make a pad.
(The pad here referred to is that used to protect the head from the load carried on it.)

58. The stranger's son makes people angry.
(Refers to foreigners offending the prejudices of natives by laughing at their customs, which the young are more prone to do than the old; hence " stranger's *son*.")

59. Talk in the house makes no man excel.
(Equivalent to, " Deeds, not words.")

60. Politeness engenders friendship.

61. An empty hand does not go to market.

{ 62. The night comes on, then runs the mouse.

{ 63. The rat does not come out in the daylight.

64. If you are an orphan, and somebody gives his child instruction, take care to listen, so that you may profit by it.

65. To the potter belong the broken pieces.

(Means that nobody buys spoiled goods.)

66. Two big fish do not drink water in the hollow of one rock.

67. The poor man gets no goods without security.

68. Rain rolls things, but not stones.

69. The last one locks the door.

70. The part of the stick that is in the fire will be burned.

(Used to mean that punishment only falls on the guilty.)

71. Two men of sense do not try to divide three cowries.

72. The cock does not crow in the desert.

(Refers to the fact that' a traveller can always know when he is approaching habitations by the crowing of cocks. This proverb and the next one are equivalent to our, "There is no smoke without fire.")

73. The palm-branch does not open its mouth without cause.

(Refers to the rustling noise made by palm-branches when agitated by the wind, which can be heard for some little distance.)

74. The diver does not know what is going on behind him.

(Used to a person who is seen without his being aware of it.)

75. Although a man looks back, he does not know what is on his back.

76. Follow the customs of your father. What he did not do, avoid doing, or you will harm yourself.

77. One man kills the elephant, and many villages eat it.

(When an elephant is killed, a rare occurrence now, as they have all been driven far inland, it is usual to divide the meat among the people of the neighbouring villages. The proverb is used to show that one person may benefit many.)

78. What went into the belly yesterday is not in the mouth to-day.

79. The eyes see things, but eat them not.

80. Where war is, there the drum will be.

81. Who wants to eat does not sit still.

82. The soup is sweet to the cat's mouth, even though she has no hand with which to raise it.

(Means, "So long as you have enough to eat, do not grumble at the mode in which it is put before you.")

83. Distant fire-wood is good fire-wood.

(Something like our, "Distance lends enchantment to the view.")

84. Nobody tells a sick man that he ought not to complain.

85. A boy looks for things, but not for *golo's* eggs.

(The *golo* is a kind of crane that builds its nest in the depths of impenetrable swamps. Means, "No one attempts the impossible.")

86. If the thief steals stolen goods, the dispute is not far off.

(Equivalent to, "Two of a trade never agree.")

87. A small thing is in your hand, but even that can make much blood flow.

(Refers to the serious injuries that may be in-

flicted with a small knife, and is used in the
sense of, "Little beginnings often have big
endings.")

88. A dog gnaws bones, but not stones.
89. Your grandmother does not correct you ; she sends
you to your mother.

(Is a mode of telling people to mind their own
business, the bringing up of a child being the
business of the mother, though here, as elsewhere, grandmothers sometimes interfere to spoil
the child.)

90. If the boy leaves his father's house, he cannot go
to that of his mother.

(Boys remain under the care of the mother
until they are old enough to be of service to
the father, when they leave the maternal roof
and live in the father's house. Is used to mean
that the past is irretrievable.)

91. He who goes to the father need not go to the
mother.

(The father being the superior.)

92. If the agriculturist does not go to his neighbour's
plantation (and see him at work), he says, " I
alone am working."

93. A seller of herbs does not sell them as grass.

(Means that nobody depreciates the value of his
own wares.)

94. He who works for himself can do as he pleases.
95. Nobody makes a bargain to take the burden and
pay the debts.

96. A small calabash does not sound like a big one.

(Is used to braggarts.)

97. Nobody eats cactus.

98. The python swallows creatures, but not porcu-
pines.

   (Used when a person is trying to make use
   of another as a " cat's-paw.")

99. The deaf and dumb man does not know when
you call him.

100. A tree lopped of its branches does not move in
the wind.

101. Blood is surely in a person's mouth before he
swallows saliva.

   (The Ewe native believes that by gathering
   saliva in the mouth he excites the blood, and
   to swallow saliva, instead of ejecting it, is a
   sign of anger or disgust. The proverb is something like our, "Coming events throw their
   shadows before them.")

102. The big water-pot goes not to the well.

   (Used in the sense of, "The more haste, the
   less speed." The big water-pot here referred
   to is the large one that is half-buried in the
   ground near the house, and which contains the
   household supply of water for the day. It is
   filled with the water brought in smaller pots
   from the well, or spring, by the women.)

103. Take care, robbers, there is a sword in Dahomi.

   (Used as a warning.)

{ 104. A boy counts things, but he does not count sand.
{ 105. A boy can count cowries, but he cannot count the
stars.

   (Sand and stars are commonly used to express
   a countless multitude.)

106. If a thorn goes into your foot, the hand pulls it out; but if a thorn goes into your hand the foot cannot pull it out.
107. If corn is put in the sun to dry, and not watched, will not the goats eat it?

   (Used to reprove carelessness or imprudence.)
108. Every palm-leaf falls separately.
109. One palm-nut spoils all the palm-nuts.

   (The red nuts of the wine-palm are used in stews, and one bad one spoils the whole mess. Used in much the same way as our, "Evil communications corrupt good manners.")
110. One belly eats something, another gets fat on it.
111. Fowls do not bring forth stones.

   (Used to a person who is handling a fragile article roughly or carelessly.)
112. The mouth talks plenty that the heart does not say.
113. Mouse sitting in the palm-oil and lizard's head suspicious.

   (The head of the male lizard is something of the colour of palm-oil. The proverb means that a suspicious person will always find something to suspect.)
114. The fruit falls under the tree.

   (Equivalent to, "As you have sown, so you will reap.")
115. An amiable person is never good-for-nothing.
116. The head does not sit under, so that a knee can put on a hat.

   (Used to check arrogance and assumption.)
117. Boy, I bind a tooth-amulet round your neck; but

you cannot trust yourself under the fangs (of a wild beast).

(The tooth-amulet is to guard the wearer from beasts of prey. The proverb is used to check rashness, or over-confidence.)

118. If the mouse gnaws stones, then the melon is frightened.

119. Respect the elders, they are our fathers.

120. Stones are heavy, but the pounding-stone is heavier.

(Refers to the stone pestle used for pounding corn, which is very heavy in proportion to its size. The proverb is equivalent to our, "Do not judge by appearances.")

The fables in vogue amongst the Ewe-speaking peoples, and of which there are a great number, are always material, and are in no way connected with metaphor. They are tales pure and simple, are not designed to account for events, or for phenomena in nature or life, and have no analogy with the moral fables which were once popular in Europe, and of which those of Æsop afford an example. They are merely stories of the adventures of beasts and birds, to whom the Ewe-speaking native ascribes a power of speech, and whose moral nature he conceives to be at least as analogous to that of man as their physical nature. This form of myth is probably primary, the allegory and moral lesson being added when a more advanced stage of civilization is reached.

These fables are usually recounted on moonlight

nights, when the young people of the town or village gather together in one of the open spaces amongst the houses. It is usual for the story-teller to be accompanied with the sound of a drum, whose rhythm occurs after each sentence. A few taps on the drum are sounded, the narrator announces his subject by saying, " My story is of so-and-so ; " the audience reply, " We hear," " We listen," or " We take it up," and the recital then commences.

<h2 style="text-align:center">I.—THE HYENA AND THE BUSH-CAT.</h2>

The hyena had a little one, and it died : the bush-cat had also a little one, and it died.

The bush-cat took a dislike to its country ; so did the hyena, and each went to seek for a better place.

When it arrived at a certain place, the hyena said, " This will do. To-morrow, at day-break, I will come and pull up the grass."

The bush-cat chanced upon the same place ; it pleased him ; he tore up the grass and went away to sleep.

Next morning the hyena returned. " Oh ! " he cried, " what a good place ! I was going to pull up the grass, and the grass has already pulled itself up."

He took possession, swept the ground, and went away.

The bush-cat came back in his turn. " Oh ! " he said, " what a good country ! I was going to sweep, and the ground has swept itself."

He cut down some poles (trees), left them on the ground, and went away.

The hyena returned, fixed the poles in the ground, and went away to sleep.

Then the bush-cat came. "The poles," he said, "have planted themselves," and he cut some bamboos and put them on the ground.

The hyena came and fastened the bamboos to the poles.

The bush-cat returned. "Ah!" he said, "the bamboos have tied themselves to the poles." And he took the grass and thatched the house.

"How is this?" said the hyena when he came. "The roof is made."

He divided the house into two parts, keeping one room for himself and leaving the other for his wife.

Then the bush-cat returned. "Good!" he said; "the house is divided into two. This part I shall keep for myself, and that I shall give to my wife. In five days I will bring my property here, and settle down."

The hyena, on his side, made the same arrangement.

When the fifth day arrived, the bush-cat took his property and came with his wife.

The hyena did the same.

The hyena went into one room, and the bush-cat into the other.

Each believed that there was nobody else in the house.

Now, at the same time each broke something, and each one said, "Who is that breaking something in the next room?"

And each one ran away.

They ran as far as from Keta to Amutino, and then they met.

PROVERBS AND FOLK-LORE. 271

"What are you doing, oh hyena?" asked the bush-cat.

"I had built a house," said the hyena, "and something drove me out. I don't know what."

"The same happened to me," said the bush-cat. "I cut down trees, and the poles planted themselves."

The hyena said, "I found a place that I liked, and I was going to pull up the grass; but when I went to do it the grass had pulled itself up."

Then the bush-cat and the hyena commenced running again.

They have never been able to look at each other since.

II.—THE MAIDEN WHO ALWAYS REFUSED.

A man, his wife, and daughter lived in one house.

The girl grew up; she grew up beautiful. Her father and mother were rich.

Then men came to ask for her, to take away and marry the maiden; but the maiden said, "Not yet."

Then, whenever men came to ask for her, she continued to refuse. She said, "My shape is good, my skin is good, therefore I shall stay," and she stayed.

Now the leopard, in the leopard's place, hears this.

He turns himself to resemble a man. He takes a *saku*[1] in his hand, he makes himself a fine young man. His shape is good.

Then he goes to the father and the mother of the maiden, and he says, "I look strong and manly, but I do not look stronger than I love."

[1] A native stringed instrument.

Then the father says, " Who looks strong, takes ; " and the young man says, " I am ready."

The young man comes in the house. His shape pleases the young girl. They give him to eat, and they give him to drink.

Then the young man asks the maiden if she is ready to go, and the maiden says she is ready to go.

Then they give the maiden things and two slaves ; one female that her mother gives, and one male that her father gives ; and goats, and sheep, and fowls.

Then the father gives a word of advice to his child ; the mother embraces her. They walk out a little way on the road with their child, and then the father and mother turn back again.

Then the young woman and her husband go. They take the road to go out. He walks with his wife's hand in his.

Presently the husband says, " I am hungry."

Then the woman says to her husband, " Here is some yam you can eat." The husband refuses it ; he says, " I am not one who eats roots."

Then the woman says, " Here are fowls," and the husband takes and eats the fowls.

Then they go again on the road, and presently the husband says, " I am hungry ; is there anything to eat ? "

Then the wife says, " Here are sheep " ; and the husband takes and eats the sheep.

Then they go up the road again a little, and the husband says directly, " I am hungry."

Then the wife says, " Here are goats."

The husband takes and eats the goats ; he eats all the flesh, only he does not eat the two slaves.

Presently again he is hungry. He says to his wife, " Is there anything to eat ? "

Then she says, " Is not everything finished ? " And he says, " No ; there are these two persons."

Then the wife weeps. She says, " Take them and cut them up, if it must be."

But to bring down this flesh to eat it, he turns back to become a leopard. Then he eats the two slaves.

Then they go again on the road. Immediately he says, " I am hungry. Is there anything to eat ? "

Then the wife weeps ; she cries loud, for everything is finished.

A hunter is in the bush ; he hears the weeping, and he comes to hide.

Then the husband says again, " I am hungry ; " and the wife says, " I have nothing in my hand. Have you not eaten all ? "

Then the husband says again, " I am hungry."

The hunter comes up close in the bush and looks.

The young woman weeps ; she throws herself down on the ground. Immediately the leopard made a leap towards her.

Then the hunter aimed his gun, and fired it. The leopard fell on the ground.

The hunter came and spoke to the young woman. He cut off the leopard's tail. He led her to come up out of the bush, and took her to his house.

This is it. This is the way of young women. The young men come to ask ; the young women meet them, and continue to refuse—again, again, again—and so the wild animals turn themselves into men and carry them off.

T

III.—WHY MONKEYS LIVE IN TREES.

Listen to the story of the bush-cat.

One day the bush-cat had been hunting all day, and had got nothing. She was tired. She went to sit down and rest ; but the fleas would not give her any rest.

She saw a monkey passing. She called to him, "Monkey, please come and flea me."

The monkey agreed, and while he was picking out the fleas the bush-cat fell asleep.

Then the monkey took the tail of the bush-cat, tied it to a tree, and ran away.

The bush-cat awoke. She wanted to get up, but she found her tail tied to the tree.

She struggled to get free, but she could not succeed. She remained there panting.

A snail came along. "Please unfasten my tail," cried the bush-cat, when she saw him.

"You will not kill me if I untie you ?" asked the snail.

"No, I will do nothing to you," answered the bush-cat.

The snail unfastened the bush-cat.

The bush-cat went home. She went and said to all the animals, "On the fifth day from now announce that I am dead, and that you are going to bury me."

All the animals said, "Very well."

On the fifth day the bush-cat lay down flat, pretending to be dead. And all the animals came, and all danced round her. They danced.

The bush-cat sprang up all at once. She leaped to

catch the monkey. But the monkey had already sprung into a tree. He escaped.

So this is why the monkey lives in the trees, and will not stay on the ground. He is too much afraid of the bush-cat.

IV.—WHY THE HARE RUNS AWAY.

This is a story of the hare and the other animals.

The dry weather was drying up the earth into hardness. There was no dew. The creatures of the water even suffered from thirst. Soon famine came, and, the animals having nothing to eat, assembled in council.

" What shall we do," said they, " to keep ourselves from dying of thirst ? " And they deliberated a long time.

At last it was decided that each animal should cut off the tips of its ears, and extract the fat from them. Then all the fat should be collected and sold, and with the money they would get for the fat, they would buy a hoe and dig a well, so as to get some water.

And all cried, " It is well. Let us cut off the tips of our ears."

They did so, but when it came to the turn of the hare to cut off the tips of his ears, he refused.

The other animals were astonished, but they said nothing. They took up the ears, extracted the fat, went and sold all, and bought a hoe with the money.

They brought back the hoe and began to dig a well in the dry bed of a lagoon. " Ha! here is water at last. At last we can slake our thirst a little."

The hare was not there, but when the sun was in the

middle of the sky, he took a calabash, and went towards the well.

As he walked along, the calabash dragged on the ground and made a great noise. It said—" Chan-gañ-gañ-gañ—Chan-gañ-gañ-gañ." [1]

The animals, who were watching by the lagoon, heard this noise. They were frightened. They asked each other, " What is it?" Then as the noise kept coming nearer, they ran away.

Reaching home, they said there was something terrible at the lagoon, that had put to flight the watchers by the lagoon.

Then all the animals by the lagoon were gone. The hare drew up water without interference. Then he went down into the well and bathed, so that the water was muddied.

When the next day came, all the animals ran to take water, and they found it muddied.

" Oh," they cried, " who has spoiled our well?"

Saying this, they went and took an image. Then made bird-lime and smeared it over the image.

Then, when the sun was again in the middle of the sky, all the animals went and hid in the bush near the well.

The hare came. His calabash cried, " Chan-gañ-gañ-gañ, Chan-gañ-gañ-gañ." He approached the image. He never suspected that all the animals were hidden in the bush.

The hare saluted the image. The image said nothing. He saluted again, and still the image said nothing.

" Take care," said the hare, " or I will give you a slap."

[1] Gañ-gañ (ñ, highly nasal) is a drum.

He gave a slap, and his right hand remained fixed in the bird-lime. He slapped with his left hand, and that remained fixed also.

"Oh! oh!" cried he, "let us kick with our feet."

He kicked with his feet. The feet remained fixed, and the hare could not get away.

Then the animals ran out of the bush, and came to see the hare and his calabash.

"Shame, shame, oh! hare," they cried together. "Did you not agree with us to cut off the tips of your ears, and, when it came to your turn, did you not refuse? What! you refused, and yet you come to muddy our water?"

They took whips, they fell upon the hare, and they beat him. They beat him so that they nearly killed him.

"We ought to kill you, accursed hare," they said. "But, no—run."

They let him go, and the hare fled. Since then, he does not leave the grass.

There are a few riddles in vogue amongst the Ewe-speaking peoples, but they are not up to the level of the folk-lore tales, which, as the foregoing examples will have shown, exhibit some ingenuity. Riddles amongst peoples in a low state of culture differ, as Dr. Tylor has shown,[1] from those in fashion in Europe, in that there is a real answer to be discovered. They are not merely "verbal conundrums, set in the traditional form of question and answer, as a way of bringing in a jest

[1] *Primitive Culture,* vol. i. p. 90.

à propos of nothing," but may be termed sense riddles. The following are examples—

Q. Broad and round—what is broad and round?

A. That is the casting-net. The fisherman casts his net in a broad round (wide circle).

Q. Fire eats the grass till it comes to the fast-runner. What is the fast-runner?

A. That is the stream : fire cannot eat water.

(The word used for "fast-runner" is *laglala*, which is also the name of an antelope.)

Q. The wanderer. What is the wanderer?

A. A river. It wanders on from place to place and never stops.

CHAPTER XVI.

HISTORY OF DAHOMI.

THE origin of the kingdom of Dahomi is involved in some obscurity, and all that is known about it is comprised in two traditions. The first of these, given by Governor Dalzel in his history (1793), says that the Dahomis were formerly called Foys, and inhabited a small territory situated about the centre of the present kingdom, whose capital, which Dalzel calls Dawhee, was situated between the towns of Calmina (Kana)[1] and Agbomi. Early in the seventeenth century Tako-donu,[2] chief of the Foys, treacherously murdered the chief of Calmina, who had come to pay him a visit at a time of festivity, seized his town, and made himself master of his territory, which he incorporated with his own. Thus strengthened, he was able, a few years later, to wage war with a powerful state which lay to the north of Foy, whose capital was Agbomi, and his arms being successful, he overran his neighbour's territory, and shut up the chief in Agbomi, to which he then lay siege. The siege was protracted through the stubborn defence

---

[1] Kana used to be called Kana Mina, of which Calmina is a corruption.

[2] More properly Dako Donun.

offered by the inhabitants, and Tako-donu, in order to expedite matters, invoked the assistance of the gods; promising, if they made him successful, to sacrifice to them the chief, whose name was Dà or Dañh. The gods hearkened to his prayer, Agbomi was captured, and Dà taken prisoner. The latter was sacrificed according to promise, and Tako-donu having determined to build a palace at Agbomi to commemorate his victory, ripped open Dà's body, and built the foundation wall upon it; from which the palace took the name of Dà-womi, *i. e.* Da's belly. The conquest of Agbomi is said to have taken place about 1625, and Tako-donu, fixing his residence at that town, assumed the title of King of Dàwomi. His subjects gradually adopted that designation, and by 1793 their original name of Foys was forgotten by all but a few of the tribes of the interior.

So far Governor Dalzel. His tradition is supported by the fact that there is at the present day a village named Dà-we (Dà's House) situated midway between Kana and Agbomi. The name Foy that he gives is apparently a corruption of Ffon, or Effon, the present name of the dialect of Dahomi, and which may well have been an old name for the tribe as well as for the language. Dà, or Dañh, signifies "Snake," and seems to show that in those days the natives, like so many other peoples, borrowed designations from animals; while the story of the foundation of the palace is quite in accordance with an old world-wide practice designed to give a building stability.

The other tradition, which is current at the present day, is slightly different. To understand it, it must be premised that at the beginning of the seventeenth century there were two kingdoms situated in the southern part of the present kingdom of Dahomi, both of which had been brought into some prominence by the slave-trade. They were (1) Juida, Ayudah or Whydah, which extended from the sea inland for about seven miles; its northern boundary being a lagoon which ran east and west beyond the town of Savi, called by Europeans Xavier, which was the capital. (2) The kingdom of Ardra, or Allada, which extended from the northern boundary of the kingdom of Whydah to the marshy belt, called the *ko*, which lies to the north of Toffo. On the east this kingdom extended to Godomi and Kotonu. Its capital was named Ardra, and seems to have been the present Allada, situated some twenty-five miles from the sea. To the north of the kingdom of Ardra lay the country of the Foys.

About 1610, according to the tradition, the King of Ardra died, without having nominated one of his three sons as his successor. Each strove to seize the kingdom for himself, and civil war raged for some months, until the second of the three brothers gained the upper hand, and ousted the others. Of these, one fled with his adherents to Porto Novo, and formed the kingdom of the same name, then called Little Ardra; while the other, whose name was Tako-donu, also accompanied by a number of partisans, crossed the *ko*, and sought a refuge in the country of the Foys; where Dà, the king of the latter, received him with great kindness, and gave him land for the support of himself and his followers. Tako-donu repaid the king of the Foys with the basest ingratitude. No sooner had he firmly established himself, than, assisted by other fugitives who had joined him from Ardra, he adopted a threatening attitude, gradually secured all the territories of Dà, and then, having succeeded in laying hands upon him, put him to death, and built upon his body in the manner set forth in the other tradition. This second tradition gains some support from the fact that the King of Porto Novo is of the royal family of Dahomi, and is called "brother" by the king of the latter.

Tradition tells us no more about Tako-donu, except that he died about 1650, and was succeeded by Adahunzu, or Adanzu. This king, whose birth-name appears to have been Aho, Adahunzu being a "strong name," is said to have instituted the Annual Customs. He subdued a number of small independent townships to the south, and died in 1680.

Wibaigah, Wibagi, or Akaba, the next king, was the brother of Adahunzu, and seized the kingdom from his nephew Abosasa, who fled to the Yorubas. He pushed his conquests to the east as far as Ewemi, and died in 1708.

The kingdoms of Ardra and Whydah were about this time at the zenith of their prosperity, and the intensest rivalry prevailed between them. They were essentially commercial states; in their towns were the only slave-markets of the Slave Coast, and thousands of slaves were supplied annually in exchange for European goods. To facilitate trade, the Europeans had establishments in both kingdoms, and, by permission of the king, they erected forts at Whydah for the protection of their goods. These forts were the French, built in 1671, the English, the Dutch, and the Portuguese. In later years the Dutch fort was replaced by the Brazilian, and

four out of the five quarters of the town of Whydah
are still named after these forts. The trade was so
considerable that it was not uncommon for ten or
twelve ships to be lying at anchor at one time off
Whydah, and in 1670 the King of Ardra despatched
an ambassador to Paris, to enter into a treaty of
commerce. These princelings even sought to make
Europeans amenable to their laws, and in 1700, Amah,
King of Whydah, in order to prevent conflicts between
his customers, which were detrimental to trade, passed
a law that all Europeans were to observe a strict
neutrality with each other, not only while on shore
or in the roadstead, but even while in sight of the
anchorage.

Wibaigah was succeeded by Guadja Trudo, as he is
commonly called by Europeans, the name by which he
is known to natives being Agaja Dosu, who was then
nineteen years of age. He occupied the early years of his
reign in extending his dominions to the north-west, and
having acquired considerable power and prestige by his
conquest, he next turned his eyes seaward. Now all
European goods landed at Whydah first passed through
the hands of the people of that kingdom, and then
through those of the Ardras, before they reached
Dahomi, so that the Dahomis had to suffer the exactions
of two sets of middlemen. Naturally Guadja Trudo
desired therefore to deal at first hand with the white
men, and as soon as he felt himself sufficiently strong
to be able to revenge a refusal, he sent ambassadors to
Ardra, requesting a right of way and free traffic to
the sea, and offering to pay such duties as the Ardras
themselves paid. This request was peremptorily refused,

and dissensions which broke out between the King of Ardra and his brother Hussa, soon gave Trudo the opportunity desired. Hussa applied to Dahomi for aid, and a large army was at once despatched to his assistance.

The people of Ardra were not warlike; possibly, years of peaceful commerce and the accumulation of wealth had tended to effeminate them; but they made hasty preparations to meet the enemy, and the king invited the King of Whydah to co-operate with him, pointing out that their mutual interests required them to combine. Blinded, however, by trade jealousy, the King of Whydah refused all assistance, and the Ardras alone faced the invaders; with the result that, after a three days' engagement, their army, said to have been 50,000 strong, was dispersed, their king slain, 8000 men taken prisoners, and the kingdom annexed to Dahomi. This was in 1724.

Amongst the prisoners taken at the conquest of Ardra was an Englishman named Bulfinch Lambe, who, having been sent by the Governor of the English fort at Whydah to the King of Ardra, had been detained by the latter as a slave for two years, on the pretext of a debt he claimed from the Royal African Company. This man was sent to Agbomi, where he was well treated, and furnished with a retinue of servants and everything he required. In a letter he wrote from Agbomi to Mr. Tinker, Governor of the English fort, dated November 27th, 1724, he gives an account of the wealth and power of the Dahomi king, whom he describes as vain, haughty, and warlike. The king had, he said, already paved two of his principal palaces with the skulls of his foes, and he prophesied that he would before long become master of all the surrounding states. In 1726 Lambe was permitted to return to Whydah. The town of Ardra, which was said to have been nine miles in circumference at the time of the conquest, was almost entirely destroyed, and has never since been more than a village.

On the downfall of the kingdom of Ardra, the chief of Jaquin, a state on the sea-board, apparently between Godomi and Whydah, who was a tributary of Ardra, sent his submission and offers of tribute to the Dahomi king. These were accepted, and the inhabitants of that state were not molested, but the Ardras themselves were all driven out, and fled to the east. There they contrived to enlist the sympathies of the King of Eyeo (Yoruba), and while Guadja Trudo was still at Ardra, establishing his authority, a large Yoruba army, with several thousand cavalry, entered Dahomi. Trudo immediately marched to meet it, and an action ensued which lasted four days, and terminated in favour of Dahomi. According to tradition, however, the battle was won by a stratagem. Finding himself hard pressed by the Yoruba horsemen, Trudo quietly abandoned his camp by night, leaving in it large quantities of brandy, which the Yorubas, who entered the camp in the morning, drank to such an excess, that the greater part of the army was soon helplessly intoxicated. At this juncture the Dahomis fell upon them, and completely routed them, only a few mounted men contriving to escape. Trudo, after his victory, prudently sent messengers to Yoruba to make peace, for he feared that hostilities with so powerful a neighbour would interfere with his cherished plan of forcing a way to the sea; and the Yoruba king, who probably had had enough of the war, accepted his presents, and abandoned the cause of the Ardras.

In 1726, Trudo, having repaired the losses in his army, recommenced his designs against the sea-coast states, and sent to Kufon, King of Whydah, who had only succeeded to the stool the year before, to demand a free passage through his territories for all merchandise. Kufon, a vain and short-sighted ruler, refused, and Trudo at once marched against him, and encamped on the banks of the creek or lagoon called the Nyin-tsi,[1] about half a mile to the north of Savi. The Dahomis had no canoes with them, and as the creek was only fordable at one point, a small force might easily have held the passage against the whole invading army; but the Whydahs had, after consulting their priests, confided the defence of the ford to their chief god, the python, and the Dahomis, discovering this, crossed over, killed the serpent, and about three o'clock in the afternoon fell suddenly upon the town. The surprise was complete; not the least resistance was offered, and the inhabitants, seized with a sudden panic, fled towards the sea. The king and some of the chiefs escaped by canoe to Grand Popo, but hundreds were drowned in the lagoons, and thousands captured or slain. Savi was pillaged and burned. This was on February 7th, 1727.

To meet the invaders, Kufon is said to have got together an army of 200,000 men, a manifest exaggeration; but the kings of Whydah were wealthy, since one of them was able, in 1722, to present Captain Chaloner Ogle, of H.M.S. *Swallow*, with fifty-six pounds weight

---

[1] Or Nyin-sin. Tsi, and sin, = water.

of gold-dust, as a reward for having captured, off Cape Lopez, the three pirate vessels under Roberts, which had lately plundered all the ships lying in Whydah roads; and Kufon could no doubt hire auxiliaries. The Whydahs excused their cowardice by charging the Dahomis with cannibalism, saying that they did not fear death in battle, but could not support the idea of being eaten. It is now difficult to say what truth there was in the allegation, but Snelgrave (1727) strongly inclines to the belief that the Dahomis were cannibals; and some of their customs, such as the pretence of eating the bodies of men killed by lightning, and the cry of the mob at the Platform Sacrifice, "Feed us, we are hungry," may possibly be survivals of such a practice.

Four thousand of the prisoners taken in the rout were sacrificed as a thankoffering to the gods, their heads being struck off by boys, whom it was desired to inure to scenes of bloodshed. Some of these boys were only seven or eight years of age, and the wretched prisoners endured protracted agonies at the hands of these child executioners, who had not sufficient strength to wield a sword. These boys, it may be remarked, were those who, by a recent order of Trudo, accompanied the fighting men in the capacity of pages, one being allotted to each man. They were paid by the king, for while it pleased the soldiers, it also provided a future supply of recruits inured to war.

Among the prisoners taken at Savi were some forty Europeans, whose trading establishment had been completely sacked and destroyed. They were sent to Ardra (Allada), where the king was, politely received by him, and set at liberty with a promise that he would make trade flourish. The trading establishments at Savi appear to have been fortified houses, dependencies of the forts at Whydah, to which the Europeans now retired. Their destruction was so complete that in 1772, when Robert Norris visited Savi on his way to Agbomi, not a vestige of them remained except the ditches which used to encompass them. According to tradition, Trudo, after this conquest, named the town of Whydah "Gle-we"—*gle* (provision-ground or plantation), *we* (house), meaning that the place must supply his needs. The English corrupted this to "Grigwhee," a name which often occurs in Dalzel's *History.*

The King of Whydah soon tendered his submission to Trudo, and offered to pay tribute; but this was refused, and the fugitive people were informed that the surrender of their king was the sole condition upon which they would be allowed to return to their own country. The Whydahs did not avail themselves of this easy solution of the difficulty, and rather than give up their king to a cruel death, remained in exile on the islands of the lagoons about Grand Popo, where they were reduced to such straits that they were obliged to sell their children to the Popos in order to obtain food.

They remained in this situation for some months, when, the Dahomi force at Savi having been greatly reduced, a former chief of that town, named Ossu, left the islands and established himself with a large body of men under the protection of the French fort at Whydah. The Dahomis at once advanced to dislodge them, and on the Whydahs taking refuge in the fort, it was carried by assault and blown up. Ossu contrived to regain his former place of shelter near Grand Popo, and the governor of the French fort escaped to that of the English.

The exiles now applied to the King of Yoruba for assistance; and he, perhaps anxious to revenge his former failure, suddenly despatched a large army, with 2000 or 3000 horsemen, against Dahomi. This was about September 1728. Trudo, despairing of being able to make head against this force, buried his wealth, and retired with all his people into the forested country to the north-west. The Yorubas followed in pursuit, but, not being able to make use of their cavalry in the forest, they were unable to gain any decisive advantage; and at last, at the commencement of the rains in March 1729, were obliged, for want of supplies, to return to their own country.

In the meantime Whydah was full of reports of reverses sustained by the Dahomis. It was believed that their power was utterly destroyed, and the Europeans therefore invited the Whydahs to return and take possession of their country, for under their rule trade had always been secure. The King of Whydah, accordingly, about August 1729, returned to his former kingdom with a following of some 15,000 men, most of whom were Popos, whose assistance he had purchased. With this force he encamped under the shelter of the French and English forts, and remained for some little time unmolested, the Dahomis being engaged in rebuilding their towns.

As soon, however, as order was restored at home, Trudo marched to the south. His army had been much reduced in the struggle with the Yorubas, so, in order to give an appearance of force, he armed and equipped

U

a number of women, whom he kept in the rear, the van being composed of what remained of his army. At the sight of this large body the Whydahs were much disconcerted, for they had imagined that Trudo's army had been almost destroyed, and they began to talk of retreating; but the chief Ossu and the Popo allies having declared their determination to fight, the Whydahs had to follow suit. In the battle that ensued Ossu and the Popos attacked the Dahomi right wing with such vigour, that for a time they carried all before them; but the Whydahs fled at the first fire, and the Dahomi left wing, swinging round, took the Popos in rear and routed them. The king took refuge in the English fort, whence he escaped to the lagoons. In this engagement the women-soldiers behaved with such unexpected gallantry that Trudo determined to maintain a permanent corps of women; and thus, it is said, originated the Amazons.

Trudo was well acquainted with the part which the English and French governors had played in this affair; but he overlooked it for politic reasons, and affected ignorance. Upon this the English governor, whom Dalzel calls Testesole, imagining that the king was afraid to interfere with him, treated Dahomis in a very high-handed manner. On one occasion he caused an influential man to be flogged, and released him with a message to the king that he would treat him in the same way if he could catch him. This message was duly conveyed to Trudo, and he determined to revenge the insult. For trade reasons he did not wish to embroil himself openly with the Europeans; so, instead of taking open action, he caused Testesole to be secretly kidnapped and carried off to Agbomi, where he was put to death with great barbarity. Fastened face downwards to the earth by wooden stakes, his arms, legs, and back were laid open in long gashes, and the wounds filled with a mixture of salt, pepper, and lime-juice. He was left in this condition for two days before an end was put to his sufferings by decapitation ; and Snelgrave says that his body was afterwards cut in pieces, boiled, and eaten.

Trudo now opened negotiations with the King of Yoruba, with a view to a cessation of the hostilities by which both parties had suffered. His presents were accepted, and peace was concluded by Trudo taking to wife a daughter of his foe. Being now relieved from apprehension of attack from the east, he turned his arms against the Mahis, or Makkis, who inhabited a forested and mountainous country to the north-west of Dahomi. The Mahis, however, adopted his own tactics. Abandoning their towns, they took refuge in the fastnesses of the mountains, with the result that, at the commencement of the rains, the Dahomi army had to retire through want of supplies, without having effected anything of importance.

The last event of Trudo's reign was the suppression of a revolt that had broken out in Jaquin. Moving suddenly upon that state with 15,000 men, he entirely defeated the rebels on 22nd March, 1731. Less than a year after this he died.

Trudo may be regarded as the true founder of the kingdom of Dahomi. An insignificant state when he succeeded to the stool, he increased its area fourfold, and by the conquest of the old mercantile kingdoms that lay between Dahomi proper and the sea, he took under control the whole of the commerce of the Slave Coast, which had been centred at Whydah.

This trade consisted of the importation of European goods, wines, spirits, tobacco, gunpowder, and muskets, and the exportation of slaves. There was at that time little, if any, legitimate export trade, and it was as a slave emporium that Whydah was celebrated. This trade had existed for some considerable time at this point, and it was on account of the facility with which cargoes of slaves were here obtained, that this part of West Africa was termed the Slave Coast; just as the Gold and Grain Coasts were named after their chief products, gold, and the malaghetta pepper, or Grains of Paradise. As the peoples of Ardra and Whydah were peaceable by disposition, and devoted to trade, it is improbable that they took in war the thousands of men who were annually shipped to the New World. They were apparently slave-dealers, but not man-hunters, and the slaves were supplied to them by the more warlike interior tribes. As long as these latter were without cohesion, and divided into a number of petty states whose mutual jealousies prevented combination, the two commercial kingdoms were safe from aggression; but as soon as one of them assumed a dominant position the situation was changed. Dahomi commenced by subjecting its weaker neighbours, a process which the mercantile states made no attempt to arrest; it gradually absorbed the surrounding populations, and kept increasing in wealth and power. The adult prisoners of war were sold in the slave-markets of Ardra and Whydah, and with the gunpowder and muskets obtained, in exchange Dahomi was able to continue its conquests, until at last it became sufficiently powerful to overthrow the maritime states and force a way to the sea. Thenceforth the slave-trade received a great impetus, for the slave-producers, the man-hunters, could now deal directly with the European slave-traders; and to supply the necessary thousands for this traffic and for the sacrifices at the Annual Customs, Dahomi entered upon a career of warfare, of predatory raids upon the surrounding tribes, which has lasted to this day. The number of human lives lost during these wars for supremacy may be estimated by Dalzel's statement that 30,000 skulls, principally those of Ardras alone, were placed by Trudo on his palace-walls.

The Megan and Mehu, on the death of Trudo in January 1732, selected as his successor Bossa Ahadi, or Tegbwesun, passing over Zinga, who was the eldest son. The latter endeavoured to foment a rebellion, but was seized, sewn up in a hammock at Agbomi, carried to Whydah thus secured, taken out to sea in a canoe, and there drowned, in accordance with the law that forbids the shedding of royal blood.

The new king soon proved himself a tyrant of the worst kind. One of his first acts was to cause every man and male child of the name of Bossa throughout the kingdom to be put to death, in order that no one should bear the same name as himself, and soon after his oppressions were such as to cause a formidable rebellion, headed by the Mehu, to break out in 1735. The Gau, however, and the army remained faithful, and the rebellion was soon crushed.

In 1737 Bossa Ahadi recommenced the campaign

against the Mahis, and the war was continued with
varying success till 1738, when the sudden advance
into Dahomi of a large army of Yorubas, called back
the Dahomis for the defence of their capital.   The
Yorubas advanced with such rapidity that Bossa Ahadi
was unable to repeat the tactics of his predecessor, by
burying his treasure and taking to the forest; the
enemy were at the very gates of Agbomi, and in front
of it the Dahomis made a stand.   The attack commenced
in the morning and was continued till nightfall, when
the Dahomis, overwhelmed by superior numbers, retired
into the town, after having, by their musketry fire,
inflicted very heavy losses on the Yorubas.   Agbomi
was undefended, except by a broad and deep ditch, and
as it contained no water supply, was quite untenable.
During the night, therefore, the wounded, women, and
children were quietly got out of the town and sent to
Zassa, a town about twenty-five miles west of Agbomi,
where the king already was ; and the Gau undertook to
hold the enemy in check till Bossa was in a place of
safety.   From Zassa, the king with the people from
Agbomi retired to an almost inaccessible fastness about
four hours' journey distant ; and the Gau, who had in
the meantime continued the defence of Agbomi, then
evacuated the place under the cover of a dark night.
Agbomi was plundered and burnt, as were Kana and
Zassa ; but the Yorubas, having devastated the entire
country, soon found themselves in want of supplies, and
were compelled to return to their own country.

The Yorubas now annually harassed the Dahomis,
and invaded the kingdom.   The latter never risked a
general engagement, feeling themselves unable to cope

with cavalry; and every year they abandoned their towns and retired into the forest till the enemy withdrew. The exiled Whydahs, and their allies the Popos, were not slow to take advantage of this state of affairs, and made frequent incursions into Whydah, interrupting trade and causing alarm. In 1741 a considerable body of them, at the invitation of the Portuguese governor, established themselves under the guns of the Portuguese fort at Whydah; but the time was ill-chosen, for the Yoruba campaign against Dahomi had just terminated for that year, and Bossa Ahadi was able to despatch an army to drive out these intruders. On the approach of the Dahomi force the Whydahs and Popos retired into the Portuguese fort, which, as it mounted thirty pieces of cannon, and was defended by a deep ditch, was a formidable obstacle to a foe without artillery. However, at daybreak on November 1st, 1741, the Dahomis advanced furiously to the assault on all sides, and though mown down by scores by the guns, they continued to press on till noon, when some gunpowder in one of the bastions of the fort exploded, and set fire to the thatched buildings in the courtyard. These blazed with such fury that in a few minutes the magazine took fire and blew up, and during the panic which succeeded this disaster, the Dahomis swarmed in at the embrasures, almost without opposition. The whole of the defenders were put to the sword.

This affair having been brought to a successful termination, the Gau moved his force to Jaquin, whose king, taking advantage of the disordered condition of the country, had ceased the payment of tribute. Guided by a woman, the army penetrated the swamps, and surprising the Jaquins in a position hemmed in by morasses, cut them off almost to a man.

In 1743, while Dahomi was again being overrun by the Yorubas, and the Mahis were creating disturbances on the north-western frontier, the Whydahs, with their allies the Popos, made another attempt to recover their lost territory. They advanced to within a mile of Whydah, where the Dahomi garrison, much inferior in numbers, gave them battle. The allies were completely victorious; the Yevo-gan, or viceroy of Whydah, and the Cakawo, or military commandant, were slain, and the Dahomi force dispersed. The victors pillaged and burned the town, and called upon the governors of the forts to make submission; but the latter had now changed their policy, and, instead of trying to reinstate the Whydahs, they refused to acknowledge any authority but that of the King of Dahomi. The allies did not venture to attack the forts; but they established a blockade which reduced them to great straits, and, at the end of three months, they were on the point of submitting; when, the Yorubas having now returned to their own country, the Gau suddenly fell upon the allies with a large army, and drove them once more to the lagoons.

In August 1745, Tauga, who had been appointed Yevo-gan of Whydah in the place of the one killed, conceived the project of making himself an independent sovereign. His plan was to seize by treachery Fort William, the English fort, which commanded the town; but his design was discovered and his attempt failed, while a force from Agbomi, sent to attack him, besieged him in his own house and killed him.

In 1747 Bossa Ahadi made terms of peace with the
King of Yoruba, by which he engaged to pay a heavy
tribute at Kana every November. The reason of Kana
being chosen seems to have been that it was formerly
settled by Yorubas, and in West Africa, when members
of a tribe migrate, the land they occupy becomes attached
to the stool of the king. Dahomi being now secured
against the annual Yoruba raids, Bossa Ahadi prosecuted
the Mahi war, which had been languishing for some
time. After four years of fighting, the Mahis were
driven to a mountain stronghold, called by Dalzel
Boagri, which the Gau then invested. The siege lasted
for a whole year, at the end of which, reinforcements
having arrived from Agbomi, the place was carried by
assault, and such of the Mahis as were not slain were
carried captives to the capital. This was in 1752.

In 1750, Akwasi, King of Ashanti, is said to have
crossed the Volta and attacked Dahomi, suffering a
severe defeat. This expedition is not mentioned by
Bowdich (1817), who was the first to give a sketch of
Ashanti history, or by Dalzel (1793) in his *History of
Dahomey.* As people are not fond of talking of their
defeats, the Ashantis might have omitted mentioning
the matter to Mr. Bowdich ; but Dalzel could hardly
have failed to have heard of the Dahomi victory, which
must have been in every respect more important than
the greater number of those he recounts. It seems to
have been first mentioned by Mr. Cruickshank [1] (1853),
who says that the Akims and other north-eastern tribes
of the Gold Coast, who had recently been subdued by

[1] In the absence of books of reference I cannot speak with
certainty.

Ashanti, having been instigated to rebel by the King of Dahomi, Akwasi of Ashanti, after having reduced his rebellious tributaries to order in a great battle near the Volta, crossed that river to punish the King of Dahomi for his interference, but met with a severe defeat, and escaped with difficulty. The distance from the Volta to Agbomi in a straight line is about 150 miles, and as the battle is said to have taken place only a few days' march from the river, the Dahomi army must have moved about 100 miles to the west to meet the invaders. But this territory, we know, was occupied by tribes hostile to Dahomi, with one of which, the nearest, it was, according to Dalzel, engaged at this very time; and we have no evidence that Dahomi was ever able to do more than penetrate into it some twenty or thirty miles. It therefore seems unlikely that the Ashanti and Dahomi armies ever met, and if the former crossed the Volta at this epoch to chastise any one, it was probably one or more of the Ewe-speaking tribes on the left bank of that river.

The Whydahs and Popos, who since their defeat in 1743 had remained quiet, now recommenced their attacks on Whydah. On several occasions they gained possession of Whydah beach, which is separated from the town by the lagoon, and the injury to trade was so great that Bossa Ahadi determined to crush these troublesome allies, and sent against Grand Popo a portion of the army that had been engaged with the Mahis. The Dahomis, unaccustomed to lagoons, did not understand warfare upon the water; but, having surprised some canoes, they crossed over the lagoon and reached the long and narrow ridge of sand which lies between the lagoon and the sea. Here Shampo, the Popo leader, artfully drew them on; and when they were at a considerable distance from their base, he suddenly threw a strong force in their rear to cut off their retreat, and simultaneously attacked them both from the sea and the lagoon. The Dahomis repulsed their adversaries, but their supplies having failed, they were compelled to retreat. The allies strove to bar the way, and when, after two days' fighting, the Dahomis forced a passage, they found their canoes gone and themselves lost in the maze of lagoons and swamps that lay between them and Whydah. Here, emaciated by famine and harassed by incessant attacks, the whole force perished, with the exception of twenty-four men whom the Popos spared to convey the news to the king, and whom Bossa Ahadi immediately ordered to be put to death, in order that they might proceed to Dead-land and inform their fallen comrades there how much he was displeased with them. To prevent the recurrence of such a disaster it was now made a law that no Dahomi warrior should set foot in a canoe, and that no military operations were to be undertaken that required transport by water.

Affairs now remained tolerably quiet till 1763, when the Whydahs and Popos once more invaded Whydah, and drove into the town the small Dahomi garrison, which retreated towards the French fort, thinking to be covered by the fire of its guns. The French governor, however, was a trimmer. He did not want to fire upon the allies lest they should gain the day and call him to account, and he dare not refuse to fire lest the Dahomis should be victorious. He accordingly fired blank charges only, hoping that the Dahomis would not discover the absence of missiles ; and the allies, advancing with great impetuosity, captured the suburb·s The Dahomis now retired under the guns of the English fort, to which the allies soon advanced, thinking there was nothing to be feared ; but the English governor, Mr. Goodson, received them with such storms of shot, that they were soon scattered in flight, and the Dahomis, falling upon them, completed the rout. Next day a relieving army arrived from Agbomi, and drove back the enemy to their lagoons.

According to local tradition, Governor Goodson had intended following the example of the French governor, but when the Popos were passing near the English fort, one of the savage warriors saw a white woman, combing her long hair, and looking out of a window to see what was going on ; and exclaiming, " What animal can that be ? " he fired his musket at her, the ball piercing her throat. This woman was Governor Goodson's mistress, and, filled with rage and fury, he then let fly that storm of grape-shot which snatched the victory from the allies. Bossa Ahadi acknowledged that he was indebted to Goodson for his success, and the memory of the latter is still gratefully preserved at Agbomi.

In 1764 the Dahomis again attacked the Mahis, who once more retired to Boagri. This stronghold was invested for twelve months without success, and the army was at last obliged to raise the siege. Disgusted with this failure, Bossa Ahadi renounced all further attempts upon the Mahis, and concluded a treaty of peace with them. In 1772, through the mediation of Mr. Lionel Abson, the English governor, peace was also made with the Whydahs and Popos.

In the early part of 1772, Mr. Robert Norris, the English governor, visited Agbomi, and had an interview with Bossa Ahadi on February 5th. He appears to have been the only European who was ever admitted to the interior of a Dahomi palace. On May 17th, 1772, Bossa Ahadi died, and was buried in a sedan-chair that had been presented to him by Norris, and in which six of his wives were entombed alive, while the bodies of 285 more women, who had been killed during the carnage in the palace that always succeeded the death of a king, were placed in the same grave. He was succeeded by Adahunzu, or Adanzu II., who is known in Dahomi by the "strong name" of Tsi-me-kpe, " Water in the rock " (*tsi*, water ; *me*, in ; *kpe*, rock or stone). According to Dalzel, he adopted the title of " The Male Oyster."

In the autumn of 1774 the king of the exiled Whydahs died, and two candidates for the succession appeared, one named Abavu (The Otter), and the other Aӯa (The Monkey). The former soon drove his rival from the lagoons, and Adahunzu II., thinking this a favourable opportunity for reducing the Whydahs to subjection, adopted Aӯa's cause, and sent an army to his assistance.

In the first compaign Abavu and his adherents were driven off the mainland, and compelled to take refuge in an island in the lagoon, called Vŏdu-kong, and known to the English as " Fetish Island." There, during the rains, they remained secure ; for the Dahomis could not, in consequence of Bossa Ahadi's law, cross the water ; but when the waters subsided, the latter, with prodigious labour, constructed a causeway of earth, and

stormed the island. Abavu and those who escaped the
slaughter retreated in a flotilla of some 800 canoes they
had with them, but only to find that they were shut in
by a palisade which the Dahomis had constructed across
a narrow part of the lagoon, some miles above. The
Whydahs remained on the lagoon, shut in between the
island and the palisade, for some months, subsisting
upon fish, and occasionally landing and beating up the
Dahomi quarters in fearch of food ; but at last, despairing of escape, Abavu surrendered himself, and his
followers submitted. The former was sent to Agbomi
and there put to death ; some hundreds of the latter
sacrificed at the Annual Customs, and the remainder were
sold into slavery.

In 1776 an abortive expedition against the Mahi
tribes to the west of Dahomi took place, which in 1777
was followed by a more vigorous invasion. The Mahis
were routed with great slaughter in a pitched battle, and
the entire district ravaged. A great number of fugitives
fled southward to Agweh, where their descendants still
live, and others escaped to the mountainous country to
the north. To strike terror into these survivors, and
to prevent them from re-occupying their territory, the
trees along the forest paths were hung with the bodies
of the slain, the heads being transported to Agbomi as
trophies.

The Ardras, who, according to the tradition, had
followed the fortunes of that candidate for the throne
of Ardra, who had fled to the eastward in 1610, and
founded the kingdom of Little Ardra, now called Porto
Novo, had always preserved amicable relations with
Dahomi, and in 1778 an alliance was formed between

them and Adahunzu II. for the subjection of " Porto
Novo, Appa, and Badagry." This Porto Novo, it is to
be observed, was on the sea-coast, and appears to have
been Kotonu, or some neighbouring town in Fra. The
present Porto Novo, the capital of the then state of
Little Ardra, was at that time called Ardra, a name
which was afterwards changed to Hogbono, and the
Porto Novo against which the alliance was directed was
styled "the sea-port of Ardra." According to existing
tradition, the Appas were those fugitives from Old
Ardra who fled to the east at the conquest of their
kingdom in 1724, and had been granted the territory
named Appa by the King of Pokra. Badagry, though
situated on the northern side of the Lagos lagoon, was
considered an Appa town. The Fras were called Wra
Jaquins, and were fugitives from Jaquin, who had settled
in the territory called Fra, after the Jaquin rebellion of
1731, and the final destruction of that kingdom by
Dahomi in 1742. In the projected expedition the
Dahomis were to attack by land, while the Little Ardras
undertook to intercept all fugitives who might cross the
lagoon.

The Dahomi army moved to the eastward from
Dahomi, and finding their progress checked by a creek
which then connected Lake Denham Waters with the
sea, closed the channel with thousands of baskets filled
with sand ; and, marching on, soon overran Fra and
Appa. A large number of prisoners were taken, but
the King of Appa, with a considerable following, forced
a way through the Little Ardras and escaped to Ewemi.
Satisfied with this success, the Gau led the army back
to Agbomi, where most of the prisoners were slaughtered

at the next Annual Customs.   Five of the women were put to death by five Amazons, in the presence of some European visitors who were at Kana.

The expedition to Appa was followed by the invasion of a territory north of Dahomi, called Agona by old writers, which at first proved disastrous; but upon the king himself taking the field with a large army, the Agonas fled northward to the Sirachis, and sought shelter with that tribe in the caves of a precipitous mountain, out of which they were driven by the smoke of fires strewn with peppers.   Two chiefs, or kings, and 1800 followers were thus taken; he of Agona died before reaching Agbomi; but the King of Sirachi was trussed like a hog, placed in a basket, and thrown from the platform at the Annual Customs.

In 1783 a party of Dahomis made a raid towards Badagry, and a few months later an army was sent to capture that town.   It marched along the sea-shore till nearly opposite Badagry, and then crossed the lagoon in the canoes of its Little Ardra allies,[1] and encamped for the night.   Early next morning, as the Dahomis were approaching Badagry, they fell into an ambuscade, and suffered so heavily that they were compelled to retire to the lagoon, where they were glad to take the canoes of their allies and return to the sea-shore.   The Gau then abandoned the campaign, and, to excuse his failure, charged the Little Ardras with having treacherously led the army into the ambuscade.

Shortly after the Customs of 1784, Adahunzu II. made a second attempt upon Badagry, this time from

[1] Dalzel. This seems to be at variance with the law that no Dahomi warrior should enter a canoe.

the north, while the King of Lagos undertook to intercept fugitives with a flotilla of canoes in the lagoon to
the east of the town. The Dahomi army moved down
in a leisurely manner through Ketu, and formed before
Badagry a camp of such an extent that four hours were
required to traverse it. The Badagrys, seeing that their
only hope of success lay in a bold stroke, unexpectedly
attacked this camp at daybreak in three divisions, and
for a time carried all before them; but the Dahomis
were eventually rallied by their leaders, the attack was
repulsed, and the foe pursued into Badagry. The
women and children, flying to the eastward, were seized
and carried off by the canoes of the Lagos people, and
the Little Ardras contrived to secure the greater part of
the plunder; but the skulls of 6000 men who had fallen
in the rout were conveyed to Agbomi. The arrival of
these skulls was signalized by public rejoicing, and the
king ordered them to be used to crown the exterior walls
of one of his palaces. When this work was completed,
it was found that the trophies had been placed too close
to one another, and that 127 more heads were still
required, to furnish which a corresponding number of
prisoners were slaughtered in cold blood.

The next campaign took place in 1786, when Ewemi
was overrun and depopulated, and Adahunzu now
meditated invading Little Ardra, whose alleged treachery
in 1784 had been left in abeyance, because the assistance
of that state had been required in the operations against
Badagry and Ewemi. A small party was first despatched
from Whydah, which kidnapped from "Porto Novo"
beach fourteen Frenchmen, a Portuguese, and a number
of Gold Coast canoe-men; and the king was collecting

an army with which to follow, when he received an order from the King of Yoruba to desist. However humiliating compliance might be, Adahunzu II. thought it best to submit, for he had no wish to call down upon himself the whole power of Yoruba. The persons kidnapped were ransomed by the governor of the French fort at Whydah for £4600.

The year 1788 was marked by a campaign to the north-west of Dahomi, and 1789 by one against Ketu. The town of Ketu, defended by a ditch and a double wall, was taken by a feint, and 2000 prisoners carried off.

On April 17th, 1789, Adahunzu II. died at Agona, of small-pox. The corpse was transported to Agbomi, and on its arrival at the palace-gates sixty-eight Ketu prisoners were sacrificed, while 595 of the king's women perished inside.

Adahunzu II. was succeeded by Winahiu, or Agongoro. His first expedition, which took place in 1790, was directed against a Mahi province, called Baigee by Dalzel. A few captives were brought back, who were slaughtered to fill up the grave of the late king. This was followed by a second expedition into the same district, which proved less successful than the first, the swollen state of the rivers compelling the army to return. The army was then sent against the exiled Whydahs, but effected nothing but the destruction of the plantations on the north side of the lagoon. A few months later a second expedition captured 300 Popos, who were also killed to fill up Adahunzu's grave.

In 1790 the governor of the French fort at Whydah, M. Gourg, offended the king, who caused him to be seized, bound, and exposed on the beach, till a canoe could be found to carry him through the heavy surf to a vessel lying in the roadstead. From the effects of this treatment M. Gourg died.

In 1791 the Grand Custom for Adahunzu II. took place at Agbomi. Mr. Hogg, governor of Appollonia Fort, on the Gold Coast, was present, and estimated the number of victims sacrificed at not less than 500.

Dalzel's *History* carries us only to 1791, and there is some uncertainty as to the events of the succeeding twenty-seven years. Winahiu, it appears, died about 1792, and was succeeded by Ebomi, his second son, the first-born being passed over on account of some deformity to his foot. Nothing is known of Ebomi's reign, but he is said to have died about 1812, and to have been succeeded by Adandosan, or Adansan.

This king soon gained such a reputation for cruelty and licentiousness that the Dahomis are even now ashamed to rank him among their former kings. His evil propensities were inflamed by habitual drunkenness, and under his rule neither life nor property were safe. All the prisoners taken in the annual raids were put to death, and the slave-traders of Whydah, who depended upon the king for their supply of slaves, found their business suspended. At this time there were two slave-traders established in Dahomi, who through their long residence, and the enormous profits of the traffic, had acquired great wealth and influence. They were Felix da Souza of Whydah, and Domingo Martinez of Kotonu. These two men, seeing their trade at a standstill, conceived the project of dethroning Adandosan, and placing his brother Gezo on the stool in his stead. Gezo lent a willing ear to these proposals, and the three conspirators set about gaining adherents.

Negotiations on such a scale as was necessary for the overthrow of a king of Dahomi could not long be kept secret, and Adandosan was soon informed of the plot; but Gezo had already gained such a powerful following that the king feared to proceed against him openly, and so sought to ruin him secretly. With this object he purposed having a slave sacrificed on the Legba of Gezo, intending either to charge his brother with endeavouring to procure his death by this offering, or with infringing the law which prohibits the taking of human life except by the king's order; but Gezo was warned in time, and the plot failed. Shortly after this an opportunity occurred of bringing matters to a crisis. One day, when Gezo was in the palace, his brother Owo's child accidentally struck the king with a pebble, and was by him ordered to immediate execution. Gezo interceded for the boy's life, but Adandosan was inflexible, and the child was on the point of being led away to death, when Gezo, encouraged by the murmurs of the spectators, rushed upon the king and felled him to the ground. A struggle ensued, and in the confusion of the moment, a crowd of Gezo's adherents burst into the palace. Such of the king's women as strove to resist were slain; and Adandosan was secured, walled up in a small chamber, and left to starve to death. This was in 1818. Gezo was at once declared king by the Megan and Mehu. A few chiefs only declined to acquiesce in the change, and they and their partisans were soon subjected. By the people generally, the downfall of Adandosan was hailed with enthusiasm.

Gezo's success was largely due to da Souza and Martinez, who had spent money freely in his cause, and he showed himself grateful. He styled them his two brothers, gave them special trade privileges, created for da Souza the title of "First of White Men," and made him Chacha of Whydah. Da Souza was a mulatto, and a native of Rio Janeiro. It is uncertain in what year he first arrived in Africa, but, from humble beginnings, he soon became the most opulent and notorious of the slave-traders, and almost monopolized the supply of slaves for Cuba and Brazil. He built an immense house near the site of the abandoned Portuguese fort at Whydah, which he filled with every luxury that money could command. The handsomest women along the coast were obtained for his harem, and when he walked out he was accompanied by a band of music and a number of retainers, who enumerated his "strong names" at the top of their voices. He affected to be an African amongst Africans, and a polished European amongst Europeans. The profits of the slave-trade, enormous though they were, were insufficient to meet his extravagance, and he did not scruple to plunder the masters of the vessels consigned to him for cargoes, either by the gaming-tables he kept up, or by means of the seductions of his wives. He kept open house, where wine and spirits flowed like water.

The break-up of the Yoruba kingdom, which gradually took place between 1810 and 1840, left Dahomi without any neighbour sufficiently powerful to cope with it. This break-up was caused by the conquest of the Houssa country by the Fulas, for the Houssas, driven southward, overran northern Yoruba. A war between the

Houssas and Yorubas continued for years, resulting in the loss to the latter of the province of Ilorin; and, about 1834, Eyeo or Oyo, the old Yoruba capital, was burned and pillaged. The northern Yorubas fled to the south and occupied their present territory, and the southern Yorubas formed themselves into several small independent states, the chief of which was Egba. Of the three great West African powers, Ashanti, Dahomi, and Yoruba, the latter seems to have been by far the most powerful; and that it was not so well known to Europeans as the two former, was simply due to the fact that until the kingdom fell to pieces there was no exportation of slaves from any of the ports of its sea-board.

The Yoruba tribute, which it seems had been regularly paid by Dahomi since 1747, was now abolished by Gezo. According to Captain Burton,[1] the Yorubas had been all this time established at Kana, where payment of the annual tribute was made, and Gezo now attacked and subdued them. Captain Burton quotes no authority, and it seems improbable that the Yorubas should have remained in occupation of a town only some seven miles distant from Agbomi; and which, lying directly south of it, and on the road to Whydah, would have to be traversed by every Dahomi army proceeding to the coast. Moreover, Norris, who stayed at Kana in 1772, describes it as being a Dahomi town, and the second in the kingdom.

One of Gezo's first expeditions to the east, into the now disorganized Yoruba country, was against Jenna, a populous town on the Yewa River, east of Ketu; his aid

---

[1] *A Mission to Gelele,* vol. ii. p. 402.

having been sought by a candidate for the succession, named Dekon, who had been ousted by his rival Achadi, on the death of Onsi, chief of Jenna. For three successive years an annual expedition was despatched against this town, without success, and Gezo thereupon made peace, and invited Achadi to visit him at Agbomi. Two years later Achadi was so imprudent as to accept this invitation, with the result that, at the Annual Customs, when he was on the Attoh platform, in company with the dignitaries of the kingdom, he was suddenly seized, thrown down to the executioners below, and beheaded.[1] At the next annual expedition Jenna was destroyed, and the survivors fled to Abeokuta.

Gezo now largely increased and improved the corps of Amazons, and, about 1839, attacked the northern Mahis, destroying, it is said, 126 towns or villages. The year following he made a successful raid against the Attakpamis, a Mahi tribe living to the west of Dahomi.

About 1846 commenced those quarrels between Dahomi and the Egbas of Abeokuta, which have continued to the present day. About that year Shodeke, chief of Abeokuta, died, and was succeeded by Sagbwa, who soon contrived to disagree with Dahomi. An Amazon force, sent to ravage Egba territory, was defeated by the Bashorun, or hereditary prime minister of the Egbas, at Ado or Odo, a frontier town north of Jenna, losing most of its officers and insignia, and Gezo swore that he would destroy Abeokuta. For the present, however, he satisfied himself with threats, and did not make any attempt against it.

[1] Commander Forbes.

In 1848, Gezo, at the request of a chief named Olikiki, attacked Okeadan, a populous town some twenty-five miles north-east of Porto Novo. Starting with a large force, as if about to march on Abeokuta, he suddenly turned southward, marched all night, and was admitted into the town by the treacherous chief. There was scarcely any resistance offered, and it is said that nearly 20,000 of the inhabitants were seized and sold, and several hundreds drowned in the Yewa while endeavouring to escape. A small octangular building in the square at Agbomi was paved with the varnished skulls of 148 of the slain.

In May 1849 the slave-trader da Souza died at Whydah, and three men were sacrificed to him on the beach, while a boy and a girl were beheaded and buried with him. The funeral ceremonies in his honour were repeated in October, when a body of Amazons was sent down from the capital to take part in it, and additional human victims and numbers of poultry and animals were sacrificed. Under da Souza and Martinez the export slave-trade from Whydah and Kotonu, which had been much crippled by the declaration of the illegality of the traffic by England and France, and the presence of the suppression squadron of the former power, took a new lease of life, and burst forth with renewed vigour. Acting in concert with the king, they were able, by the closing to the whites of certain routes, to insure the arrival of gangs of slaves undetected on the sea-shore, where they were rapidly embarked, and carried to Cuba and Brazil. The very difficulties of the traffic even made it more lucrative. A vessel would appear off the coast, arrange a day on which the cargo was to be ready, and then put out to sea till the appointed time, by which the slaves would have been secretly brought down. The roads from Allada to Lake No-we and the Okpara River were forbidden to Europeans, and by these routes caravans of slaves reached Kotonu in secret, whenever a cruiser was lying off Whydah. The English officers employed spies to report the arrival of caravans, but they were almost always bribed by the dealers, and the shipment in consequence made safely. Bad as da Souza was, he had some redeeming qualities, and it was through his influence that the death penalty for killing a python was commuted to the ordeal by fire, described in Chapter IV. On such occasions he used to send his slaves to mingle with the crowd, with orders to surround the culprit, and, while pretending to belabour him with sticks, to hustle him off to a place of safety.

In October 1849, Gezo was visited by Commander F. E. Forbes, R.N., and Mr. Vice-Consul Duncan, to endeavour to persuade him to enter into a treaty for the suppression of the slave-trade. The king told them to return at the Annual Customs, and the two envoys returned to Whydah and embarked, Mr. Duncan dying three days later. In May 1850, Commander Forbes returned to Agbomi, accompanied this time by Mr. Beecroft, Consul for the Bights. They were commissioned to induce the king to give up the slave-trade, and turn his attention to agriculture; to abolish human sacrifices, and to abandon his projected attack on Abeokuta, which he had been threatening since 1846; that town being regarded by Great Britain as the centre of missionary enterprise on the Slave Coast. The negotiations completely failed, the king saying that the

Dahomis had always been slave-traders, that his people were soldiers, that his revenue was the proceeds of the slave-trade, and that the traffic was necessary to enable him to meet the expenditure of the Annual Customs. The anxiety of the envoys to befriend Abeokuta was regarded with suspicion, and the mission terminated with but little good feeling on both sides.

In 1851 the long-threatened attack on Abeokuta took place. That town, then much talked of in English missionary circles, is situated on the Ogun River, and is about eighty miles due east from Kana. It is sixteen miles in circumference, surrounded by a mud wall six feet high, and defended by a ditch five feet wide. On the western side it is further defended by the Ogun. The normal population is about 75,000, but when threatened by Dahomi that number is probably doubled, as all the inhabitants of the surrounding country take refuge in the town. It was founded about 1820 by the remnants of a number of small Yoruba clans, who had been driven southward in the wars with the Houssas; and is really a federation, there being still seven quarters, or townships, the chiefs of which bear the title of king.

The Dahomi army, accompanied by Gezo in person, marched from Agbomi about the middle of February 1851, and on March 1st halted at Ishagga, a town about ten miles west of Abeokuta. The Ishaggas made sacrifices, and took oaths to join the Dahomis, and then treacherously misled them; persuading Gezo that the north-western gate, which he proposed attacking, and which was really the weakest, was the strongest; and advising him to attack the south-western gate, which had recently been fortified. They also induced him to alter his proposed night surprise into an attack at mid-day, saying that the Egbas would then be asleep or absent at their farms; and they finally led the army away from the proper ford, so that a large proportion of the ammunition became wetted.

On March 3rd the Dahomi army, about 10,000 strong, and consisting approximately of 7000 men and 3000 Amazons, advanced towards the Ogun in two divisions; the Egbas, who numbered about 15,000, being drawn up to receive them in three bodies—one at the ford on the Ogun, one on the right bank of the river opposite the south-western angle of the town, and the third in front of the Aro, or south-western, gate. The van of the leading Dahomi division, composed of Amazons, forming up in a dense column, crossed the ford with a rush, and scattered the Egba division drawn up to meet them; while the second division, led by Gezo, drove back the body of Egbas which was on the right bank, upon the rocks of the river. The third Egba division advanced to their support, succeeded in checking the advance for a time, and all three bodies of Egbas made good their retreat into the town.

The whole Dahomi force then advanced towards the walls, which were crowded with defenders, every one who could hold a musket being pressed into service. Each corps formed into line, that under Gezo being to the right, and attacked that part of the walls in front of them, the distance between the two points of attack being at least a mile. The first corps, the Amazons leading, advanced across the plain, and strove to carry the walls by escalade; but were met by such a merciless hail of missiles, that they soon retired to a distance of about 100 yards, whence they kept up a heavy fire. During the assault several Amazons succeeded in mounting the walls, but were at once clubbed to death. The corps under Gezo advanced against the south-western corner and the Aro gate, and opened a furious fusillade, but did not attempt to escalade. This fire was kept up by both corps for about five hours, when an American missionary in Abeokuta advised the Egbas to fire the tall, dry grass that covered the plain between the Aro gate and the river. This was done, and the wind carrying the conflagration rapidly towards Gezo's corps, it retired before the flames to about half-way between the Aro gate and the river. A body of Egbas sallied out and followed, but kept at a respectful distance.

Nightfall found the right division of the Dahomi army thus situated, and the left still in front of the walls ; and soon after dark the former retired across the river in an orderly manner, carrying off its wounded. As soon as the left division found that the right had retreated, it also crossed the Ogun, and retired along the road to Ishagga, leaving the Amazons to hold the ford and cover the retreat. The Egbas followed up, but only in a half-hearted manner, and the Amazons, retiring slowly and in good order, halted next morning at Ishagga, through which the remainder of the army had already passed. Here the Egbas made a hot attack, in the midst of which the Amazons were suddenly taken in flank by their pretended allies, the Ishaggas. They were thrown into confusion, and retired in disorder along the route taken by the army; but the Egbas had not the courage to pursue. The Dahomi loss in the attack and retreat was about 1200, the greater number being Amazons, several of whose bodies were found under the wall they had tried to scale. The Egbas showed throughout but little spirit, although their losses were trifling. Had they pursued in force and pushed home, the whole Dahomi army would probably have been routed.

In January 1852, Commander T. G. Forbes, of H.M.S. *Philomel*, visited Gezo at Kana, and succeeded in persuading him to sign a treaty for the abolition of the export slave-trade. The bombardment of Lagos by the British squadron in November 1851, no doubt counted for something in producing this concession; but the treaty was really so much waste-paper, as it was never observed.

The continued efforts made by England to suppress the slave-trade, and its open friendship for the Egbas of Abeokuta, had, however, the effect of prejudicing Gezo against the English, whose interests he had always hitherto supported, and he now turned to the French. The latter, who never lose an opportunity of pushing their interests in West Africa, seized the occasion; and Gezo was twice visited, in 1856 and 1858, by Lieutenant Wallon, of the French Navy, who conducted to Agbomi two howitzers as a present to the king from the French Government, and took away with him two boys from the palace to be educated in France.

In 1858, Gezo led an expedition against Little Popo, which did not meet with much success, and, soon after returning from it, died. He had greatly diminished the number of human sacrifices, and had also put a stop to the massacre of women that formerly used to take place in the palace when a king died. His death is generally attributed to small-pox; but it was said by the natives that he had been poisoned by the priests, on account of his reduction of the human sacrifices, and that his successor was only elected upon promising to increase the number of victims.

Gelele, whose birth-name was Badu, but who took the "strong name" of *Gelele ma nyonzi*—"Bigness that cannot be lifted"—succeeded his father in 1858, at the age of thirty-eight, to the exclusion of his elder brother, Godo, who was an habitual drunkard. During the first two years of his reign he despatched numerous expeditions against minor chiefs to the east and south-east; amongst them one against Akiaon, chief of Attako or Taccow, near Porto Novo, who, in a moment of madness, had sent an insulting message on hearing of the death of Gezo, to the effect that "all men were very glad." Attako was captured, its chief slain, and his head transported to Agbomi, where Captain Burton saw it in 1864.

In July and August 1860, Gelele performed the Grand Customs for his father, sacrificing, according to M. Lartigue, some 700 victims; and, immediately afterwards, commenced preparations for an attack on Abeokuta. The British Government at this time took a great interest in that town, on account of the highly-coloured reports of the missionaries as to the rapid strides Christianity was making in it; they sent out cannon for its defence, and the governor of Lagos sent up powder and lead to assist the Egbas during the threatened attack. Early in 1861, Gelele, having collected a large force, marched from Agbomi, and the British Government then determined to support the

Egbas with a small force. Munitions of war were sent from Sierra Leone, and five officers and 125 men of the 2nd West India Regiment had embarked at the Gambia in H.M.S. *Arrogant*, on March 6th, to take up a similar force at Sierra Leone, and proceed to Abeokuta, when the news was received that an outbreak of small-pox had compelled the Dahomi army to return. The reinforcement was consequently countermanded; but Captain A. T. Jones, and twelve gunners of the 2nd W. I. Regiment, were sent on to instruct the Egbas in gunnery. Captain Jones visited Abeokuta in May 1861, but the Egbas appeared to regard the proffered aid with suspicion, and as he died at Lagos on July 7th, the gunners returned to Sierra Leone.

In 1862, Gelele suddenly fell with 6000 men upon Ishagga, to punish the inhabitants for their treachery in 1851. The place was sacked on March 5th, the chief, Bakoko, and a large number of the people, slain, and about 500 carried off as prisoners. Eight days later Aibo was captured and destroyed.

Amongst the prisoners taken at Ishagga were seventeen or eighteen Christian converts, and a negro missionary, named Doherty, a native of Sierra Leone. Efforts to obtain their release were made, but some of them were put to death, in consequence, it was said, of an earthquake which took place on June 10th, and which was believed to indicate that Gezo required some more victims. It was reported that Doherty had been crucified, but in August 1867 he returned to Lagos safe and sound.

In December 1862, Captain Wilmot, R.N., senior naval officer on the West Coast of Africa, went to

Agbomi, and saw Gelele. He remained a month at the capital, and after endeavouring to persuade the king to abandon the slave-trade and abolish human sacrifices, returned to Whydah and re-embarked, with a promise to return.

In February 1863, the Dahomi army ravaged Egbado territory, and on March 15th captured and sacked the town of Igbara, situated about twenty-two miles to the south-west of Abeokuta, carrying off numbers of prisoners. It then moved towards the north-east, made a demonstration before Abeokuta on March 26th, and after pillaging the surrounding country, returned to Agbomi. In June of the same year it made an expedition against the northern Mahi tribes, and secured a few hundred prisoners.

Captain Wilmot's duties as Commodore preventing him keeping his promise to return to Dahomi, the British Government despatched Captain R. F. Burton, Consul of the Bights, on a mission to Gelele at the end of 1863, to confirm the friendly sentiments expressed by Captain Wilmot to the king, and to endeavour to put a stop to the slave-trade and human sacrifices. The delivery of the message was retarded for two months, during which Captain Burton remained at Agbomi; and, when finally delivered, the king replied to it that the customs of his kingdom obliged him to go to war, that the slave-trade was necessary for his expenses, and that unless he sold his captives he must kill them. With regard to human sacrifices, Gelele declared that he only slew malefactors and prisoners of war. Human sacrifices, indeed, and the annual raids could not be abolished without shaking the kingdom to its very foundations. The mission, therefore, failed in its objects, and Captain Burton re-embarked from Whydah on February 26th, 1864.

This reference to the slave-trade requires, perhaps, some explanation, the popular notion being that that traffic had come to an end some twelve or thirteen years before; but it did not really cease till 1865. As long as there was a market for slaves in the New World, the trade had continued to exist, in spite of the prohibitions of the European Powers and the presence of armed cruisers; and it was not until Brazil and Cuba effectively closed their ports against slaves that it ceased. In the later days of the traffic the dealers employed steam-ships, so as the more easily to avoid the cruisers; and the last one employed, a very swift vessel, made seven voyages before being captured, carrying each time more than a thousand slaves.

While Captain Burton was at Agbomi preparations were being made for a new attack on Abeokuta, and on February 22nd, 1864, the army left the capital. The force, about 12,000 strong, marched in four divisions, two of the right wing and two of the left. It had with it three brass six-pounder guns. Eleven days out it crossed the Yewa river, near Isume, and on March 13th encamped on the Owiwi river, about twelve miles from Abeokuta. Nineteen days were thus occupied in traversing the distance between Agbomi and the Owiwi, about ninety miles by road; but the army had spent ten days in halts and in foraging for food, with which it was scantily supplied. According to subsequent reports, the soldiery were reduced to living on parched rice and palm-nuts, and many of them ate nothing

Y

but a little cassava for tweny-four hours before the attack.

The army marched from the Owiwi by moonlight, intending to take the enemy by surprise, but they were seen by some people bathing in the Ogun, who gave the alarm. The Egbas, moreover, were well prepared, for the attack had been long threatened. All the villages between the Yewa and Abeokuta had been abandoned, and the produce of the farms removed ; while the ditches of the town had been deepened and the walls raised.

On the night of March 14th, the Dahomi army reached the Ogun, at the village of Aro, about three miles and a half south of Abeokuta ; and at 6.30 a.m. next day the vanguard crossed under cover of a thick mist. They were soon perceived, the alarm was given by the guns at the south-western or Aro gate, and in a few minutes the Egbas swarmed in thousands to their posts. The wall on the south side, from the Aro to the Agbamaya gates, was lined, that side being immediately threatened ; but, it having been reported that the Dahomis intended making three independent attacks, two divisions were kept in reserve.

The Dahomis advanced in compact order towards the Aro gate, and were met by a body of 400 Egbas, who sallied out of apertures tunnelled in the wall for that purpose ; but as the army continued advancing without returning their fire, they quickly returned. When within 200 yards of the wall, the Dahomis deployed in three bodies, one opposite the Aro gate, the other two to the left ; the whole line being about 700 yards long. They then advanced to within 100 yards, and, upon a signal being given by the Gau, opened a tremendous fusillade, and rushed to the assault. They advanced with great impetuosity, but were met by such heavy volleys from the walls, that their progress was arrested. They maintained their ground, however, at a distance of some 40 yards from the walls, and kept up a very rapid fire ; under cover of which some of the Amazons gained the ditch, and attempted furiously to scale the wall, only to be dragged over and killed ; while others hurled up large stones, and snatched away the muskets that were pointed at them. A few others tried to make a way through the holes tunnelled under the wall, but only to have their heads struck off as soon as they protruded on the inner side. Three Amazons succeeded in planting their banners on the wall, but were immediately cut down, and their heads and hands displayed on spears with shouts of triumph. One Amazon, who had lost an arm in scaling the wall, shot an Egba with her remaining hand, and fell back into the ditch, covered with wounds.

This struggle lasted an hour, at the end of which, no impression having been made, the entire line fell back to about 200 yards from the wall, where some kept up a desultory fire, and others sat down. The main body of the Egbas kept their places, fearing that this retreat was a stratagem ; but a number of men sallied out, only, however, to return with some haste, when the Dahomis turned upon them.

The Dahomi army now gradually fell back upon the valley of the Ogun, and halted for a short time at Aro, where it repulsed an attack by the Egbas. From Aro it retired in a haphazard way, no plan of retreat having been provided for ; and, about 10 a.m., when a large body of Egbas, which had sallied out of the Agbamaya gate and made a long circuit, fell upon its rear, it was thrown into confusion. One of the three divisions that had been engaged, broke through and got off; but the other two became mixed and fell into disorder. The pursuit was pressed home, the Dahomis still keeping in large bodies and occasionally turning upon their pursuers, until, when near Igbara, they were attacked in flank by another body of Egbas, who had taken a short cut across the Ogun. This completed the rout, and they here lost a brass gun and several hundreds of muskets. They attempted to make a stand on reaching their encampment near the Owiwi, but were speedily driven back, losing another brass gun and a great quantity of baggage, amongst the latter the razor-shaped weapons of the Razor Company of Amazons.

At 2 p.m. the routed army reached Ishagga, and there made a last stand, but it was overwhelmed by numbers and driven back. The Egbas, however, had not the courage to press closely in pursuit, and it was not until nightfall, when near Jiga, that the fugitives were again harried. Thence, the pursuit was continued as far as the Yewa River, thirty-five miles from Abeokuta, which the bulk of the defeated army crossed that night. The people of Okeadan had destroyed the bridge, and, after the main body of the Dahomis had passed the river, they found and slaughtered some four or five hundred fugitives who were too exhausted by hunger and their long march to stem the stream.

It is uncertain whether Gelele was present during the attack on Abeokuta. According to one report he was not with the army at all, while, according to another, he was with that division which broke through and got off. The Dahomi loss has been variously estimated ; it apparently amounted to about 3000 killed and 1500 prisoners. About 200 fell before the walls, 100 of them in the ditch ; 1000 dead were counted between Abeokuta and Ishagga, and beyond that the number of slain was said to have been still larger. The greatest loss took place during the rout, and for several days afterwards fugitives kept coming in to surrender, begging for food ; while others in a fainting condition were found in the bush along the line of retreat. A large proportion of the prisoners were put to death. The bodies of the slain were terribly mutilated, every-body, men and women, slashing and stoning every corpse they passed. The Egba loss was, it is said, only about 50 killed and 100 wounded.

The whole scheme of attack was ill-digested and badly carried out. No attempt was made to breach the walls, and to endeavour to carry the place by escalade was simply madness, since the walls were defended by at least 20,000 men, against whom the king had only 12,000. The Amazons showed their usual intrepidity, and, strange to say, suffered the least, the greater part of the killed and wounded being men. According to report, Gelele bought a number of slaves after his defeat, so as to be able to make a triumphant entry into Agbomi, and conceal his failure ; and about a month after his return to the capital, he sent a force to ravage the country to the north of Porto Novo, and obtain some victims for the Customs.

After the defeat at Abeokuta in 1864, the Dahomi army, without making any attempt upon that town, overran Ketu and the western parts of Egba every year; remaining on hostile soil till the rivers in its rear commenced to rise, and then returning to Agbomi. The Egbas never ventured to attack, and the villagers, on the report of the approach of the Dahomis, retired to Abeokuta, leaving their plantations and dwellings at the mercy of the enemy. On April 28th, 1873, the Dahomi army took up a position close to Abeokuta, and an attack on that town was expected ; but, after being encamped two days, an outbreak of small-pox caused the invaders to retire under cover of the night, leaving a number of dead and dying. In 1874 it again threatened Abeokuta, but after remaining in the neighbourhood for some days, retired without attempting anything against it. After the withdrawal of the Dahomi army, the Egbas made war on Porto Novo, which was in alliance with Dahomi, but they suffered so severely that they soon abandoned the campaign.

In 1876 Gelele brought himself into conflict with the British naval authorities on the West Coast of Africa, on account of the maltreatment and insult offered to Mr. Turnbull, an Englishman, and Whydah agent of the well-known firm of African merchants, Messrs. F. & A. Swanzy, whom he had caused to be seized and taken to Agbomi. In consequence of this outrage, Commodore Hewett, R.N., informed the king, in February, that £6000, or 500 puncheons of palm-oil, was required as compensation, and that if the amount was not paid by July 1st, the Dahomi coast would be blockaded. The sum demanded was not paid within the time stipulated, and a blockade was accordingly established ; but this action did not meet with the entire approval of the Home Government, and Captain Sulivan, H.M.S. *Sirius*, compromised the affair by accepting, in May 1877, 200 puncheons of palm-oil. A so-called treaty was signed at Whydah, by which the king engaged never to molest, interfere with, or threaten the lives of, any British subjects, or to compel any British subject to attend the Annual Custom, or witness human sacrifices. He further engaged to abolish for ever the export slave-trade, and granted to British subjects full liberty to reside, trade, and acquire property in all parts of the kingdom. In return for these concessions the fine of 500 puncheons was to be reduced to 400, and the blockade to be raised on the immediate payment of 200, and a promise of payment of the remainder within twelve months. It is doubtful if the king had any knowledge of this arrangement. Two hundred puncheons of palm-oil were paid in the name of the king, and the blockade was in consequence raised; but it afterwards transpired that these were really paid by the French house of Régis Aîné, Whydah merchants, whose business was being ruined by the blockade. The remainder of the fine was never paid, and Gelele repudiated the entire treaty, but the blockade was not re-established.

In August 1882 a Dahomi force invaded and pillaged Ewemi, and in 1883 a portion of Ketu was overrun and devastated. Just before the season of the annual raids, the Dahomis, to put the Ketus off their guard, and to lead them to believe themselves secure from invasion for that year, spread reports that they had been seriously defeated by the Mahis. The ruse had the desired effect, and the Ketus, believing that their foes were engaged elsewhere, neglected their usual precautions. In the meantime the Dahomi army left Agbomi, and advancing by forced marches at night, and lying hidden in the forested tracts during the day, arrived before the town of Ketu at night, without its presence being in the least suspected. Before daybreak the Dahomis scaled the walls, and the town was in their hands before the inhabitants were aroused. There was practically no resistance, and but few of the Ketus escaped. The town was pillaged and burnt, the aged, infirm, and sick were slain, and the remainder carried off to Agbomi as captives.

In 1884 Dahomi meditated a new attempt against Abeokuta, and spies were sent into Egba territory to gather information ; but fifteen of them being discovered and seized in Abeokuta itself, the design was abandoned, and the annual raid directed against the Mahi tribes. In consequence of the capture of these spies, and the discovery of the intentions of the Dahomis, the authorities of Abeokuta issued orders forbidding the inhabitants of the outlying agricultural villages to remain in their villages during the season of the raids ; with the result that the food supply was much curtailed, and great want, almost amounting to a famine, prevailed in Abeokuta.

In 1886 a large Dahomi army overran Ketu, Egbado, and Awori. The whole country was overrun by detached parties of plunderers, and several large villages were sacked. On this occasion the Dahomis pushed so far to the east that fugitives were pursued to within twenty miles of the Lagos Lagoon, and the town of Lagos was crowded with refugees. The alarm was so great that the town of Otta, on the Ibo River, only some sixteen miles to the north of Lagos, was abandoned by its inhabitants.

At the present time (March 1890) Dahomi is embroiled with France, the cause of quarrel being the refusal of the former to recognize the French Protectorate over Porto Novo and Kotonou. The history of this Protectorate is shortly as follows. In April 1861, the English bombarded Porto Novo, and, in February 1863, the king, to shelter himself from further attack, placed his kingdom under the protection of France. This Protectorate was abandoned, by order of Admiral de Ladébat, in December 1864, but the French still maintained friendly relations with Porto Novo. In 1878 France acquired a Protectorate over Kotonou, a small district on the sea-coast to the south of the Denham Waters; and in 1883 the Protectorate over Porto Novo was re-established.

Gelele does not appear to have made any protest at this time, or to have taken any action, and it seems probable that the present difficulty has been caused by the French having annexed territory to the north of Porto Novo. The limits of kingdoms such as this are never very clearly defined, and the French are disposed to act in a high-handed manner; for in March 1885, the French Resident at Porto Novo informed the Government of Lagos that he had placed the villages on both banks of the " Whemi River " under French protection, no matter to whom they belonged. Now this " Whemi River " is the Tochi Creek, or Ewemi Canal, the northernmost of the three creeks which connect the Porto Novo lagoon with the Denham Waters, and the northern bank is in Ewemi, which is a Dahomi province. Probably some such extension of the Protectorate has taken place north of Porto Novo, that is, into Ketu ; for in the French maps the words " Porto Novo " are made to cover territory some distance to the north of Porto Novo proper. As we have seen, the Dahomis have been accustomed to overrun Ketu in their annual raids, and in 1889 they seem to have ravaged some territory which the French now claim as belonging to Porto Novo. Several villages were burned and the inhabitants carried off, and, in consequence, the French dispatched M. Bayol to Dahomi to protest.

M. Bayol was detained at Agbomi during the Annual Customs of 1889, and, it seems, Gelele not only refused to recognize the French claim to the territory in dispute, but also declared that Kotonou belonged to him, and that the French must evacuate it. If this were not done, he threatened he would attack it at the next annual raid. Gelele died in 1889, or early in 1890, but this threat has now been fulfilled by his successor, Kudo ; and the French have been attacked, in March, at Zebo, in Kotonou, a village on the southern shore of the Denham Waters, by a force of 800 Dahomis. The Dahomis were repulsed with a loss of about 100 ; the French force, which consisted of two companies of Senegal irregulars, losing only one killed and two wounded.

Thus matters stand at present. If the French do not take aggressive action, it is probable that the annual raid will be directed against Kotonou for the next few years ; while if they invade Dahomi and occupy the capital the kingdom will probably fall to pieces ; but a force of at least 2000 men would be required for this, and the expedition would be costly. The best method of bringing Dahomi to terms would be to occupy Whydah ; but this might lead to European complications, that town being regarded by Germany as within the sphere of Portuguese influence. In the meantime, Kudo has seized and carried off to Agbomi six French residents of Whydah, traders and Catholic missionaries, and with these captives in his hands he is master of the situation, since he can declare that any advance against his territory shall be the signal for their massacre.

THE END.

CPSIA information can be obtained
at www.ICGtesting.com
Printed in the USA
LVHW090618081020
668179LV00003B/282

9 789353 956684